Using Standards and High-Stakes Testing *for* Students

EXPLOITING POWER WITH CRITICAL PEDAGOGY

Edited by Julie A. Gorlewski, Brad J. Porfilio, and David A. Gorlewski

PETER LANG
New York • Washington, D.C./Baltimore • Bern
Frankfurt • Berlin • Brussels • Vienna • Oxford

Library of Congress Cataloging-in-Publication Data

Using standards and high-stakes testing for students: exploiting
power with critical pedagogy / [edited by] Julie A. Gorlewski,
Brad J. Porfilio, David A. Gorlewski.
pages cm. — (Counterpoints: studies in the postmodern theory of education; vol. 425)
Includes bibliographical references.
1. Education—Standards—United States.
2. Educational tests and measurements—United States.
3. Educational equalization—United States.
4. Critical pedagogy—United States. I. Gorlewski, Julie A.
II. Porfilio, Bradley J. III. Gorlewski, David A.
LB3060.83.U75 371.260973—dc23 2011046863
ISBN 978-1-4331-1556-1 (hardcover)
ISBN 978-1-4331-1555-4 (paperback)
ISBN 978-1-4539-0525-8 (e-book)
ISSN 1058-1634

Bibliographic information published by **Die Deutsche Nationalbibliothek**
Die Deutsche Nationalbibliothek lists this publication in the "Deutsche
Nationalbibliografie"; detailed bibliographic data is available
on the Internet at http://dnb.d-nb.de/.

The paper in this book meets the guidelines for permanence and durability
of the Committee on Production Guidelines for Book Longevity
of the Council of Library Resources.

© 2012 Peter Lang Publishing, Inc., New York
29 Broadway, 18th floor, New York, NY 10006
www.peterlang.com

Printed in the United States of America

Contents

SECTION 2. De-standardizing Teachers and Learning

SECTION 3. Leveraging Standards in Secondary Classrooms

SECTION 4. Teacher Education: Modeling Critical Approaches

Foreword

Wayne Au

When the editors of *Using Standards and High-Stakes Testing for Students: Exploiting Power with Critical Pedagogy* first approached me to write the foreword for their book, frankly, I nearly declined. Based on the title and book description alone I had serious misgivings about what this book was trying to argue. You see, I've spent a good deal of my educational research and activist energies towards understanding high-stakes standardized tests (and, implicitly, the standards upon which they have been constructed), and their relationship to issues of social and educational inequality. Along the way, I've only found more and more ways to be troubled by testing.

For instance, historically speaking, today's high-stakes standardized tests are rooted firmly in the very racist, classist, and anti-immigrant I.Q. tests and the eugenics movement in the United States (Stoskopf, 1999). Personally I've always been struck by the ways in which today's standardized test-based disparities almost exactly mirror the I.Q. test-based disparities: For more than 100 years the poor, immigrants, and "darker-skinned" have always had disproportionate failure rates (Madaus & Clarke, 2001). Given today's test-derived achievement gaps, I remain convinced that such inequalities are embedded deeply in the structures and forms of the tests themselves, above and beyond various content issues (Au, 2009). Indeed, evidence to support this view can be found in several places, but most notably in work surrounding the SAT college entrance exam and the ways that a racial bias is built into the selection of test questions themselves (Kidder & Rosner, 2002–2003).

And then of course there are the myriad of other problems with high-stakes testing. We know about the narrowing of what is taught and the narrowing of classroom discourse and pedagogy that has followed (Au, 2007). We also know that in the process of such narrowing, multicultural, anti-racist curriculum and culturally relevant pedagogy have likewise been pushed out of classrooms, thereby squelching the efforts of teachers to best serve their students (Bigelow, 2009, 2010). We further know that such forms of "subtractive schooling" (Valenzuela, 1999) fundamentally decontextualize both knowledge and the very students the tests are supposedly measuring in an attempt to flatten schools, kids, teachers, learning, and entire communities into the easily comparable, one-dimensional numbers (Au, 2009; McNeil, 2000).

Specific policy issues abound as well, where, for instance high-stakes testing has greatly increased the number of high school dropouts—again, disproportionately students of color and working-class students (Bhanpuri & Sexton, 2006). Or that testing and standards have embodied a top-down, fundamentally anti-democratic policy movement (Au, 2010), hell bent on surveiling the work of teachers–cum–assembly line laborers (Au, 2011b) as part of a corporate reform package that is attacking public education from all angles (Giroux & Saltman, 2008). And it is a reform package that, despite the well-known technical problems (Au, 2010–2011), relies completely on high-stakes testing to do its dirty work.

Now it may be that, as Thompson (2001) argues, the standards movement had more benign, benevolent, or well-intended origins, but what is inarguable to me is that whatever their origins, standards have become the foundation for high-stakes testing. Given this reality, and given what I've analyzed in my own work, it has become clear to me that, within our current context, high-stakes, standardized tests are themselves completely corrupt and only contribute to educational and social inequality (Au, 2009). Indeed I might argue that they are tools for educational stratification and upward mobility above all else (Au, 2008).

So, when the editors of *Using Standards and High-Stakes Testing for Students: Exploiting Power with Critical Pedagogy* asked me to write this foreword, one might have forgiven me for being more than a bit skeptical.

However, the content of *Using Standards and High-Stakes Testing for Students*...reminds me of a basic point: Testing and standards are simply tools (Madaus, 1994), and what matters is to what ends we use those tools. As such, this book is not about how to use standards to better teach to the tests. Rather, in this collection high-stakes tests and standards aren't being used as assessments and are instead being used as points of study, as prisms through which to engage in critical analyses, as artifacts for the exploration of social and educational relations.

So in the case of *Using Standards and High-Stakes Testing for Students*...tests and standards are being used as tools in a different way—as tools for the development of critical consciousness about inequality and justice. And it is just this kind of use of tools that changes the nature of how we think about the world and act within it (Au, 2011a; Freire, 1974; Vygotsky, 1987). It goes without saying that using tests and standards in this way is something that I wholeheartedly support.

Using Standards and High-Stakes Testing for Students: Exploiting Power with Critical Pedagogy thus raises a continually relevant issue for all of us to consider: Recalling the spirit of sister Audre Lorde (1984), is it realistic for us to use the master's tools to tear down the master's house? Right now, tests and standards are the tools of the masters of educational corporate reform, and they are using them to push charters (vouchers if they could), Teach For America, the defunding of public education, and anti-unionism, among others.

Functionally there are only four ways the tests, as the master's tool, could be used to tear down the house of corporate reform. The first three are related and are based on the same premise: 1. If everyone passes a test (a statistical impossibility, by the way; Linn, 2003); 2. If everyone fails a test (which almost happened with the adequate yearly progress provisions of NCLB); and 3. If everyone simply opted out of taking the tests altogether. All three of these "possibilities" ultimately negate the validity of the tests because, if you can't show difference amongst test takers, then you can't make any claims to be able to compare student A to student B, teacher C to teacher D, school E to school F, and so on, for rank ordering (Au, 2009). Since high-stakes standardized tests are the keystone to current reforms, such a negation would ultimately undermine the entire systemic logics undergirding corporate-based education policy, which, as I mentioned above, requires all things education to be turned into numbers for comparison. Further, negating the tests' capabilities to differentiate individual and groups of students through total success, total failure, or total absence challenges the sifting function of testing, which by extension challenges the upward mobility strategies of the upper and middle classes. This would (and has) cause massive resistance amongst the professional middle class—usually one of the powerhouses behind such reforms (Apple, 2006).

A fourth way we might use tests and standards to potentially take down the master's house of corporate education reform would be if we use them as the focus of study to develop critical consciousness about social and educational inequality—as *Using Standards and High-Stakes Testing for Students*...suggests. While I personally might not think this is a viable long-term strategy to ultimately end high-stakes testing and challenge corporate-based reform, such a strategy does point to the power and potential of education. We may not be able to use the master's tools to tear down the master's house, but perhaps we can use the master's tools to become critically conscious of the structure of the master's house. And such critical consciousness is central to any action that has the goal of creating more just schools and society.

References

Apple, M. W. (2006). *Educating the "right" way: Markets, standards, god, and inequality* (2nd ed.). New York: Routledge.

Au, W. (2007). High-stakes testing and curricular control: A qualitative metasynthesis. *Educational Researcher, 36*(5), 258–267.

Au, W. (2008). Between education and the economy: High-stakes testing and the contradictory location of the new middle class. *Journal of Education Policy, 23*(5), 501–513.

Au, W. (2009). *Unequal by design: High-stakes testing and the standardization of inequality.* New York: Routledge.

Au, W. (2010). The idiocy of policy: The anti-democratic curriculum of high-stakes testing. *Critical Education, 1*(1), 1–16. Retrieved from http://m1.cust.educ.ubc.ca/journal/index.php/criticaled/issue/view/11

Au, W. (2010–11). Neither fair nor accurate: Research based reasons why high-stakes tests should not be used to evaluate teachers. *Rethinking Schools, 25*(2), 34–38.

Au, W. (2011a). *Critical curriculum studies: Education, consciousness, and the politics of knowing.* New York: Routledge.

Au, W. (2011b). Teaching under the new Taylorism: High-stakes testing and scientific management in the 21st century curriculum. *Journal of Curriculum Studies, 43*(1), 25–45. doi: 10.1080/00220272.2010.521261

Bhanpuri, H., & Sexton, S. K. (2006). The hidden costs of high school exit exams: A CEP policy brief (p. 10). Washington, D.C.: Center on Education Policy.

Bigelow, B. (2009). Standards and tests attack multiculturalism. In W. Au (Ed.), *Rethinking multicultural education: Teaching for racial and cultural justice* (pp. 53–60). Milwaukee, WI: Rethinking Schools, Ltd.

Bigelow, B. (2010). Those awful Texas social studies standards: And what about yours? *Rethinking Schools, 24*(4), 46–48.

Freire, P. (1974). *Pedagogy of the oppressed* (M. B. Ramos, Trans.). New York: Seabury Press.

Giroux, H., & Saltman, K. J. (2008, December 17). Obama's betrayal of public education? Arne Duncan and the corporate model of schooling. Retrieved December 21, 2008, from http://www.truthout.org/121708R

Kidder, W. C., & Rosner, J. (2002–2003). How the SAT creates "built-in headwinds": An educational and legal analysis of disparate impact. *Santa Clara Law Review, 43*, 131–212.

Linn, R. L. (2003, July). Accountability, responsibility and reasonable expectations. *Center for the Study of Evaluation, National Center for Research on Evaluation, Standards, and Student Testing, Graduate School of Education & Information Studies, University of California, Los Angeles.* Retrieved February 27, 2006, from http://www.cse.ucla.edu/products/reports_set.htm

Lorde, A. (1984). *Sister outsider.* Berkeley, CA: Crossing Press.

Madaus, G. F. (1994). A technological and historical consideration of equity issues associated with proposals to change the nation's testing policy. *Harvard Educational Review, 64*(1), 76–95.

Madaus, G. F., & Clarke, M. (2001). The adverse impact of high-stakes testing on minority students: Evidence from one hundred years of test data. In G. Orfield & M. L. Kornhaber (Eds.), *Raising standards or raising barriers?: Inequality and high-stakes testing in public education* (pp. 85–106). New York: Century Foundation Press.

McNeil, L. M. (2000). *Contradictions of school reform: Educational costs of standardized testing.* New York: Routledge.

Stoskopf, A. (1999). The forgotten history of eugenics. *Rethinking Schools, 13*(3), 12–13.

Thompson, S. (2001). The authentic standards movement and its evil twin. *Phi Delta Kappan, 82*(5), 358–362.

Valenzuela, A. (1999). *Subtractive schooling: U.S. Mexican youth and the politics of caring.* New York: SUNY Press.

Vygotsky, L. S. (1987). Thinking and speech (N. Minick, Trans.). In R. W. Rieber & A. Carton (Eds.), *The collected works of L.S. Vygotsky: Problems of general psychology including the volume thinking and speech* (Vol. 1, pp. 37–285). New York: Plenum Press.

1. Introduction

Julie A. Gorlewski, Brad J. Porfilio, & David A. Gorlewski

Students and teachers in the United States today, at all education levels, face a range of challenges associated with neoliberal capitalism. The social landscape is characterized by increasing disparities in income, corporate control over knowledge production, a waning political commitment to meeting the needs of citizens, and escalated accountability pressures for our students to perform as well as their global counterparts (Carr & Porfilio, 2011; Porfilio & Malott, 2008; Saltman & Gabbard, 2011). Corporate-inspired educational initiatives have come to dominate life in classrooms. The influx of standardized tests, test-prep materials, and "accountability" pressures by corporate and professional organizations have resulted in narrowed curriculum, deprofessionalization of teachers, and educational experiences that are commodified, alienating, and exploitative of student and teacher labor.

The infiltration of corporate ideologies, practices, and policies in America's K–12 public schools ensures that the vast majority of young people in this generation who graduate from these schools will have experienced a limited standards-based curriculum. Current reform initiatives reinforce this approach above all others. And, because nearly 90% of students in the fall 2010 school year attended public schools (U.S. Department of Education Institute of Education Sciences, 2011), this situation is likely to have a significant effect on the practices and philosophies of future educators. If educators do not learn about the socially constructed nature of the standards-based curriculum and explore ways to get beyond promoting indoctrinating forms of education (Kincheloe, 2007), they may be inclined to embrace dominant drill and kill pedagogies, demonize students for their lack of enthusiasm or engagement in the classroom, or drop out of the profession entirely (Toppo, 2007).

Standards, themselves, are not malevolent. Like anything socially constructed, standards manifest the values and beliefs of their developers. To meet the needs of our diverse population, standards tend to be written in general terms—broad strokes intended to address knowledge and skills that are virtually unassailable in their suitability. For example, the Common Core Standards for K–5 English Language Arts (which were, as of July 2011, adopted by 44 states), state that students should be able to: Prepare for and participate effectively in a range of conversations and collaborations with diverse partners, building on others' ideas and expressing their own clearly and persuasively (Council of Chief State School Officers & National Governors' Association, 2010, p. 22). Few people, regardless of educational background or political ideology, would argue about whether or not this is a worthwhile aim. Moreover, standards often represent cultural commonality: who among educators would promote principles that call for *lowering* expectations for students?

However, even well-constructed, carefully written standards become problematic when they are operationalized into high-stakes assessments (Garrison, 2009). The harmful effects of such assessments are well documented. They include:

- Narrowed curricula,
- Commodification of learning,
- Alienation of students and teachers from their own labor,
- Demoralization and deprofessionalization of educators,
- Inequitable consequences (students in schools serving poor and working-class communities suffer more harmful effects of standardization than students in schools serving middle- or upper-class communities).

As resources for public education have diminished, government control has increased, specifically in the form of common standards and high-stakes assessments. This has been tolerated by the public, at least in part, because current educational reform initiatives have been presented using rhetoric that *promotes* the very opposite of their actual consequences. No Child Left Behind (NCLB) and Race to the Top (the federal legislation that is the face of the accountability-based reform movement) claim to alleviate social and economic inequities by providing all children with educational opportunities that will foster success. Supporters of standardized reform maintain, incorrectly, that accountability measures based on high-stakes assessments will improve public schools, particularly for poor and minority students. However, decades of research reveal evidence that contradicts this assertion: students in schools serving poor and working-class communities are more likely to be harmed by high-stakes assessment-based reform (Au, 2008; Hursh, 2011; Kozol, 2005; Porfilio & Malott, 2008).

As standardization begins to permeate public education from pre-K through post-secondary teacher education programs (particularly through accreditation processes), critical educators are attempting to engage in pedagogical endeavors that incorporate the regulatory requirements without alienating or marginalizing students. The challenge, then, is to construct and implement curricula and instructional activities that *exploit* the possibilities of standards (and their corollary assessments) while simultaneously fostering critical thinking and student efficacy.

One of the aims of this book is to provide a deepened awareness of how educators can alleviate the negative effects of standardization, especially for students who populate poor and working-class communities. As teachers negotiate their roles in this new environment, it is essential for them to maintain and model a critical stance toward curriculum and instruction. Educators must explicitly seek to provide transformative experiences within the constraints of high-stakes accountability measures. In the chapters that follow, critical schoolteachers, teacher educators, and scholars provide concrete examples of how to use the power embedded in standards and assessments to meet the goals of critical pedagogy, i.e., empowerment, self-efficacy, and social justice.

In addition, the editors of the volume believe it is imperative for educators to engage continually in critical scholarship and pedagogical initiatives to uncover the often hidden forces that give rise to developments inside and outside of their learning communities. This reflective process is necessary to generate dissent-oriented projects that are capable of remaking the world on the ideas of love, justice, freedom, and equity—instead of reproducing the dominant values and relationships associated with the nearly 40-year neoliberal experiment. Several contributors engage in historical analysis, tap theoretical insights, and generate empirical research in order to guide educators and their students in understanding the socially constructed nature of the accountability and standardization movement.

Content and organization of this book

In addition to this introductory chapter, the book consists of four main sections and 15 chapters. The first section, *Standards, Schools, and Society*, provides a deeper understanding of the social, economic, and political forces behind why the standards and accountability movement is supported by the two major parties in the U.S., many schoolteachers and teacher educators, and many U.S. citizens. The second section, *De-standardizing Teachers and Learning*, offers insights as to how educators can hijack dominant discourses and practices aligned with the standards and accountability movement in order to promote critical forms of pedagogy and curricula within K–12 schools.

The third section, *Leveraging Standards in Secondary Classrooms*, documents how critical educators act strategically to employ instructional strategies, develop positive relationships with students, and generate transformative experiences, while concomitantly ensuring that students perform well on high-stakes examinations. The final section, *Teacher Education: Modeling Critical Approaches*, highlights how critical educators are able to exploit corporate mandates (such as the teacher education accreditation process) to model emancipatory forms of teaching and learning, to institutionalize standards, policies, and programs linked to promoting a critical agenda, and to prepare students to understand the social nature of the standards and accountability movement invading all levels of education.

Standards, schools, and society

In the first chapter of this section, "Academic Labor as Alienated Labor: Resisting Standardized Testing," Joshua Garrison provides a theoretical rationale for why the standards movement must be resisted by educators, students, and concerned citizens. Specifically, he draws upon the work of Karl Marx, Michel Foucault, and Jacques Rancière to argue that "standardized tests constitute a form of alienation that breaks students' intellectual will and forces upon them a regimen of compulsory labor" (p. 13). He also follows Chantal Mouffe, by arguing that "student opposition to those tests is a legitimate, and necessary, form of democratic expression" (p. 13). He concludes the chapter by illustrating how student organization and activism have the power to dismantle the bipartisan support in the U.S. for "a system of assessment mechanisms that alienates students, deadens their intellectual will, and forces upon them work responsibilities that should be undertaken by professionals in social, economic, and political sectors" (p. 24).

In the second chapter of this section, "Teachers as Professionals: Owning Instructional Means and Negotiating Curricular Ends," Ted Purinton suggests that the accountability and standardization movement is narrowing the ability of progressive educators and scholars to implement subversive policies, practices, and pedagogies at all levels of education. Specifically, the author links the New Public Management (NPM) approaches to schooling, which were generated during the 1980s by neoliberal politicians and business leaders, to the forces behind progressive philosophies being unwelcomed in most educational contexts. Next, Purinton demonstrates how numerous professionals, such as educators, have witnessed an incredible erosion of their occupational powers as "neoliberal tendencies have encouraged the centralization of rewards to managers as opposed to the dispersion of rewards to a wider professional base" (p. 29). To gain power in this debilitating context, Purinton suggests that educators focus their energies on controlling the means (methods of instruction) of their work, instead of fighting a losing battle with trying to contest the ends (curriculum and exams) supported by politicians, business leaders, and many citizens. He concludes the chapter by proposing steps that need to be taken in order to stimulate movement toward a professionalized educational system that permits and encourages progressive instructional methods.

In the next chapter of this section, "Speaking Empowerment to Crisis: Unmasking Accountability through Critical Discourse," P. L. Thomas illustrates how the standards and accountability movement, which has come to dominate educational institutions at all levels, reinforces the power of corporate and political elite at the expense of educators and their students. Thomas begins the chapter by arguing that the political and corporate elite have historically concocted the false trope that schools are in crisis in order to control the education agenda. More important, the crisis trope has also blocked "critical calls for critique and reform of public schools" (p. 47) from larger public conversations. Next, the author documents how the elite have shifted their tactics for controlling life in schools. Over of the past decade, they have controlled mainstream media outlets to generate a "consistent (but false) narrative about failed schools, bad teachers, corrupt teachers' unions, and the need for U.S. schools to make the country competitive internationally" (p. 49). As a result, a group of corporate education saviors, such as Duncan, Gates, Canada, and Rhee, are considered experts who have lulled many citizens into believing, incorrectly, that schools will be improved by implementing standards and accountability measures, rather than by eliminating unjust social forces and inequalities. The author concludes his chapter by not only pointing to numerous problems associated with using standards but also by capturing how critical educators must collectively raise their opposition to "the false prophets now dominating the debate over reform" (p. 58).

In the final chapter of this section, "Teaching *through* the Test: Building Life-Changing Academic Achievement and Critical Capacity," Victor H. Diaz posits that progressive educators can "teach through the test" in order to enact a curriculum and pedagogy that fosters students' critical consciousness and encourages their participation in a democratic society, in spite of the unjust pressures, sanctions, and alienation fueled by standards and accountability measures. As a teacher educator in Phoenix, Arizona, for the past four years, the author explains how he has mentored middle and high school English/Language Arts teachers to create units of instruction that have the power to spark students and teachers' critical consciousness. The author acknowledges that his approach is not a magic bullet; rather, he reveals the "complexity of the tensions between critical pedagogy and increasingly stringent accountability measures placed on teachers and students" (p. 68). He concludes the chapter by providing a clear path for educators to promote critical pedagogy amid standards and accountability measures. He states:

We must forge a fourth path, where the goals of critical pedagogy and accountability policies are not seen as a false binary, but rather a dialectic that offers hope and casts school success as a potent weapon in our students' struggle for liberation. Teaching through the test offers an example of such a path, which is increasingly needed as the accountability noose tightens on social justice educators worldwide. (p. 82)

De-Standardizing teachers and learners

In the first chapter of this section, "Just What Is Response to Intervention and What's It Doing in a Nice Field Like Education? A Critical Race Theory Examination of Response to Intervention," Nicholas Daniel Hartlep and Antonio L. Ellis "use critical race theory as an analytical lens to examine response to intervention's (RTI) (in)ability to reduce disproportionality in special education" (p. 87). Their critical analysis illustrates that RTI has not reduced disproportionality in special education in U.S. schools. The authors also shed light on how RTI is linked to the standards and accountability movement in that it provides data for schools to meet requirements under the No Child Left Behind (NCLB) Act, rather than eliminate disproportionality of minority youth in special education. The authors conclude the essay by providing policy recommendations that they believe "can help reduce overrepresentation in special education" (p. 89).

In the second chapter of this section, "The Yoga in Schools Movement: Using Standards for Educating the Whole Child and Making Space for Teacher Self-Care," Andrea Hyde details how, paradoxically, progressive educators have the ability to use dominant discourses generated by the standards and accountability movement to take part in conversations "involving national accountability in the U.S." as well as to make the yoga in schools moment available to more and more students. The author then highlights some of the aims behind the yoga movement in order to illustrate how it offers schools a socially transgressive pedagogy. She concludes the chapter by drawing upon Palmer's concept of the "movement approach to educational reform" to suggest that the yoga movement is vital to social justice educators because it has the power to transform "the purpose and structure of institutions from within, making use of whatever resources are currently available and working within and through whatever conditions are at hand" (p. 122).

In the next chapter, "Students with Learning Disabilities Writing in an Inclusion Classroom," Patricia Jacobs and Danling Fu share their findings from a qualitative case study that examined whether Learning Disabled (LD) students were able to progress as writers in a high-stakes test environment. The study took place in a K–4 school located in an impoverished rural section of north-central Florida. Despite the pressure of having to prepare LD students for the high-stakes writing examination, the students' grade 4 teacher was able to alleviate "the stress of the test by helping the children connect writing with their life experiences, and empower(ing) them to find their own voices while learning to be skilled and competent writers" (p. 129). Specifically, the authors focus on how the teachers' pedagogical approach to writing impacted two LD students who struggled with language processing and learning. Through digital storytelling, tapping students' lived experiences, and being part of a supportive writing community, "these two students were *enabled* users of 21st-century literacies that combined print, visuals, and sound—rather than disabled learners who struggled with language and learning" (p. 137). The authors conclude by suggesting additional ways educators can alleviate the pressures of high-stakes examinations to assure success in a writing curriculum.

In the third chapter of this section, "'Standardized' Play and Creativity for Young Children? The Current Climate of Increased Standardization and Accountability in Early Childhood Classrooms," Lindsey Russo, through her personal experiences in early childhood classrooms and a review of the literature surrounding the standards and accountability movement, captures how the over-emphasis on academics in early childhood education has placed "young children...under pressure to meet inappropriate expectations, including academic standards, that until recently were reserved for older children" and upper grades (p. 142). This "academic focus" has concomitantly shunted "important pedagogical dimensions and instructional activities from the classroom, including the elimination of play." In the remaining part of the chapter, the author documents how one learning community in New York City, the Blue School, has successfully juggled "the needs of the children and families with the pressures of accountability" (p. 145). She also suggests how other early childhood programs can follow in the schools' successful footsteps:

> We need to use authentic assessment methods that are not characterized by the risks and limitations of standardized testing practices. We cannot make life-changing decisions based exclusively upon standardized tests. We must use a triangulation of methods while observing and reflecting upon the process rather than the product. This is the model being explored by Blue School's recursive model of assessment and it results in the development and implementation of curriculum and practice that fit the needs of each and every child. (p. 154)

Leveraging standards in secondary classrooms

In the first chapter of this section, "Occupying the Space for Change: The Effects of Neoliberalism in a Public School in Metro Buffalo," Shawgi Tell examines how neoliberal reform measures, such as high-stakes testing, are designed to "justify and facilitate the upward distribution of operational and financial control of schools, leaving students, teachers, administrators, parents, and community residents with less decision-making power" (p. 163). The author notes that the increasing commercial control of K–12 schools has not only positioned many teachers to drop out of the profession but has also made many of his pre-service and in-service teachers question whether it is worth entering or remaining in the profession. In light of the socially degenerative environment wrought by corporate imperatives in K–12 schools, Tell highlights how it is possible for secondary teachers to balance "the demands of high-stakes testing and accountability with a more genuine, holistic, critical, relevant, and meaningful approach to educating" students through the narratives of one experienced ESL teacher (p. 164). Tell concludes by arguing that, in addition to persevering and trying to implement humanizing methods and pedagogies, educators must work toward eliminating unjust policies and practices "through the reclaiming of education reform discourse using a human rights perspective" (p. 174).

In the second chapter of this section, "The Race to Somewhere: Experiential Education as an Argument for Not Teaching to the Test," Rosemary A. Millham provides a reflective narrative of her own teaching practices when she was an earth science teacher in a high school located in the Mid-Hudson Valley in New York State. She documents how she was able to "practice critical pedagogy and create transformative experiences for [her] students, and still have students succeed on high-stakes tests" (p. 180). The author begins by articulating what transformative learning means through the lens of three leading transformative educators. Next, she pinpoints the process of how she was able to implement critical pedagogy in her classroom. She concludes the chapter by documenting how her teaching "guided students to think, to reason, and to participate in discourse as part of a comfortable classroom community" (p. 194).

In the next chapter, "Making Writing Matter: Creating Spaces for Students in the Research Process," Katie Greene and Peggy Albers illustrate how they ground their teaching practices in critical pedagogy in order to guide students to become transformative researchers. The authors begin by explicating the importance of grounding the research process in the ideals of critical literacy. Critical literacy, when linked to the research process, helps students understand "the context of important societal issues," prepares them to read and write, and engages them in "examining and writing about their world and its assumptions about learning" (p. 199). Next, the authors illustrate how they linked professional standards to an action research project in which students addressed "social issues of importance to them and, through reading and exploring their topics via a variety of viewpoints, collaborate with one another" (p. 201). The authors conclude the by evaluating whether the project guided students to become transformative researchers, and they suggest additional ways to improve their own instructional practice.

In the fourth chapter of this section, "Traditional Language Arts Viewed through a Media Lens: Helping Secondary Students Develop Critical Literacy with Media Literacy Education," Kathy Garland and Marion (Marty) Mayer provide two examples of how professional standards can be leveraged to foster students' critical consciousness of self and their social world. One of the authors, Marty—a teacher in a rural high school in north Florida—created an honors English language arts elective called Literature in the Media. She did so to allow students to "participate when formally studying popular culture text" (p. 213). Through the students' narratives, Garland and Mayer demonstrate how the course nudged their participants to realize that to be "literate requires one to read different types of texts that may include visual images," to use "visual images to convey messages...and to see how literacy is socially and culturally constructed" (p. 221) The authors then argue that each state's Common Core Standards can provide a pathway to use the mass media to foster critical literacy.

Teacher education: Modeling critical approaches

In the first chapter in this section, "Teaching *from* the Test: Using High-Stakes Assessments to Enhance Student Learning," Julie A. Gorlewski explores "how the typically negative effects of standardization on curriculum and instruction can be used to develop critical pedagogies intended to advance student empowerment and promote social justice" (p. 227). Specifically, the author illustrates how she worked in a private/accelerated teacher education program in western New York State to foster critical pedagogies, while simultaneously preparing students to pass a high-stakes teaching certification examination. Gorlewski then highlights some of the central elements that assisted her in making "standards as something we can use *with* and *for* our students (rather than *on* or *against* them)" (p. 237). Her work preparing pre-service teachers to employ information from the New York State content examination assured both success in passing that test and in developing personal and transformative skills.

In the second chapter of this section, "Standardizing Effective Pedagogical Practices," David A. Gorlewski argues that modeling good pedagogy is probably the impost important trait "a teacher educator possesses because, within that context, a continuous examination of what we teach, how we teach, and how we assess can occur" (p. 238). The author was guided by this belief when his teacher education department went through an accreditation process three years ago. Faculty members were compelled to standardize all courses in terms of objectives, benchmarks and assessments. By outlining an array of carefully selected reading, writing, listening, and speaking activities, Gorlewski documents how he tried to model good pedagogy in this standardized environment and assuring that "the accreditation mandates to standardize course objectives and assessments did *not* result in the standardization of [his] course but, rather, were used to help students gain a deeper understanding of the content and concepts related to the objectives" (p. 240).

In the final chapter of this volume, "A Counternarrative of Subversion and Resistance: Hijacking NCATE to Promote Equity and Social Justice in a

College of Education," Lauren P. Hoffman and Brad J. Porfilio open the chapter by capturing what are some key constitutive forces "behind the marginalization of critical multicultural education educators and their ideas, beliefs, and scholarship" (p. 255). Despite the commercialized and political pressures to dismantle teacher education and remove socially generative policies, practices, and pedagogies, the authors provide a critical narrative of " how the national teacher accreditation process provided fertile ground" (p. 255) to transform a conservative and commercialized college of education. The authors conclude the chapter by highlighting how additional pressures, as well as their clinical colleagues, made it difficult for them to sustain the critical framework they instituted during the national accreditation process.

References

Au, W. (2008). *Unequal by design: High-stakes testing and the standardization of inequality*. New York: Routledge.

Carr, P. R., & Porfilio, B. J. (2011). *The Phenomenon of Obama and the agenda for education: Can hope audaciously trump neoliberalism?* Charlotte, NC: Information Age Publishing.

Council of Chief State School Officers & National Governors' Association. (2010, July 2). *Common Core State Standards Initiative*. Retrieved June 6, 2011, from Common Core State Standards: http://www.corestandards.org/assets/CCSSI_ELA%20Standards.pdf.

Garrison, M. (2009). *A measure of failure*. New York: SUNY Press.

Hursh, D. (2011). More of the same: How free market-capitalism dominates the economy and education. In P. R. Carr & B.J. Porfilio. *The Phenomenon of Obama and the agenda for education: Can hope audaciously trump neoliberalism?* (pp. 3–22). Charlotte, NC: Information Age Publishing.

Kincheloe, J. (2007). City kids—not the students you'd want to teach. In J.L. Kincheloe and K. Hayes (Eds.). *Teaching city kids: Understanding and appreciating them* (pp. 3–40). New York: Peter Lang.

Kozol, J. (2005). *The shame of the nation: The restoration of apartheid schooling in America*. New York: Three Rivers Press.

Porfilio, B. & Malott, C. (Eds.). (2008). *The destructive path of neoliberalism: An international examination of education*. Rotterdam, New York: Sense Publishers.

Saltman, K. & Gabbard, D. (Eds.). (2011). *Education as enforcement: The militarization and corporatization of schools* (2nd ed.). New York, NY: Routledge.

Toppo, J. (27, September, 2007). Kozol holds fast to "no child' protest." *USA Today*. Retrieved from: http://www.usatoday.com/news/education/2007–09–17-kozol-nochild-protest_N.htm?loc=interstitialskip.

U.S. Department of Education Institute of Education Sciences. (2011). *IES National Center for Education Statistics*. Retrieved September 10, 2011, from Fast Facts: http://nces.ed.gov/fastfacts/display.asp?id=372

SECTION 1.

Standards, Schools, and Society

2. *Academic Labor as Alienated Labor: Resisting Standardized Testing*

Joshua Garrison

In 2008, former schoolteacher turned radical educational critic John Taylor Gatto announced The Bartleby Project, an "open conspiracy" that aimed to enlist "60,000,000 American students, one by one, to peacefully refuse to take standardized tests or to participate in any preparation for these tests" (Gatto, 2008). For Gatto, the standardized test is an "ugly phenomenon" and a "weapon of social control" that that causes great "personal and social damage." Convinced that standardized tests are firmly entrenched in the American political and educational system, and that students cannot expect the testing industry to relent any time in the near future, Gatto urges students to take a revolutionary step and embark upon a movement that has only one aim: "test destruction" (Gatto, 2008).

The Bartleby Project is a heated polemical manifesto. And though well intentioned, Gatto fails to provide a theoretical rationale for his project. This essay builds upon his premise that resistance to standardized tests by students is necessary, but adds to that premise a theoretical justification not found in the Bartleby document. Drawing upon the work of Karl Marx, Michel Foucault, and Jacques Rancière, I argue that standardized tests constitute a form of alienation that breaks students' intellectual will and forces upon them a regimen of compulsory labor. And following Chantal Mouffe, I put forth the argument that student opposition to those tests is a legitimate, and necessary, form of democratic expression.

I.

The moral dimension of the Progressive Era's crusade against child labor was well summarized by the National Child Labor Committee in its "Declaration of Dependence," a statement that outlined the rights of "helpless and dependent" children everywhere:

> Childhood is endowed with certain inherent and inalienable rights, among which are freedom from toil for daily bread; the right to play and to dream; the right to the normal sleep of the night season; the right to an education, that we may have equality and opportunity for developing all that there is in us of mind and heart. (McKelway, 1918, p.)

Reformers routinely condemned industrial and agricultural interests that profited by exploiting the young. They issued protectionist injunctions that intended to save "child-nature" from the avaricious capitalist, and at the heart of their arguments lay the premise that capitalist production and childhood were mutually exclusive. Indeed, the insertion of a child into the capitalist workforce at too young an age was tantamount to stripping that person of her very childhood, and constituted for reformers a kind of social and developmental death: "Child labor means moral impairment and physical destruction and it is the duty of the state to protect the tender childhood, and not allow the young lives to be sacrificed at the altar of greedy employers, or even by selfish parents" (Seligman, 1909, p. 19). The aim, in the words of the National Child Labor Committee's chairman, was to "save child life" (Seligman, 1909, p. 19). And this was accomplished via a cultural and legislative campaign that "universalize[d] the middle class ideas of childhood as a period devoted to play and education" (Mintz, 2004, p. 184).

This rationale for the de-proletarianization of childhood was clearly articulated in the early, more humanistic writings of Karl Marx. And though the Progressive Era reformers were by no means Marxists in the formal sense, their arguments paralleled Marx's in important ways. Specifically, we find in the reformist literature a recapitulation of Marx's thesis of alienation. Obviously, the Progressive Era child savers' critique of industrial capitalism was narrower than Marx's, focused as it was on only the most vulnerable members of the workforce. Still, in order to effect a cultural shift in which children were reconceived as a protected population rather than a "useful" one (Mintz, 2004), the movement did need to level a radical critique upon the deleterious effects of capitalist production on human development. Following Marx, they argued that work under capitalism deprived the childworker of her most essential nature, that of being a free and creative human. In essence, reformers put forth the provocative claim that capitalism separated the child from childhood. And in so doing, they spoke in tones that were decidedly Marxian.

Marx's concept of alienation is developed in his *Economic and Philosophical Manuscripts* (1844). For Marx, humans are naturally productive beings—they produce objects, communities, and selves. Production is the "life activity" of the "species-being," and humans fulfill their nature when production is voluntary, free, and spontaneous. Whereas animals produce only from instinct and need, Marx's ideal human "is motivated by nothing more than the need to create, to express oneself, to give oneself external embodiment" (Schacht, 1970, p. 78). But under capitalist modes of production, the worker loses control of his productive capacities as the "means of his existence and his activity are increasingly concentrated in the hands of the capitalist" (Marx, 1844, p. 72). No longer does production lead to individual satisfaction or creative expression; instead, production no longer bears any meaningful relation to the individual whatsoever—the object of his production becomes alien to him:

> The worker puts his life into the object, and his life then belongs no longer to himself but to the object….What is embodied in the product of his labour is no longer his own….The *alienation* of the worker in his product means not only that his labour becomes an object, assumes an *external* existence, but that it exists independently, *outside himself,* and alien to him, and that it stands opposed to him as an autonomous power. The life which he has given to the object sets itself against him as an alien and hostile force (Marx, 1844, pp.122–123).

The worker's estrangement from the object produced is attended by an alienation from the labor process itself and, ultimately, he finds himself alienated from his nature as a productive being. When imposed, work becomes "miserable," unfulfilling, and to be avoided since it is "external to the worker [and] not part of his nature" (p. 124). For Marx, capitalist production constitutes a "mortification" and a "vitiation" of the human and, with the loss of control over one's own productive activity, the human-as-laborer is dehumanized and forced into a condition of oppression.

For the Progressives, the freest and most natural activity for children was play. Psychologist G. Stanley Hall, founder of the American child study movement, promoted the idea of free play during the Progressive Era and wrote extensively about play being essential to a child's well-being. For Hall, play was the child's proper productive activity and too soon an introduction to the world of work was anathema, as it deprived the young of exercising their most basic instincts and interests (Hall, 1906, pp. 68–74). The opponents of child labor, along with Marx and Hall, recognized that the working child was alienated from her own being, prevented from engaging in free and voluntary expression, and compelled to produce for the benefit of another.

The de-proletarianization of Progressive Era children was guided by an attempt to remove young people from a world in which they were alienated from their natural state of being. And the reformers' rescue plan involved the creation of protective institutions that would ensure proper development for the young and vulnerable. Compulsory schooling was intended to provide a legal and institutional guarantee that children would be temporarily blocked from exposure to the harsh realities of the capitalist order. In reality, however, mass schooling constituted a *re*-proletarianization of childhood and within schools children remained economic subjects—educational institutions delayed entry into zones of economic production, but only because they offered a greater economic promise: well-trained and prepared workers. As vocationalization came to dominate the educational establishment, the school became no less alienating than the regimen of the workplace, this despite the child labor reformers' goal to free young people from the interests of the capitalist class. This Progressive Era legacy is the one that resounds most loudly today.

Slavoj Žižek has argued recently that the idea of the proletariat needs to be expanded. Following Marx's idea that the proletarian is that being who is alienated from his own being, Žižek worries that we are all in danger of becoming proletarianized:

> What unites us is that, in contrast to the classic image of the proletariat who have "nothing to lose but their chains," we are in danger of losing *everything*: the threat is that we will be reduced to abstract subjects devoid of all substantial content, dispossessed of our symbolic substance, vegetating in a unlivable environment. The triple threat to our entire being renders us all proletarians, reduced to "substanceless subjectivity," as Marx put it. (Žižek, 2009, p. 92).[1]

A broadly conceived notion of the proletariat requires that we move beyond Marx's focus on the workplace and become open to the possibility that alienation occurs in spheres of life that are not explicitly economic. The subject of our inquiries, then, should be all of the domains in which humans "produce." If the "life-activity" of the "species-being" is productive activity, as Marx argues, then there is no reason why that need occur only in spaces of material manufacture. This move allows for the application of Marxian alienation to a number of productive zones, the school included.

Many critical educators hold that the educational process should allow people to produce knowledge and understanding in an environment that is free, voluntary, and spontaneous. Inspired by a Marxian reading of human nature, Paulo Freire held that education should be unshackled from the interests of the ruling class, that only a pedagogy based on a liberatory praxis would produce non-alienated people: "For apart from inquiry, apart from the praxis, men cannot be truly human. Knowledge emerges only through invention and re-invention, through the restless, impatient, continuing, hopeful inquiry men pursue in the world, with the world, and with each other" (Freire, 1970, p. 58). In Freirean/Marxian terms, the free student is motivated to generate knowledge and understanding by an internal desire to act as a free, producing subject; when the student becomes proletarianized, however, the motivating force for knowledge production is imposed from without, and for purposes that are not the student's own. "If [man] is related to his own activity as to unfree activity," wrote Marx, "then he is related to it as activity in the service, and under the domination, coercion and yoke, of another man" (Marx, 1844, p. 139). From this theoretical perspective, academic labor in the postmodern age is no less alienating than the industrial labor experienced by young people in the modern period. It is from this perspective that our critique of standardized testing will develop.

II.

Under capitalism, labor undergoes two radical transformations: first, the "worker works under the control of the capitalist"; second, "the product is the property of the capitalist and not that of the worker, its immediate producer" (Marx, 1867, pp. 291–292). In exchanging his labor power for a wage, the productive process is commodified; in essence, the worker sells his labor power as a commodity on the market in exchange for a wage, and in doing so, he loses ownership of his own productive capacity. The capitalist, meanwhile, "wants to produce a commodity greater in value than the sum of the values used to produce it, namely the means of production and the labour-power he purchased with his good money in the open market" (Marx, 1867, p. 293). Production is conceived, then, as a "process of creating value."

Academic labor can be thought of in much the same way. Divested of their labor power by Progressive Era reformers, young people were moved en masse to another productive domain: the school. There children engaged in a different kind of labor, although, in actuality, "school work" followed exactly the logic of wage work: students worked under control of the teacher, and their "products" became the property of the educational institution—in exchanging their academic labor for a grade, students, like workers, lost ownership of their own productive capacities. Academic and wage labor, then, are analogous and this should come as no surprise, as the modern school was envisioned as the place of incubation for future capitalist producers (Spring 1972). To clarify and elaborate on this point, however, we must move beyond Marx, turning instead to Michel Foucault.

The product of academic labor power is the completed examination, which Foucault regards as a disciplinary device that both subjugates and objectifies. Disciplinary procedures constitute techniques of power that sort individuals into hierarchies, evaluate them according to standards and norms, and turn them into analyzable units through the processes of examination and documentation. According to Foucault, under the regime of modern disciplinarity, "the school became a sort of apparatus of uninterrupted examination" (Foucaul, 1977, p. 186). The examination "is a normalizing gaze, a surveillance that makes it possible to qualify, to classify and to punish. It establishes over individuals a visibility through which one differentiates them and judges them" (p. 184). As the architecture of the modern school was transformed into "an apparatus of observation" in which the "gaze" of schoolmaster was able to see everything that occurred within the school's walls, the examination served the purpose of exposing the student's internal workings. Compelled to work under "a principle of compulsory visibility," students became objectified subjects to be seen, documented, and analyzed. Visibility assured the teacher's power over the student by investing in the former absolute evaluative power.

If production under a system of wage labor creates material objects that enhance the wealth of the capitalist, academic production produces through the examination knowledge about the student that is owned and used by the professional class of educators. In Foucault's words, the "examination enabled the teacher, while transmitting his knowledge, to transform his pupils into a whole field of knowledge" (Foucaultm, 1977, p. 186). The examination quantifies the student's abilities and transforms her into a documented case, "making it possible to classify, to form categories, to determine averages, to fix norms" (p. 190). The graded student is placed on a continuum and receives her identity, as an academic being, only after her work has been compared to, and integrated into, the whole. Placing students within hierarchies has, for Foucault, a "double effect":

> It distributed pupils according to their aptitudes and their conduct, that is, according to the use that could be made of them when they left the school; it exercised over them a constant pressure to conform to the same model, so that they might all be subjected to "subordination, docility, attention in studies and exercises, and to the correct practice of duties and all the parts of discipline." So that they might all be like one another. (p. 182)

From a Marxian perspective, then, the examination alienates on two levels. First, the result of the student's academic labor in no way relates to his own "creative powers and interests," nor is it an "expression of his personality," necessary conditions for Marx's fully authentic human (Schacht, 1970, pp. 85, 90). Second, the labor expended in the examination process is not made by an autonomous will. Consider how well our notion of academic labor conforms to Marx's comments about alienated labor: "He does not choose to make it, but rather is directed to do so. He does not even choose *how* to make it; he is compelled to suppress all individuality in the course of its production. In reality, it never is *his* product at all; he is merely the implement of its production. In a word, it is alien to him" (p. 85). The labor of students, then, not only contributes to their own oppression (a topic to be explored below), but it also is done for the sole benefit of another; the product generated by the examination (the score) belongs not to the student, nor is that product to be used for her own satisfaction or well-being. Instead, the scores are owned by various external agents—educators, politicians, business leaders—and used for purposes that are entirely alien to the student herself.

In contemporary discourse about standardized examinations, it is abundantly clear that the fruits of student testing labor are used for a variety of purposes that are external to the individual, giving credence to the claim that standardized testing constitutes a form of alienation. Indeed, standardized testing places responsibility for various educational, social, and economic reforms upon the backs of laboring students, whose performance on those tests provides politicians and educators with data that are used to make important decisions. Secretary of Education Arne Duncan, for instance, has urged schools leaders to use student testing data in their evaluation of teachers. Speaking at a National Education Conference in 2009, Duncan stated, "Data can also help identify and support teachers who are struggling. And it can help evaluate them. The problem is that some states prohibit linking student achievement and teacher effectiveness" (U.S. Department of Education, 2009). Thus, work forced on students at school is done so for purposes other than intellectual development, self-expression, the satisfaction of a curiosity, or the pursuit of an interest. Rather, student work is conducted with the other aims in mind: determining teacher merit and effectiveness (Ballard & Bates, 2008); demonstrating that states, districts, and schools are eligible for federal funding (Austin, 2005); ensuring that the United States will retain competitive footing in the "global economy" (Levin, 1998); and bridging the achievement gap between "racial majority and minority students" (Hunter & Bartee, 2003, p. 153). In one publication, *The Survival Kit for the Elementary School Principal*, administrators learn that the "purposes of standardized tests" include assessing "general school effectiveness," providing "insights into curriculum content," determining "areas of strength and need in the instructional program," measuring "individual student achievement," and making "multiyear comparisons of student achievement within a school" (Bergman, 2010, pp. 113–115).

When students test, students work. And these examinations constitute, in the Marxian sense, an alienation of the student's academic labor. And though we must examine the injustice of robbing the student of the opportunity of engaging in meaningful intellectual work, requiring instead that she labor for the benefit of educational, political, and economic establishments, it first behooves us to examine the deleterious impact that the subjugation of one's academic labor has on one's own sense of self. For, as Marx noted, alienated labor dehumanizes the individual and reduces her to a combination of animal, machine, and slave (Marx, 1844). Such is the insidious power of the examination, as Foucault so clearly illustrated.

III.

For Marx, alienation involved the twin process of "separation and surrender," an idea taken from Hegel. But unlike Hegel, Marx, along with Foucault, showed that alienation was the result of a compulsory dynamic: the separation of an individual from his productive capacity was concomitant with surrender to another person (Schach,t 1970). As Marx wrote, "Just as [the worker] creates his own production as a vitiation, a punishment, and his own product as a loss, as a product which does not belong to him, so he creates the domination of the non-producer over production and its product. As he alienates his own activity, so he bestows upon the stranger an activity which is not his own" (Marx, 1844, p. 131). Likewise, for Foucault, the examination—that disciplinary technique in which the individual is forced to produce a visible and documentable self that is compared to a set of standards or norms—results in a condition of alienated disempowerment. But Foucault further expands upon the idea of surrender found in Marx's work on alienation: not only does an individual surrender to the empowered stranger, as Marx noted; she also internalizes and reinforces a self-imposed sense of inferiority and volunteers her powerlessness to the other:

> He who is subjected to a field of visibility, and who knows it, assumes responsibility for the constraints of power; he makes them play spontaneously upon himself; he inscribes in himself the power relation in which he simultaneously plays both roles; he becomes the principle of his own subjection. (Foucault, 1977, pp. 202–203)

If Foucault's analysis is correct, then we should find among test takers a sense of educational helplessness and a feeling that intellectual work is alienating, unfree, and in conflict with the interests of one's academic being. Further, once alienation is fully inscribed, the student will no longer critically engage with the testing-based status quo. When students no longer question the belief that testing is part of the natural educational order, then academic alienation reaches its terminus.

These conclusions can be explored in greater depth by examining Jacques Rancière's text *The Ignorant Schoolmaster* (1991). Rancière elaborates upon both Marxian and Foucauldian notions of alienation and applies those ideas to the pedagogical context with greater focus than did either Marx or Foucault. In *The Ignorant Schoolmaster*, Rancière develops the idea that the institution of schooling inflicts upon students a condition of intellectual "stultification." The school exercises its power by deploying various apparatuses and mechanisms, including grades and tests, that debilitate student will, interest, and, ultimately, the very desire to exercise the intellect. If academic labor renders learning "miserable," as Marx would say, then the individual's intellectual development becomes calcified.

Rancière posits that stultification is the inevitable result of any educational enterprise that positions the "master" over the student. The problem with all pedagogies, methodologies, and evaluative practices, he argues, is that they place two intelligences in opposition to each other. On the one hand, we find the teacher or evaluator—that privileged being who is already in full possession of intelligence and answers; on the other, there is the student—lacking in knowledge, deficient in intelligence, and in need of guidance. This unequal relationship constitutes for Rancière the fundamental "myth of pedagogy": "the parable of a world divided into knowing minds and ignorant ones, ripe minds and immature ones, the capable and incapable, the intelligent and the stupid" (Rancière, 1991, p. 6).

In the universe of traditional teaching and assessment methodologies, the teacher is the "master explicator," and is responsible for determining what is to be learned, how learning occurs, and when learning has taken place; meanwhile, the assessment mechanism becomes the "sole judge" of learning. Together, the teacher, evaluative apparatus, and student are fixed upon a hierarchical scheme of power relations in which the teacher is placed in control over the student's intellectual development, while the test, in a decentered and seemingly objective fashion, renders judgment on both the student and the teacher's activities. Thus, we should add to Rancière's position that teaching is a stultified act of stultification—testing alienates both students and teachers from their productive capacities. When two intelligences are positioned in opposition to each other, as they are in the traditional educational and evaluative context, a belief in the superiority of certain minds and techniques over others is structured into the most fundamental beliefs about learning, teaching, and their institutional relationship.

For Rancière, the dominant pedagogical model rests upon the idea that children are intellectually inferior to adults. (Indeed, Rancière's philosophical program is dedicated to the premise that all minds are equally intelligent.) It is unsurprising that the child's intelligence is considered by adults to be deficient, unformed, immature, and incomplete, as these beliefs inform an entire vision of childhood that is reinforced by virtually all social, political, and cultural institutions. As Allison James and James Prout have argued, the "implicit binarism" inherent in the adult-child relationship forces young people into a subservient social position in which their ultimate educational and developmental assignment is to efface their own childishness by incorporating assimilative strategies:

> Socialization is the process which magically transforms the one into the other, the key which turns the asocial child into a social adult. The child's nature is therefore assumed to be different; for the model to work this must be the case. The child is portrayed like the laboratory rat, as being at the mercy of external stimuli: passive and conforming. Lost in a social maze it is the adult who offers direc-

tions. The child, like the rat, responds accordingly and is finally rewarded by becoming "social," by becoming adult. (James and Prout, 1997, p. 13)

While James and Prout deal expressly with childhood, Rancière argues that ours is a "society of contempt," in which every individual, not just the old and young, are positioned along various continua in which they are ranked—superiority and inferiority are the two points on a social-measuring spectrum that can be escaped by no one. "It is easier to *compare* oneself," he writes, "to establish social exchange as that swapmeet of glory and contempt where each person receives a superiority in exchange for the inferiority he confesses to" (Rancière, 1991, p. 80). This confessional is only possible after one accepts the premise of intellectual inequality that is, in Rancière's view, one of the primary lessons taught by the school, for it is there that young people most directly encounter their own intellectual inferiority. Ranked first against their teachers, then with one another, and finally in relation to all of those mass-produced data points that represent childhood as a national and global whole, the young are taught a single, simple message: intellect is structured comparatively and relationally according to external norms and standards that have no intrinsic interest or value for one's creative and spontaneous "species-being."

In the end, Rancière argues that conventional pedagogy cripples student will. Trapped in a relational world in which knowledge has no independent worth, where the exigencies of measurement take precedence over the exercise of interest, where the content of curricula is always determined from above and from without, and where assessment focuses not on growth or satisfaction but on the degree to which one approximates a given standard, we find that learning takes place in an environment that alienates the individual from her intellectual product. The consequences of this bleak picture are twofold. First, academic alienation leads naturally to a condition of anti-intellectualism and self-defeatism. As Marx noted, the "worker, therefore, feels himself at home only during his leisure time, whereas at work he feels homeless" (Marx, 1844, p. 125). If intellectual pursuits are recast as alienated labor, for which standardized testing is the best example, academics will suffer from the same fate that "work" met when it was reconstituted under capitalist production. Second, the alienated individual is easier to control and, thus, is more likely to direct his academic labor to an imposed end, one that benefits the dominant interests and not those of the student herself. As is evident from a variety of contemporary sources, including President Obama's *Blueprint for Reform* (U.S. Department of Education, 2010), the purpose of schooling in America is to promote a neoliberal agenda that privileges economics over politics, individuals over communities, competition over collaboration, and a consumer mentality over an intellectual one (Giroux, 2010). Standardized testing is one component of a system that intentionally alienates students in order to make them more governable. And developing a program of resistance to a system that produces academic and intellectual alienation should be a priority for critical scholarship.

IV.

It is curious that today's liberal establishment has embraced the educational platform espoused by American conservatives in the 1980s, a signal that Democratic politics has moved rightward over the last several decades. Barack Obama's claim that increased standards are needed to bolster the United States' position in the global economy hearkens back to *A Nation at Risk,* the famous report published during the Reagan presidency. The claim made in *A Nation at Risk* that America's "once unchallenged preeminence in commerce, industry, science, and technological innovation is being overtaken by competitors throughout the world" (NCEE, 1983) is echoed by Obama, who recycles the old trope of decline: "America was once the best educated nation in the world. A generation ago, we led all nations in college completion, but today, 10 countries have passed us" (U.S. Department of Education, 2010, p. 1). For both Obama and the 1980s conservative, the overarching concern is global economic dominance: "the countries that out-educate us today will out-compete us tomorrow," worries the president (p. 1).

Further, Obama's belief that improving student performance on standardized tests will contribute to a program of social justice, in which the achievement gap between minority and majority students will be closed, leading to a more just and equal society, was a popular conservative position in the 1980s, and one that the Left routinely rejected as too absurd to be taken seriously. The reemergence of this idea, which was articulated in E. D. Hirsch, Jr.'s book *Cultural Literacy* (1987), demonstrates that the Left's imagination and integrity have become impoverished. As Democratic politics chases the Right in its move to the conservative extreme, it can be said with confidence that there no longer remains a strong, Leftist agenda in mainstream educational politics. That there is currently no legitimate political alternative to the stranglehold that standardized tests have on American students is a point made forcefully by John Taylor Gatto, who noted that the testing industry is "immune to reform" and that the American political system has no intention of freeing students from this unnecessary burden (Gatto, 2008). In his call for "test destruction," Gatto argues that "nobody should believe that this step can be taken politically—too much money and power is involved to allow the necessary legislative action" (Gatto, 2008). But even if the impediments are great, Gatto's solution is relatively simple: standardized testing can be defeated if students just refuse to take the tests.

Pockets of resistance do seem to be developing, though Gatto's goal of enlisting America's 60,000,000 students in a mass movement remains a lofty dream. Still, there are signs of promise. In 2008, for instance, some 160 students at a Bronx middle school "pulled off a stunning boycott against standardized testing" when they refused to take a state social studies exam. Said one student, "They don't even count toward our grades. The school system's just treating us like test dummies for the companies that make the exams" (Hinckley, 2008). A more forceful statement about the alienating nature of standardized tests would be difficult to make. Other protests have occurred over the last decade, but they by no means constitute a critical mass.

Many critical theorists have applied Marx's claim that antagonism is an inherent characteristic of capitalism to the context of schooling (Allman, McLaren, & Rikowski, 2005; Giroux, 1989). Several noteworthy political philosophers, meanwhile, have argued that an antagonistic social order should be met with by an equally antagonist politics. In *The Democratic Paradox* (2000), for instance, Chantal Mouffe outlines a program of democratic praxis that allows outsiders the opportunity to challenge hegemonic power structures. Rather than embrace a conventional democratic paradigm in which conflicting parties seek unity through compromise and deliberation, Mouffe argues that unresolved conflict between adversaries is a necessary condition for a legitimate democratic politics. Her notion of an "agonistic" democracy "requires accepting that conflict and division are inherent to politics and that there is no place where reconciliation could be definitively achieved as the full actualization of the unity of 'the people'" (Mouffe, 2000, pp. 15–16).

For Mouffe, efforts to "negate the ineradicable character of antagonism and to aim at a universal rational consensus [are] the real threat to democracy" (Mouffe, 2000, p. 22). Our nation's bipartisan support of a system of assessment mechanisms that alienates students, deadens their intellectual will, and forces upon them work responsibilities that should be undertaken by professionals in social, economic, and political sectors also constitutes a threat to democracy, and it should be resisted. Coupled with Gatto's call for mass resistance, and the arguments put forth here, Mouffe's political model of adversarial resistance can and should be taken up by those students who find themselves stultified, alienated, and disempowered by the imposition of standards and norms that limit their intellectual growth and creative being. Academic labor need not remain miserable, but change will require that students activate and organize. Gatto was right: political interests are too entrenched to expect radical change. Emancipation depends upon the students themselves.

Note

1. Guy DeBord made a similar point in *The Society of the Spectacle* (New York: Zone Books, [1967] 1995). Translated by Donald Nicholson-Smith. See page 21.

References

Allman, Paula, Peter McLaren, and Glenn Rikowski. 2005. "After the Box People: The Labor-Capital Relation as Class Constitution and Its Consequences for Marxist Educational Theory and Human Resistance." In *Capitalists and Conquerors: A Critical Pedagogy against Empire*. Peter McLaren (ed.). Lanham, MD: Rowman and Littlefield.

Austin, Gina. 2005. "Leaving Federalism Behind: How the No Child Left Behind Act Usurps State's Rights." *Thomas Jefferson Law Review* 27 (Spring): 337–370.

Ballard, Kelli, and Alan Bates. 2008. "Making a Connection between Student Achievement, Teacher Accountability, and Quality Classroom Instruction." *The Qualitative Review* 13 (December): 560–580.

Bergman, Abby Barry. 2010. *The Survival Kit for the Elementary School Principal*. Thousand Oaks, CA: Corwin.

Foucault, Michel. [1977] 1991. *Discipline and Punish: The Birth of the Prison*. New York: Vintage Books. Translated by Alan Sheridan.

Freire, Paulo. [1970] 1984. *Pedagogy of the Oppressed*. New York: Continuum. Translated by Myra Bergman Ramos.

———. [1984] 1986. *The Care of the Self: The History of Sexuality, Volume III*. New York: Vintage Books. Translated by Robert Hurley.

———. 2008. *The Birth of Biopolitics: Lectures at the Collège de France, 1978–1979*. New York: Palgrave Macmillan. Translated by Graham Burchell.

Gatto, John Taylor. 2008. "The Bartleby Project." http://bartlebyproject.com/gatto.html. Accessed January 23, 2011.

Giroux, Henry A. 1989. "Schooling as a Form of Cultural Politics: Toward a Pedagogy of and for Difference." In *Critical Pedagogy, the State, and Cultural Struggle*. Henry A. Giroux and Peter McLaren (eds.). Albany, NY: State University of New York Press.

Giroux, Henry A. 2010. *Youth in a Suspect Society: Democracy or Disposability?* New York: Palgrave Macmillan

Hall, G. Stanley. [1906] 2006. *Youth: Its Education, Regimen, and Hygiene*. Middlesex, UK: The Echo Library.

Hinckley, David. 2008. "Bronx 8th-graders Boycott Practice Exam but Teacher May Get Ax." *New York Daily News*. May 21. http://articles.nydailynews.com/2008–05–21/local/17898868_1_practice-exam-standardized-testing-blank-exams. Accessed March 15, 2011.

Hirsch, E.D., Jr. 1987. *Cultural Literacy: What Every American Needs To Know*. New York: Houghton Mifflin.

Hunter, Richard C., and RoSusan Bartee. 2003. "The Achievement Gap: Issues of Competition, Class, and Race." *Education and Urban Society* 35 (February): 151–160.

James, Allison, and Alan Prout. 1997. "A New Paradigm for the Sociology of Childhood? Provenance, Promise and Problems." In *Constructing and Reconstructing Childhood*. Allison James and Alan Prout (eds.). Bristol, PA: Taylor & Francis: 7–32.

Levin, Harvey. 1998. "Educational Performance Standards and the Economy." *Educational Researcher* 27 (May): 4–10.

Marx, Karl. [1844] 1963. *Economic and Philosophical Manuscripts: First Manuscript*. In *Karl Marx: Early Writings*. T.B. Bottomore (ed.). London: C.A. Watts & Co. Ltd.

———. [1867] 1990. *Capital: A Critique of Political Economy, Volume I*. London: Penguin Books. Translated by Ben Fowkes.

McKelway, A.J. 1918. "Declaration of Dependence by the Children of America in Mines and Factories and Workshops Assembled." *The Child Labor Bulletin 7*.

Mintz, Steven. 2004. *Huck's Raft: A History of American Childhood*. Cambridge, MA: Harvard University Press.

Mouffe, Chantal. 2000. *The Democratic Paradox*. London: Verso.

The National Commission on Excellence in Education. 1983. *A Nation at Risk: The Imperative for Educational Reform*. Washington, D.C.: U.S. Government Printing Office. http://reagan.procon.org/sourcefiles/a-nation-at-risk-reagan-april-1983.pdf

Rancière, Jacques. 1991. *The Ignorant Schoolmaster: Five Lessons in Intellectual Emancipation*. Stanford, CA: Stanford University Press. Translated by Kristin Ross.

———. 1999. *Disagreement: Politics and Philosophy*. Minneapolis, MN: University of Minnesota Press. Translated by Julie Rose.

Schacht, Richard. 1970. *Alienation*. Garden City, NY: Doubleday & Company.

Seligman, Issac N. 1909. "Duty of a Rich Nation to Take Car of Her Children." In *The Child Workers of the Nation: Proceedings of the Fifth Annual Conference on Child Labor, Chicago, Ill. January 21–23*.

Spring, Joel. 1972. *Education and the Rise of the Corporate State*. Boston: Beacon Press.

U.S. Department of Education. 2009. "Secretary Arne Duncan Speaks at NEA Conference, Invites Comments About Test Scores and Teacher Evaluations." http://www.ed.gov/blog/2009/07/secretary-arne-duncan-speaks-at-nea-conference-invites-comm/. Accessed February 15, 2011.

———. 2010. *A Blueprint for Reform: The Reauthorization of the Elementary and Secondary Education Act*. Alexandria, VA: Educational Publications Center. http://www2.edgov/policy/elsec/leg/blueprint.pdf

Žižek, Slavoj. 2009. *First as Tragedy, Then as Farce*. London: Verso.

3. *Teachers as Professionals: Owning Instructional Means and Negotiating Curricular Ends*

TED PURINTON

Progressive educators face increasingly hostile political and organizational environments. Their visions of enacting critically focused, emancipatory curricula are steamrolled by the incentives that teachers are increasingly given to the punishments—such as closure or principal reassignment—that schools increasingly endure. Clearly, in a political sense, progressive educators are on the losing side of a battle, one which David Labaree (2004) suggests has been stacked against them for most of the 20th century. Indeed, the struggle for political influence is likely to become more intense as citizens are increasingly informed about the wastefulness of government schools, the selfishness of teacher unions, the harm of social justice curricula, and the impracticality of education theorists.

From a socio-political perspective, however, specific organizational and inter-organizational tools provide the possibility of resurrecting a movement that has at its core the social justice and emancipatory values that progressive educators hold dear. In particular, a socio-political perspective, which provides a lens on the ways in which the political sphere reflects a society's values, can help us to determine the role of the educator within society. With that role defined, how the educator is structured in relationship to society will determine the extent to which the values of progressive educators can be fulfilled. In this chapter, I begin by briefly outlining the primary types of organizational and inter-organizational arrangements available to educators, schools, the public, for-profit companies, and politicians for the purpose of defining the educator's role in society. Then, I turn directly to the main purpose of this chapter, which is to identify a key strategy that progressive educators can use to assert their vision into the discussions about the future of public primary and secondary schooling. I do not intend to promote a subversive backlash against educational standardization, as an outright rejection of standardization today is both untenable and perhaps strategically unhelpful. As Lagemann (1989) famously has said, "One cannot understand the history of education in the United States during the twentieth century unless one realizes that Edward L. Thorndike won and John Dewey lost" (p. 185). Indeed, after decades of fighting neoliberal reforms in education, progressives are no closer to their cause, universally. Instead, I propose that progressive educators must work directly within political systems to demonstrate the values of their philosophies, while compromising where necessary in order to move education away from its present parochial and polarized state.

Methods of occupational organizing

Educators who serve in government primary and secondary schools—funded by taxpayers, many of whom do not directly benefit from free enrollment—are subservient to wider political systems. Because educators work in organizations (specifically, schools), they are provided three occupational-organizational options, each one defining the extent to which they enjoy control over the means of their work: bureaucratic, New Public Management (NPM), and professional (Gruening, 2001). Generally, bureaucracy attempts to assess compliance; NPM (modeled on markets) attempts to assess outcomes; professionalism attempts to assess practice (though with an eye toward outcomes).

Until fairly recently, modern school systems have operated mostly as loose bureaucracies: local boards, state organizations, or national systems translate local voter intent into school action; full enactment of political intent is usually muted by resulting bureaucracies. Max Weber (1962) argued that bureaucracies were essential elements of governance within democratic systems because politicians are unable and ill-equipped to carry out recurring tasks, even ones specifically mandated by voters. Thus, the bureaucracy is a common approach to policy implementation. Because schools meet multiple societal purposes, organizational theorists often say that bureaucratic structures are indeed ideal, as outcomes are obviously contested within political environments and the means to reach them are often technically vague (Ouchi, 1980). Because all bureaucracies are shaped not only by policy but by the interpretations of "street-level" workers (Lipsky, 1980), progressive educators were, for quite a while, able to inch their values forward, though usually in a relatively underground fashion: the very popularity of books such as Postman and Weingartner's (1971) *Teaching as a Subversive Activity* or networks such as the North Dakota Study Group is a testament to the values of large groups of educators who were never able to widely scale up their methods as politically desirable practices.

Since the 1980s, educational systems, particularly in the U.S., Canada, and the UK, have moved steadily toward NPM approaches, as seen through accountability mechanisms (Fusarelli & Johnson, 2004). NPM seeks to install quasi-market systems on public bureaucracies to ensure that certain outcomes are met. In some arenas, the outcomes are negotiated; in education, however, outcomes have been essentially determined by parties operating outside the schools, such as textbook and testing firms (e.g., the College Board had a major role in developing the U.S. Common Core Standards). In attempting to insert elements of NPM to the already-bureaucratically organized school systems, countries have sought to encourage competition as a way to promote efficiency and increase quality. Reformers assert that market-like features might counteract the rigidness of bureaucratic structures (Leicht, Walter, Sainsaulieu, & Davies, 2009). When progressive educators protest recent educational reforms that prevent them from applying their educational philosophies, those reforms can be said to be a part of the larger NPM framework. Indeed, because NPM demands strict performance on narrow measures and seeks to align all other processes with those measures, including worker compensation, it would appear that progressive philosophies are unwelcome.

Professionalism, as evidenced in such occupations as law, engineering, medicine, and academia, is a negotiated contract (informal from a cultural sense; formal by way of state oversight of certification and practice) whereby the means of production remain the property of the professional while the outcomes belong to society, politics, or the marketplace (Freidson, 2001). For instance, society (and the marketplace) would have little use for the medical profession if it did not deliver expected results. From a Marxian viewpoint, the knowledge and skill of a professional are the "capital" by which the profession maintains its legitimacy with the public, and thereby the right to control, through state oversight, the terms of its own work (Abbott, 1988). And in cases where the public or the marketplace acknowledges the need for a specialized skill—particularly a skill that is not easy for average citizens to grasp—additional monetary or status rewards are granted to the professionals (Freidson, 2001). Indeed, professionals in the last few decades have witnessed an incredible erosion of their occupational powers to both corporations and politicians as neoliberal tendencies have encouraged the centralization of rewards to managers as opposed to the dispersion of rewards to a wider professional base (Braverman, 1974; Leicht & Lyman, 2006). When such deskilling occurs, in both highly trained professionalized fields and trade-based craft fields, unions form as a political response to lowered wages and working conditions (Larson, 1980). Physicians have, for instance, debated unionization off and on for a couple decades. On one hand, it creates solidarity of labor against undesirable management decisions; yet, on the other hand, it sends a message of defeat of cost efficiency over specialized skill (e.g., Aton & Connolly, 2001). Nonetheless, the call for unionization increases within fields that once were secure by virtue of those specialized skills either because the skill is less valued or because it can be performed by a technology or a cheaper alternative occupation (e.g., nurse practitioners who can write prescriptions have taken some business away from traditional physicians). Thus, an autonomous profession proves its worth to society—within markets or political systems—as a result of the perceived value of its trademark skill, developed through intense training. De-skilling, then, is the natural consequence of neoliberalism, which seeks occupational deregulation in favor of flexible employment. A profession controls employment through training, credentialing, and performance monitoring and then obtains certification granting rights from the state. Flexible employment markets allow for quicker induction into a field, as well as simpler firing by managers and fewer certification constraints from the state.

Before turning to specific strategies for instituting progressive values through K–12 educator professionalism—especially in light of the current neoliberal context—it is important to understand why they previously failed to obtain occupational autonomy: First, most obviously, teaching rarely is perceived as highly skilled work. Second, educational researchers have not developed fail-proof research-based solutions to educational problems—or at least they have not been able to communicate effective solutions to practitioners and politicians. Third, even if there were research-based solutions, educators, parents, and citizens have forced conflicting demands on schools, causing schools to pursue idiosyncratic goals. The move toward NPM partially acknowledges the specialized skill in teaching in that it seeks (though usually only in theory, not as much in practice) organizational autonomy in exchange for accountability; however, it also upholds the view that teachers need carrots and sticks to carry out specific, culturally inspired wishes.

Both NPM- and professionally-oriented organizations demand specific work outcomes, and both are afforded some level of autonomy in their pursuit of those outcomes; in other words, both provide leeway on the means as long as the anticipated ends are achieved. The primary difference, however, is in the ways the work processes are judged and the performances documented. Market-oriented organizations must respond quickly to customer influence; yet customer influence can be problematic, so such organizations are accustomed to risk. A simple example comes from American automobile makers: For a few decades, car sizes kept increasing, as petrol prices remained relatively stable. When prices in 2008 spiked, American companies found it rather difficult to continue selling the large trucks that had sustained them in the previous years, and—as quickly as they could re-tool—they met new customer demands with smaller cars. Professionally oriented organizations operate with greater stability in that their work and performance rewards are centered on associationally accepted methods. They do not turn on a dime, like automobile companies, to meet customer demands, because ultimately—and loyal customers of established professionally oriented organizations, such as hospitals, law firms, and universities, generally know and accept this—their performance is predicated on the knowledge and skills embodied in the professionals that these organizations hire. Rapidly accommodating a trend or a customer interest, while possibly paying short-term dividends, may quickly result in long-term negative consequences. Autonomy in professionalized systems, thus, supports mechanisms that allow for internal work processes to be judged only by fellow trained professionals. For example, in the field of academia, peer review of research or academically governed curricular processes, while less efficient than what a for-profit university might support by employing few or no tenure-track professors, preserves the association-sanctioned work of academia. Of course, it must be noted that even non-profit universities that once supported a strong academic profession have been affected by NPM values, demonstrated by markedly fewer tenure-track professors being hired, as well as by the greater number of institutional rewards going to professors whose research generates larger amounts of money.

Turning back to K–12 education, in NPM-oriented systems, progressive educators feel the pinch of time and the strict demands of testing; by contrast, if K–12 educators worked in a professionalized system, outcomes would still be important (perhaps similar to outcomes expected in an NPM-oriented system), but they would be negotiated within the realities and constraints that well-trained educators can meet, while the means would be left entirely in the hands of those educators. This arrangement would permit progressive educators to craft systems that unite a skills-based curriculum with social justice, progressive, child-centered instructional approaches. Yet, as in the cases of medicine and academia, cost tends to be a greater concern to politicians and corporations. Thus, as we have noticed over the last decade in the U.S. in regard to the results of No Child Left Behind, test-based accountability (the instrument of NPM in education), while perhaps cheaper than a professionalized system, has not improved outcomes to any expected level (Lee, 2008a; Price, 2010).

Acknowledging that NPM and neoliberalism are still massive forces in the developed world, continuing to impact educational institutions, the balance of this chapter proposes steps that would need to be taken in order to stimulate movement toward a professionalized educational system that permits—and possibly encourages—progressive instructional methods. Though the effort is not a short-term endeavor, a professionalized system would foster better research that would in turn become the skill base of educators, offering them greater opportunities for autonomous work processes. In fostering such a system, progressive educators need to mobilize on issues of practice more than on issues of politics (Ball & Forzani, 2009). Teaching practice must be seen, both within and outside the profession, as the safeguard of autonomy from political or corporate interests. Indeed, progressive educators have few other options if they wish to make their values relevant to larger and more diverse populations.

Distinguishing curriculum from instruction methods

Elsewhere, I have argued that the quality and use of practitioner-focused evidence and theory are essential factors in establishing educational professionalization (Purinton, 2010, 2011); research is most often utilized in education for political, organizational, and market-based purposes, not for practitioner purposes—mainly because there has not been a market for thorough practitioner-based evidence. My argument in this chapter, however, is that educators sabotage their opportunity to take greater control over their work because they have continually sought control over curriculum, not instructional methods. This is most evident among the far right and far left: Curriculum, politically, is assumed to be a vehicle for the transmission of values, occasionally at the expense of labor-related skill building. In sum, the widespread direct promotion of progressive, emancipatory, social justice education as curriculum—rather than instructional method—will continue to alienate progressive educators from politics and markets, essentially because it is the curriculum that is the publicly acknowledged outcome for which taxpayers fund.

Therefore, what is needed is a route by which progressive educators can permit the political system to continue pushing for standardized outcomes—though perhaps negotiated—while still employing classroom strategies that empower students and give them critical tools to analyze and interpret the world. If curriculum is a politically compromised feature of the school system, instruction should be the province of professional educators. Indeed, professional jurisdictional theory (Abbott, 1988) suggests that competing occupations or interests will seek to overtake the methods by which certain societal problems are solved. Clearly, non-school organizations, such as textbook companies, have co-opted methods by which education is delivered in developed and developing countries alike by designing and marketing scripted materials. By ensuring, instead, that progressive philosophies are utilized as *instructional methods*, rather than as curriculum, standards can be met, taxpayers can be assured, and educators can gain greater recognition for their indispensable skills. If the professional has full responsibility for the means of the work, then the organization, the politician, or the voter can judge the outcome and then choose whether or not to further support the profession. In other words, the profession must first determine what the public wants; second, tell the public what it can provide (or negotiate with the public on what it can and perhaps should have); and third, deliver. If the public either does not want what the profession provides, then skill and knowledge development provided in K–12 settings will either continue to be further de-skilled or outsourced to alternative models or occupations (see Christensen, Johnson, & Horn, 2008, for a plausible prediction of how technology may begin to appeal to cost-conscious politicians—larger classes, fewer certified teachers, more technology, and more low-paid classroom assistants). So, it is therefore incumbent upon the profession to provide the public what it wants and, in education, the negotiating point should be the curriculum.

Curriculum has been defined in many ways, from macro-level goals to textbooks and lesson sequences. In distinguishing curriculum from instruction, Laska (1984) identifies seven components to the instructional process: (1) source of instruction, e.g., teacher or book; (2) instructional or curricular goal; (3) instructional method, broadly conceived, e.g., presenting new material, self-discovery, reinforcement; (4) curricular content, e.g., material employed as instructional method to help meet instructional or curricular goal; (5) instructional approach, which is defined as the delivery system; (6) student characteristics; and (7) instructional context. In this sense, macro-level curriculum is the instructional or curricular goal, while micro-level curriculum is the curricular content or the materials through which the goals are reached.

By comparative advantage, micro-level curricular goals should ideally be made—given student characteristics and instructional contexts—as close to the classroom as possible. That they are occasionally made at the school level is a testament to productive norms of collaboration, usually benefiting teachers by way of planning efficiencies and principals by way of oversight. That they are quite often made at the district/regional/national level or integrated into textbook packages or mandated programs is the result of three efficiencies: First, textbooks—particularly in more advanced educational systems—are used as supplement for learning that is managed by teachers (Heyneman, 1997). In theory, they serve to reduce the time teachers must devote to culling materials on their own, something they presumably *could* do on their own if they had the time and resources (Purinton, 2011); for instance, a textbook that lasts five to seven years may be less expensive than a similar number of photocopies reproduced each year. Second, management of classroom practice within and across schools is presumed to be more efficient if the material items are similar. Third, political accountability appears more straightforward if stakeholders either know about or can have a say in the selection of the materials used to presumably guide or focus instruction.

Aside from the first efficiency, there is little reason to believe that micro-level curriculum is best determined far from the classroom: attending to issues of academic engagement, culturally relevant pedagogy, or appropriate scaffolding by selecting the right materials to enhance learning (for instance, specific textual sources, video sources, novels, websites, or audio sources) is an essentially relational aspect of the instructional process. Thus, inter-school collaboration (as well as common assessments, common text selections, and so forth—e.g., when a secondary school English department jointly makes a decision to purchase a set of a specific novel) can provide teachers with technical support on instructional practice. Yet, that support is close to the classroom and involves the effort and input of the teacher. Alternatively, a mathematics teacher may work within the constraints of the available or chosen textbooks for the mere purpose of expediency in providing students with practice opportunities and textual explanations. Explanations, however, can and likely should be supplemented with other multisensory materials, all additional elements of the micro-level curriculum.

With this sort of view of the micro-curriculum, we come to a specific understanding of the macro-curriculum: the anticipated or expected outcomes—the knowledge and skills displayed by students—as a result of a sustained program of instruction. Two examples may be helpful: A university's liberal arts curriculum on a macro-level is the assumed skills and knowledge that its students should have upon graduation, usually organized by requirements in physical science, written communication, visual arts, and so forth. The layer of curriculum below those requirements—the specific classes taken—is often determined by individual students. Yet, the macro-level curricular requirements are assumed to yield "well-rounded" individuals (though this may not actually occur; see Arum & Roksa, 2011). A more relevant way to conceive of this is by comparing a particular standard to a way in which it is operationalized in the classroom. The following are two entries from the 9th–10th grade Language Arts Common Core Standards from the U.S. Council of Chief State School Officers (CCSSO):

> RI.9–10.1. Cite strong and thorough textual evidence to support analysis of what the text says explicitly as well as inferences drawn from the text.

> RI.9–10.9. Analyze seminal U.S. documents of historical and literary significance (e.g., Washington's Farewell Address, the Gettysburg Address, Roosevelt's Four Freedoms speech, King's "Letter from Birmingham Jail"), including how they address related themes and concepts.

With a mobile population, such age-level standards may actually be quite appropriate to maintain continuity of learning between schools within a system, such as a state or country. Additionally, they codify expected outcomes in a way that is transparent to outsiders and instructive to insiders. Where they are inappropriate, however, is in their lack of developmental sensitivity, which will be discussed below. Yet in analyzing these two standards above, we see one skill-level macro-curricular standard that is material-neutral and one that provides material direction. The former is skill based; the latter is canon based. Both could serve simplistic ends (particularly with the aid of poorly designed tests) if teaching methods consider the former as a discrete skill and the latter as canonical knowledge. They could, conversely, serve progressive ends if teaching methods consider, for instance, the former as academic discourse community skill and the latter for critical-historical purposes. The difference to the public is subtle; but, to a progressive educator, it is critical.

The development of the Common Core Standards (National Governors Association, 2009) provides a good example of how curricular outcome expectations may be out of line with reality: A review of the development team members reveals that while some educators were represented—particularly in the feedback teams—non-educators were greatly over-represented, especially during early phases of development. A common complaint from American educators is that standards at particular grade levels may not be appropriate to students' abilities. While there are very simple ways around this that schools and teachers can employ, such as targeted tutoring (Shanahan, 1998; Wasik & Slavin, 1993), what is more problematic is the lack of educator input. In the medical field, for instance, policy makers, hospital administrators, patients, and insurance providers might all prefer flawless cures for certain diseases, but trained physicians provide a check on appropriate expectations; indeed, in return for their expertise, they place significant burden on patients for their role in the healing process (Cohen, 2005).

It is this disconnect that has muddied the waters of curriculum, standards, outcomes, and instructional practice. If the public assumes that careful monitoring of the curriculum either through materials, standards, tests, or incentives is sufficient to yield specific outcomes, and conversely, if educators assume that the curriculum, embodied in materials, standards, and tests, constrains their ability to apply expert or progressive practice in their classrooms, then the understood problems and available solutions are clearly not aligned. To help clear this up, I offer a set of boundaries around definitions and roles regarding curriculum (macro) and instruction (which, for purposes of the following discussion, will also include the micro-curriculum, as well as actual instructional methods, which will include all efforts that a teacher employs to design an inviting, caring, supportive, and challenging classroom environment). I also attempt to align these boundaries to three specific areas: (1) the now two-decade-old conception of systemic reform (O'Day & Smith, 1993) that has provided conceptual guidance behind the NPM approaches; (2) the tenets of professional jurisdiction that shape levels of autonomy over work; and (3) the conceptions of academic engagement and culturally relevant pedagogy consistent with progressive, political, and/or constructivist views of education. The aim in this analysis is not to devise a way to undermine public input into the educational process; rather, it is to find room for public input and political accountability (which may very well be unsuitable to progressive educators) alongside progressive methods of teaching by defining curriculum and instruction, on the one hand, and determining roles, on the other.

New public management versus professionalism

In the United States, the idea behind systemic reform, proposed in various ways in the early 1990s, was that schools as links on bureaucratic chains were unresponsive to achievement gaps, as well as new knowledge regarding teaching and learning. Instead of blaming only teachers or schools, all stakeholders involved were encouraged to step up: education colleges, researchers, school board members, politicians, parents, and test and textbook publishers. Schools were to be given the freedom from bureaucratic constraints but were, in turn, expected to produce certain results. O'Day and Smith (1993) indicated that this arrangement was a step toward professionalism in education, as it provided the space for schools to innovate or to deviate from prior practices—so long as standards were met. This sentiment made its way, ultimately, to No Child Left Behind. Thus, given the troubling record of this law's performance (Lee, 2008b), a critique of systemic reform is warranted. While the plan demanded that all parties improve quality, accountability methods primarily targeted schools; in fact, there was no conceptual linkage between other institutions' responsibilities and the accountability systems ultimately designed for schools. Consequently, tests were poorly designed, education colleges refrained from reform, and politics remained tied to parochial notions of schooling. Additionally, the idea that systemic reform increased professionalism was proffered, as schools were supposed to function as autonomous organizations. However, either schools were unable to break free from the bureaucracies of states and districts or they were ill-equipped to carry out functions that previously were housed in centralized offices. The very insinuation of professionalism, in fact, is misleading, as organizations are never thought to be professional, themselves—only the people within them. No profession-building apparatus resulted from systemic reform, and by many accounts—two decades later—educator professionalism seems much more elusive.

Additionally, the reformers refused to understand fully the extent to which various stakeholders still demanded their own visions of schooling. In theory, competition crafted from school choice would encourage greater school-level autonomy and parental "shopping," yet parents were not always interested in the outcomes by which schools were judged, and states, the federal government, local businesses, and taxpayers all expressed some level of stake in the educational system, as well, resulting in additional expectations.

So it is worth asking what the public, generally speaking, desires from publicly funded education. And whether educators could reliably provide that without constant fear of criticism. And, ultimately, can the values of progressive educators ever be in line with populations that generally are more conservative? The answer to the first question is complicated, yet a general direction seems quite plausible. Despite some parochial notions of education (e.g., religious values, athletics, patriotism), education in most advanced countries has focused on collective economic growth, individual economic opportunity, and citizenship development (e.g., Bushaw & Lopez, 2010). With this general goal, let us, for just a moment, assume that academic standards (i.e., subject-specific classifications of learning goals, organized by disciplinary features and developed in light of any range between work and college readiness) either provide or have the potential to provide macro-curricular guidance. I claim that the answers to the second and third questions above are resoundingly yes: progressive educators can, if various preconditions are met, implement their practices, safe from political or family interference, and still meet political goals for economic outcomes of education. To illustrate the road map, I utilize as an example higher education and the debates about academic freedom.

Educational professionalism and progressive values

Though a thorough argument about why most progressive values of education are complementary to the standards movement is beyond the scope of this chapter, a brief delineation on progressive education is still necessary. Drawing upon Dewey and a variety of other sources, Kohn (2008) summarizes progressive education as comprising the following:

attention to the whole child

community

collaboration

social justice

intrinsic motivation

deep understanding

active learning

taking kids seriously

Kohn cautions that the caricature of progressive education as being too easy—or conversely, of traditional education as being too challenging—is misleading. Fundamentally, progressive education is attuned to good pedagogy that simultaneously challenges and motivates students to learn in ways that are natural reflections of ideal social relations (Cohen, 1998). A focus on social justice is not so much a deviation from academic learning as much as it is a deliberate concentration on diversity and social care through classroom norms; indeed, as Banks (2004) argues, social justice education prepares children to participate responsibly in diverse environments; though, in practice, progressive methods have never been widely used (Hayes, 2006), I argue that the academic standards movements, and the corresponding accountability movements, are either agnostic in regard to progressive philosophies or unintentionally supportive of them. Indeed, many educators have casually noted that despite the draconian nature of No Child Left Behind in the United States, more attention has been paid to the achievement gaps as a result. Considering that educators are more likely to view social justice curriculum as oppositional to standards, a re-framing of the concept of curriculum, as discussed in an earlier section of this chapter, provides us with a means-ends model to achieve both value systems, not one or the other. And ultimately, the way progressive education is sold to the public is problematic: How supporters talk about it internally only provides more skepticism of it externally. Perhaps the public is skeptical of certain methodologies because it does not understand how goals, even ones that they, themselves, may have, are achieved. For instance, if the public desires "21st-century skills" but then also eschews certain proven yet seemingly progressive reading and mathematical teaching strategies, communication failure may be to blame. After all, other professionals are fairly clear with the public what the methods they use can do and cannot do—and they are willing to educate the public to earn the trust and respect necessary to utilize those skills.

The established profession of academia (though, like teaching, academia is also experiencing an erosion of public support) provides a useful analogy: Given the societal and individual benefits accrued from college education, concerns about the process, until very recently, have been limited to rather extremist ideologues. Even quite conservative individuals have tended in the past to overlook what are thought to be the liberal tendencies of universities, mainly because universities have for so long provided a service assumed to be highly valuable to society and to individuals, and because universities tend to temper political polarization with mainstream values when necessary. My claim that universities are left alone to do their work is, of course, slightly problematic in that (a) many publicly funded universities are increasingly having to cope with less support and (b) the courts and the newspapers are filled with cases of contentions about academic freedom. But compared to other social institutions in developed countries, universities—and especially the professors that fill them—still obtain significant leeway to fulfill what society and individual tuition payers expect from them. If that means that a stronger bias toward politically liberal views is present, well then, the public for the most part has been okay with that, as the profession of academia seemingly has contributed widely to many of the economic and social benefits experienced in advanced nations. This arrangement makes academia a quintessentially professional occupation: the ends are negotiated and lean toward societal or tuition-payer expectations (i.e., universities give the public what it wants), but the means are controlled by the professionals, mediated by professional peer review, and deemed socially inappropriate for average citizens to perform on their own (e.g., universities like to show off the percentage of faculty with terminal degrees). That fewer tenure-track professors are hired (and conversely, that more adjunct professors are employed) is just one signal that though the profession may still have some clout within non-profit institutions of higher education, it is considered to be costlier to society than the benefit society receives in return.[1]

The debates over academic freedom serve as an ideal analogy to the curriculum-instruction division proposed for a professional system of teaching. Rights to academic freedom, though occasionally used as defense in individual cases of errant judgment, are provided to academics for the sheltering of their professional means of work. Legal rights to academic freedom become hazy by how they are lumped together with the general nature of free expression (Schauer, 2006). Yet, organizationally, the modern university is structured in such a way as to protect academics from criticism over the means of their work so that they can, ultimately, produce the expected ends. And actually, rather than a legal qualification, academic freedom is an organizational arrangement that seeks to encourage better outcomes. The various arguments for academic freedom, including intellectual truth searching, democratic exchange of ideas, and autonomous action, define the means of academic work—in other words, the anticipated outcomes cannot be achieved any other way (Andreescu, 2009; Tierney & Lechuga, 2008). But again it is the professionalized organizational form, not any legal right, that maintains the social defense against market or bureaucratic takeover of university-based academic operations (Krause, 1996). And for the most part, despite moderately weak protections in some European countries and high-profile incidents in the United States, academics are still accorded with academic freedoms, as the products of academia (knowledge, degrees, patents) are still in strong demand (Karran, 2007; Tierney & Lechuga, 2008). As Cole (2009) has argued, the professionalized academic model has been so thoroughly institutionalized in modern culture that we barely notice how important it is to a developed country's way of life. Nonetheless, because it is centered on an organizational form, not a legal right, the forces of NPM have already eroded its impact: universities, as organizations, have made decisions that prioritize cost effectiveness (hiring more adjunct professors than tenure-track professors) over the outcomes that we have come to expect from universities.

To consider academic freedom as a process tool that allows desired production of knowledge and knowledge dissemination is to explicitly define the distinctions between ends and means. While a great many conservative U.S. citizens, for instance, disapprove of certain lines of research or even broad academic subjects, they have still enjoyed the advancements cultivated from university research, and they often send their children to universities to obtain degrees and credentials. Despite shrinking numbers of tenure-track faculty, highly ranked universities continue to hire into tenure tracks, as doing so increases reputation. In sum, given all the recent pressures on universities, academics are much more autonomous in their work than are primary and secondary school teachers, mainly because the outcomes of higher education enjoy greater respect than do K–12 schools.

Yet, higher education has recently faced major criticisms: the costs to society (through loans) and families (through tuition) are increasingly assumed to be too great for the return; assessments demonstrate little student learning (Arum & Roksa, 2011); and jobs may not even be available for many college students on the other side of graduation. Some political solutions, naturally, have focused on New Public Management/quasi-market models that increase the amount of testing and overly simplistic outcome-based measures. Indeed, academic freedom has been blamed (see Nelson, 2010). Yet to listen to the criticisms about academic freedom from outside higher education is to recognize that the public, as well as specific clients of higher education, is marked by confusion about the role of academic freedom, particularly when caricature-like stories of seemingly silly research projects or courses are highlighted. Under this view, if higher education is facing a challenge to academic professionalism, then the academic professionals have not communicated with and built trust among the public and their specific clients enough so that all parties understand the values of academic freedom—or in other words, so that all parties regain trust that the means of the work of academic professionals will help society and individuals attain expected ends.

What would it take for progressive primary and secondary educators to obtain autonomy over their work so that their philosophies might be incorporated into the regular process of schooling? Given the above discussion, educators must better conceptualize the differences between instructional methods (and micro-curriculum) and broader curricular goals. This is an essential step to a political platform that would divvy up responsibilities to appropriate stakeholders. In higher education, academic freedom is assumed to provide the organizational structure by which academics can expertly perform their work so that society ultimately benefits, by way of new knowledge and an educated workforce and citizenry. By not maintaining dialogue with the public on the value of academic freedom, the public has begun to feel that higher education is irrelevant to many of its societal goals. In the same way, K–12 educators—by not building consistency within their practice across classrooms, districts, states, and regions—have bolstered the view that the value of a skilled, certified, and well-compensated educator with autonomy over practice is unnecessary to achieve certain goals. Thus, educators must dialogue about curricular ends at the same time that they seek to encourage autonomy (and consistency) over the means of instruction.

A few words about the negotiation of curricular ends: progressive educators undermine their own democratic cause when they seek to co-opt broad curricular goals; negotiation is crucial in the development of trust. Educators must amass and utilize evidence—in ways the public demands it—to demonstrate the value of certain instructional methodologies. In particular, educators must learn to speak the language of politics; to refrain will only serve to marginalize them further. Perhaps this is also a central downfall to the profession of academics: If the public perceives that academic freedom is an end in itself (e.g., when legal rights are invoked), not enough negotiation over what sort of knowledge creation and dissemination society wants has occurred.

Educators must also attend to the politics of educational economics. Whether the issue is unions, pensions, teacher performance pay, or educator certification, teachers cannot ignore that their current forms of occupational organizing are harming their collective ability to sell a skill that demands autonomy. Central to this is initial training, professional development, and performance monitoring. Central to these mechanisms is a common framework—a set of principles about instruction (and its relationship to politically mediated broad curricular goals) that is accepted and practiced by members within the profession. Thus, likely the most challenging message of this chapter is this: Progressive values will continue to be underground and ultimately irrelevant to most of the world's children and adolescents if progressive educators do not aim for *entire systems* within and across countries. Of course, educators must temper their personal aspirations (e.g., higher pay, greater respect) with their professional aspirations (e.g., a focus on public service and student development); we currently live in a time that, strangely, sees teachers characterized by laziness or greed. As progressive educators fight new battles for work-related autonomy, they must keep their initial focus central, demonstrating what William Sullivan (2004) labels *civic professionalism*. In other words, their task is to show the way toward expected outcomes—they must teach the public about good teaching, if you will.

Such a campaign is long overdue, for it is quite a misconception to believe that in an era of great standardization that most children and adolescents in the developed world actually are receiving a standardized education. Sure, they take standardized tests, and their teachers are supposed to follow standardized curricula (often macro and micro). But teaching quality and practice vary considerably. Ultimately, in this view, progressive educators are not fighting the right fight: While they are busy critiquing standardization, most of the world's teachers are doing what they know how to do and what they believe is right. Could it, instead, be the teachers, themselves, that progressive educators must target? After all, if they care about instituting their ideas into classrooms of a couple or more dozen students, should they not desire to see their ideas instituted in millions of classrooms producing tens of millions of students who think deeply and broadly, express care for others and the planet, accept and celebrate human differences, contribute to fair and just economic advancement, and desire political ownership of their communities and nations?

Note

1. The issue of for-profit universities in the U.S. complicates this picture. For-profit universities have generally been developed so to skirt professional academic practices. Now that they are under greater scrutiny by the U.S. federal government for luring more students into degree programs than plausible for the job market, initial signs of concern regarding NPM approaches are starting to be noticed.

References

Abbott, A. (1988). *The system of professions: An essay on the division of expert labor*. Chicago: The University of Chicago Press.

Andreescu, L. (2009). Foundations of academic freedom: Making new sense of some aging arguments. *Studies in Philosophy and Education, 28*(6), 499–515.

Arum, R., & Roksa, J. (2011). *Academically adrift: Limited learning on college campuses*. Chicago: University of Chicago Press.

Aton, A.M., & Connolly, H.S. (2001). The debate over the unionization and collective bargaining of private physicians. *Hofstra Labor and Employment Law Journal, 18*(2), 657–686.

Ball, D.L., & Forzani, F.M. (2009). The work of teaching and the challenge for teacher education. *Journal of Teacher Education, 60*(5), 497–511.

Banks, J.A. (2004). Teaching for social justice, diversity, and citizenship in a global world. *Educational Forum, 68*(4), 296–305.

Braverman, H. (1974) *Labor and monopoly capital*. New York: Monthly Review.

Bushaw, W.J., & Lopez, S.J. (2010). A time for change: The 42nd Annual Phi Delta Kappan/Gallup Poll of the Public's Attitudes Toward the Public Schools. *Phi Delta Kappan, 92*(1), 9–26.

Christensen, C., Johnson, C.W., & Horn, M.B. (2008). *Disrupting class: How disruptive innovation will change the way the world learns*. New York: McGraw-Hill.

Cohen, D.K. (1998). Dewey's problem. *The Elementary School Journal, 98*(5), 427–446.

Cohen, D.K. (2005). Professions of human improvement: Predicaments of teaching. In Nisan, M., & Schremer, O. (Eds.), *Educational Deliberations*, pp. 278–294. Jerusalem: Keter.

Cole, J.R. (2009). *The great American university: Its rise to preeminence, its indispensible national role, and why it must be protected.* New York: Public Affairs.

Freidson, E. (2001). *Professionalism, the third logic: On the practice of knowledge.* Chicago: University of Chicago Press.

Fusarelli, L.D., & Johnson, B. (2004). Educational governance and the new public management. *Public Administration & Management: An Interactive Journal, 9*(2), 118–127.

Gruening, G. (2001). Origin and theoretical basis of new public management. *International Public Management Journal, 4*(1), 1–25.

Hayes, W. (2006). *The progressive education movement: Is it still a factor in today's schools?* Lanham, MD: Rowman & Littlefield.

Heyneman, S.P. (1997). The quality of education in the Middle East and North Africa. *International Journal of Educational Development, 17*(4), 449–466.

Karran, T. (2007). Academic freedom in Europe: A preliminary comparative analysis. *Higher Education Policy, 20*(3), 289–313.

Kohn, A. (2008). Progressive education: Why it's hard to beat, but also hard to find. Independent School, 67(3), 18–30.

Krause, E.A. (1996). *Death of the guilds: Professions, states, and the advance of capitalism, 1930 to the present.* New Haven, CT: Yale University Press.

Labaree, D.F. (2004). *The trouble with ed schools.* New Haven: Yale University Press.

Lagemann, E. C. (1989). The plural worlds of educational research. *History of Education Quarterly, 29*(2), 185–214.

Larson, M.S. (1980). Proletarianzation and educated labor. *Theory and Society, 9*(1), 131–175.

Laska, J.A. (1984). The relationship between instruction and curriculum: A conceptual clarification. *Instructional Science, 13*(3), 203–212.

Lee, J. (2008a). Is test-driven external accountability effective? Synthesizing the evidence from cross-state causal-comparative and correlational studies. *Review of Educational Research, 78*(3), 608–644.

Lee, J. (2008b). Two takes on the impact of NCLB on academic improvement: Tracking state proficiency trends through NAEP versus state assessments. In G.L. Sunderman, (Ed.), *Holding NCLB Accountable: Achieving Accountability, Equity, and School Reform*, pp. 75–90. . Thousand Oaks, CA: Corwin.

Leicht, K.T., & Lyman, C.W. (2006). Markets, institutions, and the crisis of professional practice. *Research in the Sociology of Organizations, 24*, 17–44.

Leicht, K.T., Walter, T., Sainsaulieu, I., & Davies, S. (2009). New public management and new professionalism across nations and contexts. *Current Sociology, 57*(4), 581–605.

Lipsky, M. (1980). *Street-level bureaucracy: Dilemmas of the individual in public services.* New York: Russell Sage Foundation.

National Governors Association. (2009). News Release: Common core state standards development work group and feedback group announced. Retrieved from: http://www.nga.org/portal/site/nga/menuitem.6c9a8a9ebc6ae07eee28aca9501010 a0/?vgnextoid=60e20e4d3d132210VgnVCM1000005e00100aRCRD

Nelson, C. (2010). *No university is an island: Saving academic freedom.* New York: New York University Press.

O'Day, J. A., & Smith, M. S. (1993). Systemic reform and educational opportunity. In S. H. Fuhrman (Ed.), *Designing coherent education policy: Improving the system.* San Francisco: Jossey Bass.

Ouchi, W.G. (1980). Markets, bureaucracies, and clans. *Administrative Science Quarterly, 25*(1), 129–141.

Postman, N., & Weingartner, C. (1971). *Teaching as a subversive activity.* New York: Delta.

Price, H.E. (2010). Does No Child Left Behind really capture school quality? Evidence from an urban school district. *Educational Policy, 24*(5), 779–814.

Purinton, T. (2010). Quintessential acts of inquiry in educational practice: Delineating inquiry and interpretation in the pursuit of teacher professionalization. *Inquiry in Education, 1*(2), article 3. Retrieved from: http://digitalcommons.nl.edu/ie/vol1/iss2/3.

Purinton, T. (2011). *Six degrees of school improvement: Empowering a new profession of teaching.* Charlotte, NC: IAP.

Schauer, F. (2006). Is there a right to academic freedom? *University of Colorado Law Review, 77*(4), 907–927.

Shanahan, T. (1998). On the effectiveness and limitations of tutoring in reading. *Review of Research in Education, 23,* 217–234. Washington, DC: American Educational Research Association.

Sullivan, W.M. (2004). Can professionalism still be a viable ethic? *The Good Society, 13*(1), 15–20.

Tierney, W.G., & Lechuga, V.M. (2008). Academic freedom in the 21st century. *Thought and Action, 21,* 7–22.

Tierney, W.G., & Lechuga, V.M. (2010). The social significance of academic freedom. *Cultural Studies Critical Methodologies, 10*(2), 118–133.

Wasik, B., & Slavin, R.E. (1993). Preventing early reading failure with one-to-one tutoring: A review of five programs. *Reading Research Quarterly, 28,* 178–200.

Weber, M. (1962). *Basic concepts in sociology by Max Weber* (H.P. Secher, Trans.). New York: The Citadel Press.

4. *Speaking Empowerment to Crisis: Unmasking Accountability through Critical Discourse*

P. L. Thomas

> *Because curriculum is not a neutral entity, because it is always ideo-*
> *logically inscribed, educational purpose is always a political question.*
> —Joe L. Kincheloe (Kincheloe & Weil, 2001, p. 16)

A graduate student who is an early-career ELA teacher in a school serving students from high-poverty backgrounds sent me an e-mail about an argument she was having with a colleague concerning the current state of education in the U.S.:

> I was arguing with a teacher (who also happens to be my best friend of 9 years) about education. She used the word "crisis" last night over drinks and I told her how we should avoid using that word because of how long the failure has been going on. She argued that it is a crisis (and that I was being picky over semantics) because students today are not being substantially prepared for society. She claimed that school was a better place when our parents went. I disagreed with her that school was not any better—we only think it is because of what things like AYP and standardized tests are making it seem like today—on top of all the other bullshit pouring out of every politician's mouth.

In this brief statement, this excellent and rightly frustrated teacher has captured the current and historical failure *associated* with universal public education in the U.S. But that failure is not educational; it is political, bureaucratic, and social.

Kincheloe and Weil (2001) offer a framework for the dynamics creating the marginalization of educators (and thus the frustration expressed above) while reinforcing the power of the political and corporate elite who are using education reform and the accountability movement as a tool for maintaining, ironically, the status quo:

In such an insidious and covert context, power wielders shape our "democratic" schools with little democratic participation. In this political domain, those with the most power dictate purpose. Hinchey argues that in the contemporary United States, those with the most power are business and corporate leaders and their political allies who in the language of standards specify the types of workers they want....Control of schooling is in the process of passing from internal to external forces such as corporations and businesses. (pp. 12, 18)

Kincheloe's words, written a decade ago, are even more accurate today as political and corporate leaders have accelerated claims of educational crises paired with Utopian goals for what those same failing schools *could* accomplish if only standards were higher, accountability mandates were tighter, and teachers were better (and unions were eliminated).

The powerful but ultimately bankrupt (Freire, 1993) playbook of political and corporate calls for standards-based education reform has positioned a few non-educators as reformers (Secretary of Education Arne Duncan, Michelle Rhee, Bill Gates, and Geoffrey Canada)[1] and mislabeled critical educators as defenders of the status quo (Bessie, 2011; Kohn, 2010a; Peters, 2011; Thomas, 2011d). Here, the historical and current flaws with calls for national standards and greater accountability are placed within the public and political failure to heed critical voices that call upon critical educators to speak empowerment to crisis.

In this chapter, I unveil how the collection of false prophets at today's historical movement serve a corporate agenda by crying educational crisis at one moment and promising Utopian outcomes at another. I also argue that the reformers persist in calls for changing the status quo by offering the same responses to educational reform we have been implementing for three decades, and the entire process is driven by the tired refrains of crisis and Utopian promises that reach back a century. Also, I will illustrate how dominant media outlets have become chief supporters of the refrains of crisis and Utopian promises in education today and, as a result, more U.S. citizens believe incorrectly that corporate educational policies and practices have the power to improve, rather than circumscribe, student educational performance. I will conclude the chapter by offering three broad policy considerations that have—unlike the dominant, tired corporate narrative generated by the ruling elite—the power to promote student engagement in their social world.

Technical standards—ignoring critical voices for reform

Over the past few years, I have increased my commentary work as a writer/scholar, feeling that speaking from a position of expertise to the public is central to my role as a scholar (a role often insular since scholars tend to publish for scholars in publications read exclusively by other scholars). In one piece addressing the current state of belief culture in the U.S., I asserted about our political system:

> In the second decade of the 21st century, we do not have liberals and conservatives vying for the votes and minds of America; we have corporate Democrats and corporate Republicans vying through a false dichotomy for the votes and minds of American consumers who are too often eager to hear what they already believe. (Thomas, 2011c)

Taken a step further and narrowed to the education debate, the belief culture of the U.S. is absent a critical voice, as Kincheloe explains:

> Decontextualized technical standards that are easy to statistically manipulate for good public relations perfectly fit the needs of the reeducators....The public buys into "simplistic answers to complex problems," and as long as it does, technical standards will remain extremely popular....Reductionism, thus, helps create an illusion of educational improvement in the minds of citizens. (Kincheloe & Weil, 2001, pp. 20, 70)

The history of proclaiming that public education in the United States is in crisis, of calling for wide-scale education reform, and of offering simplistic templates for that reform is long and essentially monolithic (Kincheloe & Weil, 2001; see vol. 3, *Historical Timeline for Educational Reform and Standards*, pp. 1137–1149). One element of that history is the false tension between the political Left and Right—essentially two sides of the same corporate-driven coin—that combines to silence the critical calls for critique and reform of public schools. The education policies grounded in accountability, standards, and testing have remained essentially the same regardless of political party in power since the early 1980s, revealing the hierarchical and mechanistic assumptions taken from corporatism and imposed on education by bureaucracy and legislation.

Critical educator Paulo Freire passed away just before co-teaching a graduate seminar at the Harvard Graduate School of Education with Donaldo Macedo (Freire, 1998). While Freire raised a powerful and critical voice for decades, his final proclamations came well into the current standards and accountability movement begun by *A Nation at Risk* (Bracey, 2003; Holton, 2003; Ravitch, 2010). Merely a decade and a half into the contemporary standards era, Freire recognized the false dichotomies of education reformers and politicians along with the inherent flaws of technical standards:

> If education cannot do everything, there is something fundamental that it can do. In other words, if education is not the key to social transformation, neither is it simply meant to reproduce the dominant ideology....The freedom that moves us, that makes us take risks, is being subjugated to a process of standardization of formulas, models against which we are evaluated....We are speaking of that invisi-

ble power of alienating domestication, which attains a degree of extraordinary efficiency in what I have been calling the bureaucratizing of the mind. (pp. 110, 111)

The bureaucratizing of the mind is the best and most chilling characterization of what educators and students face as we move into the second decade of the 20th century—just ten years removed from a powerful warning offered by critical educators concerning technical standards.

As noted above, Kincheloe (Kincheloe & Weil, 2001), like Freire (1998), stood at the cusp of the dramatic turn that the standards movement took in 2001 with the bipartisan support behind No Child Left Behind (NCLB). But neither could have anticipated what lay ahead, namely that the driving force behind even greater folly would be a Democratic president and secretary of education—President Obama and Secretary of Education Arne Duncan.

One of the central problems with the standards and accountability movement has been repeated over the past ten years—the failure of the media to report accurately the complexity of both education problems and needed education reform: "[T]he quality of the standards conversation itself has been disappointing to many scholars, educators, and citizens" explains Kincheloe (Kincheloe & Weil, 2001, p. 1). The simplistic claims of crisis and promises of technical responses to those crises have resonated with the public, fueling greater and greater dependency on this dynamic by politicians seeking power and status. Kincheloe's argument, then, stands ironically *against* technical standards (touted as raising expectations) because those technical standards are reductive and speaks *for* critical calls that are ignored but do seek more challenging expectations for academics, justice, and agency.

In the current climate, however, as I have noted, those critical voices opposing the current self-appointed education reformers (Secretary Duncan, Bill Gates, Michele Rhee, and Geoffrey Canada) are labeled as defenders of the status quo, implying a resistance to change and challenging expectations. Critical educators have spoken and practiced *against* the norms of traditional schooling for decades. Despite those same educators' and scholars' highlighting the flaws inherent in the accountability/standards approach to reform, the technical standards movement has not only survived, but also thrived.

And at the forefront of the powerful but flawed technical standards movement is a collection of false prophets serving the corporate agenda by crying crisis at one moment and promising Utopian outcomes at another.

False prophets of education reform—crisis discourse, utopian promises

While nearly two decades of standards- and accountability-based initiatives driven by state bureaucracy fulfilled virtually none of the promises that came with the mandates, NCLB became law and shifted the standards and account-ability movement to the federal government, ironically under a Republican president who built a substantial amount of his political clout on education reform in Texas that has been subsequently discredited (Hacker, 2009; Klein et al., 2000; Thomas, 2004). Then, over the next eight years, federally driven standards and accountability—overlaid on the state systems—failed to produce positive results as well (Hout & Elliott, 2011).

So, while the election of Barack Obama and his appointment of Secretary of Education Arne Duncan may have raised hopes for change, instead, the federal government is doubling-down by masking corporate agendas and technical assumptions in the convenient sheep's clothing of crisis discourse and Utopian promises—led by Duncan and other new reformers, billionaire Gates, entrepreneur Canada, and ex-chancellor (and Teach For America alum) Rhee. Sirota (2010) offers this characterization of neoliberal educational reformers:

> Of course, 30 years into the neoliberal experiment, the Great Recession is expos-ing the flaws of the Washington Consensus. But rather than admit any mistakes, neoliberals now defend themselves with yet more bait-and-switch sophistry—this time in the form of the Great Education Myth.

All of the new reformers work through an uncritical media by weaving a con-sistent (but false) narrative about failed schools, bad teachers, corrupt teach-ers' unions, and the need for U.S. schools to make the country competitive internationally. The narratives are a mix of insincere civil rights references, alarmist claims, and Utopian promises that contradict each other. Here, I want to catalogue snapshots of the celebrity tours by Duncan, Gates, Canada, and Rhee to expose the flaws in their calls for technical standards as a panacea for not only schools but also the entire country.

Arne Duncan—authority through appointment

Secretary of Education Duncan has capitalized on his political appointments to create the perception that he is a leader, a reformer, and an educator; but, like Gates, Canada, and Rhee, Duncan is inexpert—all rhetoric and no cred-ibility. He is adept at speeches that hide corporate agendas and technical views of teaching and learning beneath civil rights discourse (Thomas, 2010b). Duncan's speeches highlight the flaws of his claims and his solutions.

Duncan is proving to be a master of crisis discourse, cloaking his corporate com-mitments in the language and settings of authentic civil rights. In Arkansas, for example, Duncan spoke on behalf of the Obama administration at the Bill Clinton Library as part of his tour to gain feedback on education in the U.S. There, he reminded his audience of Dr. Martin Luther King Jr. and Central High. Duncan (2010c) made his case by crying wolf[2] about the need to focus on teacher quality:

> The big game-changer for us, however, in terms of both formula and competitive programs, revolves around the issue of teacher quality....Nothing is more important and nothing has a greater impact on the quality of education than the quality and skill of the person standing in the front of the class—and there is so much that needs to change in the way that America recruits, trains, supports and manages our teachers.

In this speech, Duncan mentioned teachers more than four dozen times, but he never mentioned poverty, racism, sexism, or homophobia as the central forces impacting student achievement. And while he waves his arms and draws our eyes toward the claimed failure of teachers in our failed schools, invoking a crisis in teacher quality (which fits well into the public's acceptance of the drop-out crisis and the achievement gap crisis), the truth about what matters in student achievement remains ignored (Berliner, 2009; Hirsch, 2007; Rothstein, 2010).

While Duncan (2010b) has repeatedly characterized public schools (and their teachers) as abysmal failures, he simultaneously promotes a Utopian promise of what schools can do if reformed as he prescribes (framing all of this in nostalgic views of when schools were successful despite the contrary evidence that in the past similar cries of crisis in education were common). Duncan suggests:

> The promise of universal education was then [1945] a lonely beacon—a light to guide the way to peace and the rebuilding of nations across the globe. Today, the world is no longer recovering from a tragic global war. Yet the international community faces a crisis of a different sort, the global economic crisis. And education is still the beacon lighting the path forward—perhaps more so today than ever before.
>
> Education is still the key to eliminating gender inequities, to reducing poverty, to creating a sustainable planet, and to fostering peace. And in a knowledge economy, education is the new currency by which nations maintain economic competitiveness and global prosperity.

This public and political discourse portrays public education as both in crisis *and* capable of miracles.

While a failing teacher corps is not central to the conditions he labels "crisis," Duncan (2010a) persists in his claims of crisis, expressed in a flawed use of international test scores, Program for International Student Assessment (PISA):

> Here in the United States, we have looked forward eagerly to the 2009 PISA results. But the findings, I'm sorry to report, show that the United States needs to urgently accelerate student learning to remain competitive in the knowledge economy of the 21st century. The United States has a long way to go before it lives up to the American dream and the promise of education as the great equalizer. Every three years, PISA assesses the reading, mathematics, and scientific literacy of 15-year-old students. It provides crucial information about how well our

students are prepared to do the sorts of reading, mathematics, and science that will be demanded of them in postsecondary education or the job market, and as young adults in modern society. Unfortunately, the 2009 PISA results show that American students are poorly prepared to compete in today's knowledge economy.

Just as Duncan ignored poverty while blaming teachers in Little Rock, here he offers a simplistic ranking of PISA scores to mask the facts of what those scores actually reveal:

> The problem is not as much with our educational system as it is with our high poverty rates. The real crisis is the level of poverty in too many of our schools and the relationship between poverty and student achievement. Our lowest achieving schools are the most under-resourced schools with the highest number of disadvantaged students. We cannot treat these schools in the same way that we would schools in more advantaged neighborhoods or we will continue to get the same results. The PISA results point out that the U.S. is not alone in facing the challenge of raising the performance of disadvantaged students. (Riddile, 2010)

In fact, when U.S. students' PISA scores are compared to the rest of the world by taking into account poverty levels, Riddile displays, the U.S. exceeds and matches all of the countries that Duncan often cites as surpassing the U.S.— including Finland and Korea.

As an education reformer, Duncan reveals that his authority rests solely on his being appointed through political connections. He expresses contradictory themes, inaccurate claims about the causes of student achievement gaps, and simplistic conclusions drawn from complex data that he seems not to understand.

Bill Gates, wealth trumping expertise

Another powerful but misguided reformer is Bill Gates, who conjures expertise on education (and everything it seems) merely by his status as a billionaire. *Newsweek* journalist Daniel Lyons (2010) posed a series of questions to Gates and Randi Weingarten, president of the American Federation of Teachers. The questions focused on the problems with the U.S. educational system and what is needed to fix it. This interview exposes Gates's lack of credibility when famed against Kohn's (2010a) unmasking the new reformer movement dominating public discourse about education and education reform:

> For a shrewd policy maker, then, the ideal formula would seem to be to let people enjoy the invigorating experience of demanding reform without having to give up whatever they're used to. And that's precisely what both liberals and conservatives manage to do: Advertise as a daring departure from the status quo what is actually just a slightly new twist on it.

But conservatives have gone a step further. They've figured out how to take policies that actually represent an *intensification* of the status quo and dress them up as something that's long overdue. In many cases the values and practices they endorse have already been accepted, but they try to convince us they've lost so they can win even more.

The *Newsweek* piece, perpetuated in the Education section of *The Huffington Post*, is flawed from the start, with each question framing the potential answers within misinformation and distortion. For instance, Daniel Lyons presupposes that U.S.'s schools will be improved by the policy measures touted by Gates and other elite figures when he states that the notion of giving tenure to teachers is "ridiculous" and implies Gates should be frustrated by the fact that schoolteachers are afforded pensions, health care, and a good salaries without holding them accountable for students' performance through high-stakes testing. Furthermore, we cannot discount that the entire discussion is also framed among the elites themselves—authorities who have benefited well from the current system, leaving us to wonder why they would want to change anything. The interview works within the crisis assumptions and offers Gates an opportunity to confirm by simply responding that all the new reformers' claims are true—the U.S. "lag[s behind] the rest of the world" in education, schools are failing due to bad teachers and corrupt unions, education reform must include national standards and accountability, and teacher tenure is an outdated process of protecting those bad teachers (Lyons, 2010).

Gates builds his case for international comparisons with discourse about investment and return, but he fails to identify the impact of poverty (again, see Riddile, 2010) and avoids making an international comparison based on childhood poverty that is central to educational outcomes in the U.S.: The U.S. ranks at the bottom with respect to childhood poverty rates when compared against the same countries Gates and others use for claiming relative crisis in our schools (Adamson, 2005, 2007). For example, Finland has about 3–4% childhood poverty (and a population of about five million people) while the U.S. has about 21% childhood poverty (and over three million teachers) (Thomas, 2010a).

The misrepresentation of teacher quality, teachers' unions, and tenure iscentral to Gates's focus on the workforce and the dangers of labor negotiations; however, his claims mask the facts. The myth of the bad teacher (Bessie, 2010) is couched within subtle statements identifying in-school factors impacting student performance, while avoiding the overwhelming influence of out-of-school factors (Berliner, 2009). This union bashing (Thomas, 2011b) is designed to trigger the populist turn against unions at the heart of movements such as the Tea Party phenomenon, but it ignores the strong correlation between test scores and union presence—notably that low-scoring states such as South Carolina are non-union states (Thomas, 2011a)—and that praised countries such as Finland have a teacher workforce that is essentially 100% unionized.

As the interview ends, the topic turns to teacher tenure—which has been commonly portrayed as guaranteeing a job for life instead of properly characterized as integral to academic freedom and the application of due process to termination—but when Weingarten attempted to justify and clarify tenure, Gates interrupted, suggesting again a failure in the investment/return dynamic of education:

> No, we spend more on professional development than they do. We spend more on salaries than they do. We spend more on pensions than they do. We spend more on retirement health benefits than they do. But we have less evaluation than they do. In many districts you have to give advance notice before anybody can come into your classroom. That's part of the contract. So there are some real differences in terms of the personnel system in these other countries. (Lyons, 2010)

This inaccurate use of terminology represents a central flaw with the narratives weaved by the false prophets—they don't add up. In order to demonize teachers' unions, Gates must misrepresent tenure and then attack his misrepresentation. Therefore, once each of the foundational claims is refuted, the final call for higher standards and more accountability falls flat.

Geoffrey Canada—benevolent reformer

The celebrity tour during Obama's first years in office included entrepreneur Geoffrey Canada on Comedy Central's *The Colbert Report* (Geoffrey Canada, 2011). Canada made his second appearance with Colbert as the face on the Harlem Children's Zone (HCZ)—mislabeled as a "miracle" (Thomas, 2010c) and representing the selective corporate model for school reform (since Canada serves as an entrepreneur supplanting the role of government to provide education and social services). Canada kept the drum beating by opening on *Colbert* with a sweeping claim that would make Duncan blush: America, it seems, is for the first time in 30, 40, or 50 years taking education seriously.

Like Duncan, Gates, and Rhee, Canada promotes claims and recommendations about education that are offered in a historical and research vacuum—appealing to the ahistorical perspective that blinds public opinion (Meier, 2011). The truth is that assertions made by Canada and all the new reformers are the same narrative that has been driving political discourse about schools for a century—simplistic international comparisons, crisis discourse about graduation rates, discrediting teachers and teaching as a profession, and a complete failure to mention or address social inequities and childhood poverty.

And here, once again during the celebrity tour, Canada makes a plea *for a group of children who couldn't fit into the economy* (Canada's characterization), lamenting the high prison rate in the U.S. But, like Duncan in his speeches about education reform, Canada never mentions poverty directly.

Worse still, by implication, Canada places the focus on the children themselves for not "fitting in"—never raising questions about the U.S. economy or the social inequities that result from neoliberal policies. It appears to be acceptable to demonize schools, teachers, and above all else teachers' unions (one joke toward the end of the interview resulted in Canada saying "both" to Colbert's satirical question about whether we should blame teachers or teachers' unions). However, it is beyond reproach even for Canada, a man who came from poverty himself, to say "poverty" or to challenge the status quo of American politics and corporate consumerism.

Instead, Canada evokes his goal of a 100% graduation rate at the HCZ (not evidence of what has been accomplished, but a Utopian promise about what could be), rails against the achievement gap (conveniently omitting that the achievement gap reflects the social equity gap), repeatedly endorses the credibility of testing, and builds to the most powerful distortion of all coming from the new reformers: "We've got to hold the adults responsible....We've allowed our schools to fail these kids with no consequences."

These charges sound compelling and echo America's faith in myths about rugged individualism, pulling one's self up by one's bootstraps (for which Canada stands as a shining example of making the exceptional the norm against which we are all judged), and rising tides lifting all boats. Ironically, the new reformers are calling for accountability from perches upon which they themselves face no accountability—wealth (billionaires in some cases), political appointments, and celebrity. Calling for *other* people to be held accountable while ignoring context and standing outside the accountability machine is a hollow and cowardly call—even when people have the best of intentions.

Michelle Rhee as authoritarian ideal

The U.S. is floundering at the bottom of international comparisons of education. What makes this worse is that in the often-idealized 1950s, the U.S. was at the top—at least that is one story offered by Rhee on another episode of *The Colbert Report*. Like Canada, Rhee has attained celebrity status as an education reformer. In her case, this status is two-pronged, having arisen partially from the media fawning over her since she left as chancellor of Washington, D.C., schools and partially through the misleading documentary *Waiting for "Superman"* (Dutro, 2011).

Rhee's celebrity tour raises some real problems about not only what the false prophets are saying about education, but also how the so-called left-wing media helps (directly and indirectly) to perpetuate misinformation about the education system—misinformation that is being promoted to mask the real issues about poverty in our culture that the political and corporate elite do not want to face. Rhee, in her interview with host Stephen Colbert, makes several sweeping claims about schools, and, as is the nature of contemporary media (recognizing, of course, that Colbert is satire), she is allowed to make those claims without any evidence to support them.

As an example, I will unpack the claim about the U.S. being number one in education and graduation in the 1950s. First, Rhee is following a clever playbook of the new education reform movement: Make partial claims that few people will question because they sound true. In this case, the claim itself is masking; even if the claim is factually correct, Rhee is referring to the U.S. public education system *before* integration and the civil rights movement impacted a public education system that had closed doors to many American citizens. In short, the education system of the 1950s was an incomplete one that shunned many people marginalized by race and poverty.

Rhee trusts that most people embrace a misguided nostalgia for the past, a nostalgia lacking evidence for such faith in a better time. However, once we actually return to that Golden Era, the message then is somewhat confusing in the light of Rhee's claims.

The full truth, of course, is that corporate and political elites have been making the same exact unwarranted charges heard from Rhee, Secretary Duncan, Gates, and Canada without much resistance for at least half a century. Rhee's misinformation is nothing new, but it is finding renewed traction because these messages are being reinforced through the cult of celebrity, and that cult of celebrity is being driven by the so-called left-wing media just as easily as anywhere else—*Oprah*, Bill Maher's *Real Time*, *The Colbert Report*.

It is negligent to allow—and even embrace—the distortions driving the new educational reform movement being fueled by false prophets who have no business representing the education agenda of a free society that claims to value academic freedom, human agency, and the hope of democracy not yet fulfilled. The narrative replayed over and over by Duncan, Gates, Canada, and Rhee falls apart at each claim. Thus, their conclusion (higher standards and greater accountability are the reform our schools need) necessarily does not follow.

Common standards—misinformation equals wrong solution

The new reformers persist in calls for changing the status quo by offering the same responses to educational reform we have been implementing for three decades, and the entire process is driven by the tired refrains of crisis and Utopian promises that reach back a century. And the critical argument for rejecting the siren's call of accountability and standards persists as well (Kohn, 2010b; Mathis, 2010; Kincheloe & Weil, 2001).

In the second decade of the 21st century, with the blessing and encouragement of the nation's president and secretary of education, the U.S. is pursuing "common core standards" to address the historical claim that our public schools are failures. In the 1890s, a similar lament was voiced by the group known as the Committee of Ten:

> When college professors endeavor to teach chemistry, physics, botany, zoology, meteorology, or geology to persons of 18 or 20 years of age, they discover that in most instances new habits of observing, reflecting, and recording have to be painfully acquired by the students—habits which they should have acquired in early childhood. (Report of the Committee of Ten on Secondary School Studies, 1894)

Their solution? Almost exactly what the current common-standards pursuit offers us. In fact, the bureaucratic and technical approach to schools—establish content, prescribe content, and measure student acquisition of that content—has been visited and revisited decade after decade for more than a century now. It has always failed, and it always will.

This time around, educators and the public must use the creation of, and debate about, national standards to reject a failed solution for the ignored problems facing public schools—and U.S. society. Today's attempt at national standards, the recently released work of the Common Core State Standards Initiative (2010) in English language arts and mathematics that is being adopted separately by states, fails for numerous reasons. First, the standards are based on two flawed assumptions: that educators, in the 21st century, don't already know what to teach (they do and have for decades); and that, somehow, a standard body of learning matches what humans need and what a democracy that values human agency wants (the simple pursuit of standards doesn't necessarily support either [Kincheloe & Weil, 2001]).

Next, the standards further deprofessionalize teaching at the K–12 level. Chemistry professors in college do not need a set of standards to teach chemistry; part of the appropriate expectations for their job is to be scholars of their field and adept at teaching that body of knowledge. (In fact, a central problem to address is that, at the K–12 level, the need for teachers to be knowledgeable is trivialized, and at the college level, a professor's need to be skilled at teaching is trivialized. Educators need both.) To standardize and prescribe expectations is, in fact, to lower them (Kincheloe & Weil, 2001).

Common standards also devolve into asking less, not more, of students once those standards are reduced to assessments used for accountability since those are invariably tied to the most efficient types of assessment. Some clichés have become clichés because they are true. The truism "Give people a fish and they eat for the day; teach people to fish and they eat forever" captures perfectly the flaw with a standards approach to education: Prescribed standards of learning are giving children fish, not teaching them to fish. Standards-driven education removes decisions from teachers and students and renders classrooms lifeless and functional, devoid of the pleasure and personal value of learning, discovering, and coming to be.

Further, common standards begin by assuming that the content is all that matters in learning. To create a standard body of knowledge is to codify the belief that the students themselves do not matter—at least in any humane way. The standards movement envisions children as empty vessels to be filled by the prescribed knowledge chosen for them (Freire, 1993)—certainly a reductive view of humans in a free society.

A call for "higher standards" speaks to our human quest for improvement, but that call conflates "standard" with "expectation," and the two terms are not synonymous in the way needed for empowering education. Yes, high expectations are needed for teachers and students, but those expectations can never be and will never be any more *standard* than one human to the next. In fact, to standardize and prescribe expectations is to lower them.

Offering national standards as a solution for the failure of public education implies that a lack of standards exists, and that this assumed deficiency is somehow the cause of our educational problems. And that central fallacy is at the heart of what is most wrong about the new common core standards: The creation of national standards is drawing our attention away from the actual causes of educational problems (specifically achievement gaps) primarily driven by poverty and other forms of social inequalities impacting the lives of children.

Therefore, focusing on national standards is a political veneer, a tragic waste of time and energy that would be better spent addressing real needs in the lives of children—safe homes, adequate and plentiful food, essential health care, and neighborhood schools that are not reflections of the neighborhoods where children live through no choice of their own.

Speaking expert to celebrity—challenging false education reform

Perrillo (2010), writing about the Editorial Project at the West Texas Writing Project, "presents a strategy for countering contemporary political mandates that threaten teacher professionalism as a whole" by arguing for the power of teachers' voices, specifically in the form of editorials addressed to the public discourse surrounding education reform:

> The process by which the fellows wrote their editorials was important for fostering simultaneously the questioning frame of mind associated with inquiry and the confidence associated with claiming one's expertise. In contrast to the way in which many of the fellows were used to writing academic papers, we completed a great deal of focused freewriting and other prewriting for the draft in class and we shared this writing publicly....In all, this process encouraged the fellows to embrace inquiry and revision while writing in a genre that privileges argument and certitude. The combination was important; by holding both intellectual work and education advocacy at its center, the Editorial Project pushed the fellows to investigate their

ideas and account for their beliefs. This was a different model of professionalism than many were used to, particularly in a political climate that often requires teachers to subsume both their ideas and beliefs to following the program. For this reason, writing editorials stands to provide teachers with a fuller and richer understanding of how and why they teach and, to paraphrase the teacher in *Tested* (Perlstein, 2007), why they seek graduate training. As many of the editorials that came out of this project reflected, the stakes of thinking more critically about the profession and their role in it are as high for teachers today as ever. (pp. 10, 11–12)

A tension exists between traditional and technocratic views of educators (that teachers are to be unbiased, apolitical, objective, and essentially quiet) and critical views of educators (that educators are necessarily political and subjective, thus both must be embraced), as expressed here:

> Thus, proponents of critical pedagogy understand that every dimension of schooling and every form of educational practice are politically contested spaces. Shaped by history and challenged by a wide range of interest groups, educational practice is a fuzzy concept as it takes place in numerous settings, is shaped by a plethora of often-invisible forces, and can operate even in the name of democracy and justice to be totalitarian and oppressive. (Kincheloe, 2005, p. 2)

The antidote, then, to technical standards that are reducing the opportunities of schooling, deprofessionalizing teachers, and codifying public education as a vehicle for preparing a compliant workforce is the voice of expertise raised by educators at all levels against the false prophets now dominating the debate over reform. Educators must speak against the false dualities of conservative/liberal and traditionalist/progressive, to speak expert to celebrity as radicals, as Howard Zinn (1994) implores in his memoir *You Can't Be Neutral on a Moving Train*:

> From that moment on, I was no longer a liberal, a believer in the self-correcting character of American democracy. I was a radical, believing that something fundamental was wrong in this country—not just the existence of poverty amidst great wealth, not just the horrible treatment of black people, but something rotten at the root. The situation required not just a new president or new laws, but an uprooting of the old order, the introduction of a new kind of society—cooperative, peaceful, egalitarian. (p. 173)

As I have worked as an educator and scholar—writing about and examining the rise of new reformers (Duncan, Gates, Canada, and Rhee)—I have been struck by another formative influence on my life, George Carlin (2004), specifically this rant about "zero tolerance" (Ayers & Dohrn, 1999) from *When Will Jesus Bring the Pork Chops?*:

> I get weary of this zero tolerance bullshit. It's annoying. To begin with, it's a fascist concept; it's what Hitler and Stalin practiced. It allows for no exceptions or compassion of any kind. All is black and white—no gradations. But even more

important, it doesn't solve anything. The use of such a slogan simply allows whichever company, school or municipality is using it to claim they're doing something about a problem when, in fact, nothing is being done at all and the problem is being ignored. It's a cosmetic non-solution designed to impress simpletons. Whenever you hear the phrase zero tolerance, remember, someone is bullshitting you. (p. 84)

Parallel to Carlin's distrust of "zero tolerance," I find the relentless calls for "accountability" and "standards" to be hollow. Those calling for accountability—from student accountability at the beginning of the standards era in the early 1980s to the more recent mantra about "bad teachers" and teacher accountability—are billionaires, celebrities, politicians, and political appointees—all of whom through their affluence and status tend to live outside anything resembling accountability.

In 2011, after a year of the new reformers speaking celebrity to the mythologies driving public opinion and masking evidence about the reality of U.S. public education and the reform that system does need, educators have an obligation to speak expert to celebrity by refuting the false prophets consistently and by offering a critical and nuanced voice for what our schools need to reform in order to address their role for a free and empowered people.

Education reform must include three broad categories: acknowledging and addressing out-of-school factors that constitute the bulk of causes behind education outcomes; reforming public education and teacher education/certification; and confronting in order to change both our political/public discourse about education and our assumptions about teacher, learning, and human nature.

How can educators acknowledge and address out-of-school factors burdening education?

- Create and fully fund as a high priority social programs through federal and state agencies that address the identified out-of-school factors that are strongly linked to education achievement: "(1) low birth-weight and non-genetic prenatal influences on children; (2) inadequate medical, dental, and vision care, often a result of inadequate or no medical insurance; (3) food insecurity; (4) environmental pollutants; (5) family relations and family stress; and (6) neighborhood characteristics" (Berliner, 2009). The evidence for more than a century shows that we must accept that the idealistic claim education will solve poverty is Utopian and ultimately counterproductive, and education reform must be supported by social and political commitments to eradicate childhood and family poverty in the U.S as stated by Martin Luther King Jr. from his "Final Words of Advice" (1967):

I am now convinced that the simplest approach will prove to be the most effective—the solution to poverty is to abolish it directly by a now widely discussed measure: the guaranteed income....We are likely to find that the problems of housing and education, instead of preceding the elimination of poverty, will themselves be affected if poverty is first abolished.

- Design and implement a home library program that begins for every child at birth and continues until graduation. This home library program should provide for every child 20 books a year—authentic books, not textbooks—divided evenly between 10 books selected for the child and 10 books selected by the child/family. This program should be organized through local libraries and public schools, and federal and state governments should call on corporate America (Amazon, Barnes and Noble, Scholastic) and billionaire education hobbyists to partner with federal and state agencies to fund this program. Access to books in the home will provide a greater boost to student achievement than any accountability, standards, or testing mandate—and at a fraction of the costs in time and money.

How can educators and political leaders reform public education and teacher education/certification?

- Reduce dramatically, and even eliminate, accountability, standards, and testing mandates and structures. We have 30 years of high accountability as proof that the accountability/standards/testing paradigm does not work (Hout & Elliott, 2011); in fact, evidence (Amrein & Berliner, 2002) shows that this paradigm narrows learning, squelches teaching and learning, and exacerbates negative outcomes such as dropping out of school.

- Confront and reform teaching assignments. After excessive testing and misguided accountability, the next worst fault of our public schooling is the teacher assignment dynamic that tends to reward teacher experience and expertise by giving those teachers the smallest classes with the most elite students. Peske and Haycock (2006) have exposed that children living in poverty, children of color, and ELL students disproportionately sit in classrooms taught by the least experienced and often under- and un-qualified teachers. This dynamic results in schools perpetuating the inequity of students' lives instead of confronting them.

- Recognize the professionalism and empowerment of teachers by supporting their right to create and implement the education that each unique student and class of students bring to the classroom. We must drop the historical view that teaching can be scripted independent of real students sitting in a classroom. Standards (state or national) that can be packaged and imposed on any child or group of children are counter to the knowledge base about teaching, learning, human nature, and individual freedom. Teachers should be supported and expected to design and make transparent rich learning experiences that are unique to the needs of students currently in their care.

- Reduce and eventually eliminate stratified course offerings— tracking and elite programs of study that allow gate-keeping mechanisms to privilege some students over others.

- Increase significantly the role of active learning by students. Most of the school day is dominated by teachers talking and doing *to* and *for* students; students make few decisions and remain silent, still, and compliant—as required by the demands of those teachers. Passivity, silence, and compliance are enemies of deep and genuine learning.

- Restructure high school requirements and paths to graduation, including the elimination of exit exams and standard requirements for a high school diploma. The U.S. Department of Education should solicit a national study of drop-outs throughout the U.S. to confirm causes in order to redesign high school to address our role in creating drop-outs, particularly as that is related to bureaucracy and accountability.

- Redesign teacher certification to increase the focus on education as a field and to reduce and even eliminate the bureaucracy of teacher certification. During my path to teacher certification and advanced degrees, every moment spent fulfilling certification bureaucracy has impeded my quest to be an effective teacher, while my scholarship related to the field of education has been invaluable to my growth. The problem with education preparation is certification being too bureaucratic and prescriptive, not that the field is flawed. Teachers as scholars are likely to raise the quality of the field while bureaucratic mandates designed to label and punish teachers are destined to lower the quality of the teaching.

How can education experts confront and change our political/public discourse about education and our assumptions about teaching, learning, and human nature?

- Confront and challenge crisis discourse and Utopian expectations for education. The record of history shows that conditions we often label as "crisis" are persistent throughout the past 100 years—students not being ready for college work, drop-outs, test scores. And expecting through mandate 100% success by any organization dealing with humans can achieve only failure.

- Reject the flawed assumption that learning is linear and sequential. Humans are natural learners, but cognitive growth is bound by brain development and easier to describe after the fact than predict. Our faith in and pursuit of "scientific" has its strengths, but ultimately we have failed "scientific" by reducing that to "mechanistic" and "prescriptive."

- Acknowledge that traditional views of schooling and current accountability mandates and practices are *counter* to the claimed goals of public education for individual empowerment and democracy. The discourse and the practices involving education are in direct contrast, and allowing this to persist erodes the quality of public schools and democracy.

- Reject an authoritarian view of children and humans. Public education has done more to demand compliance over the past century than to support human agency, which should be at the center of a people who value freedom and democracy.

- Expose and change our deficit views of children and especially children who happen to live in poverty (Dudley-Marling, 2007). We tend to measure and evaluate children—and impoverished children more harshly—by what we identify as missing against cultural norms. These deficit views place unfair burdens on those children and honor norms as "right," leaving those without power silenced and unable to challenge those norms. Concurrently, we must confront and reject the claims of a "culture of poverty"—which distorts human conditions through stereotyping (Gorski, 2008).

Of course, social and education reform can and should include more than I have offered here. But the current reform movement, guided by false reformers, has created a manufactured dichotomy between them as change agents and all others as "defenders of the status quo." While I feel educators are obligated to offer expertise as rebuttals to repeated faith in technical standards, educators must begin to be more diligent about offering alternatives to reform because the U.S. is faced with social and public education failures that are inexcusable, but change will not occur until leaders and the public admit that the current state of society and public education *is due to the efforts of the privileged and the powerful*—who thus have the same ability to bring change if they truly seek the ends they claim publicly.

A critical call to action among educators must rise from and work against the status quo of privilege. The corporate and political elites do maintain their privilege and could bring about equity, but they likely never will risk their privilege for equity. Thus, social and education reform must spring from a critical commitment among educators and fostered throughout our society, acknowledging that social change and education are inextricably tied to a shared cultural commitment to equity and justice—not competition, capital, or systems blind to the dignity of human agency.[3]

Notes

1. These reformers have either no or very little education, credentialing, or experience as classroom teachers, but have built credibility from primarily bureaucratic appointments.
2. In folklore, a shepherd discovers that repeated false cries of wolf led to his being disregarded when a real wolf appears. Duncan has lost credibility with educators since he claims teacher quality to be the most important factor in student achievement despite overwhelming evidence that out-of-school factors account for about 60–85% of measurable achievement; thus, his false cry about teacher quality erodes his future credibility.
3. Sections of this chapter have been adapted from the following commentaries:

   Thomas, P. L. (2011, January 20). Speaking expert to celebrity in 2011—The education reform debate. *OpEdNews.* http://www.opednews.com/articles/Speaking-Expert-to-Celebri-by-Paul-Thomas-110120–684

   Thomas, P.L. (2011, January 10). Supermen or kryptonite?—Legends of the fall, pt. V. *The Daily Censored.* http://dailycensored.com/2011/01/10/superman-or-kryptonite%E2%80%94legend-of-the-fall-pt-v/

   Thomas, P.L. (2010, December 28). Wrong questions = wrong answers: Legends of the fall, pt. IV. *The Daily Censored.* http://dailycensored.com/2010/12/28/wrong-questions-wrong-answers-legend-of-the-fall-pt-iv/

   Thomas, P.L. (2010, December 2). The education celebrity tour: Legend of the fall, pt. II. *The Daily Censored.* http://dailycensored.com/2010/12/02/the-education-celebrity-tour-legend-of-the-fall-pt-ii/

   Thomas, P.L. (2010, August 11). Why common standards won't work. *Education Week, 29*(37), 33–34. http://livinglearninginpoverty.blogspot.com/2010/08/9-august-2010-op-ed-at-edweek.html

References

Adamson, P. (2005). Child poverty in rich countries 2005. Innocenti Report Card (6). United Nations Children's Fund Innocenti Research Centre. Florence, Italy. http://www.unicef-irc.org/publications/371

Adamson, P. (2007). Child poverty in perspective: An overview of child well-being in rich countries. Innocenti Report Card (7). United Nations Children's Fund Innocenti Research Centre. Florence, Italy. http://www.unicef-irc.org/publications/445

Amrein, A.L., & Berliner, D.C. (2002, March 28). High-stakes testing, uncertainty, and student learning. *Education Policy Analysis Archives, 10*(18). Retrieved 1 November 2009 from http://epaa.asu.edu/epaa/v10n18/

Ayers, W., & Dohrn, B. (1999, November 21). Resisting zero tolerance. Milwaukee, WI: Center for Education Research, Analysis, and Innovation. Retrieved 22 June 2011 http://nepc.colorado.edu/files/cerai-00-01.htm

Berliner, D. C. (2009). Poverty and potential: Out-of-school factors and school success. Boulder and Tempe: Education and the Public Interest Center & Education Policy Research Unit. Retrieved 25 August 2009 from http://epicpolicy.org/publication/poverty-and-potential

Bessie, A. (2010, October 15). The myth of the bad teacher. *Truthout.* Retrieved 10 January 2011 from http://www.truth-out.org/the-myth-bad-teacher64223

Bessie, A. (2011, January 22). Let's not "reform" public education. *Truthout.* Retrieved 8 February 2011 from http://www.truth-out.org/lets-not-reform-public-education67006

Bracey, G. W. (2003). April foolishness: The 20th anniversary of *A Nation at Risk. Phi Delta Kappan, 84*(8), 616–621.

Canada, Geoffrey. (2011, January 4). *The Colbert Report* [TV]. Retrieved 21 June 2011 from http://www.colbertnation.com/the-colbert-report-videos/369836/january-04-2011/geoffrey-canada

Carlin, G. (2004). *When will Jesus bring the pork chops?* New York: Hyperion.

Common Core State Standards Initiative. (2010). Washington, DC: National Governors Association. Retrieved 10 February 2011 from http://www.corestandards.org/

Dudley-Marling, C. (2007). Return of the deficit. *Journal of Educational Controversy, 2*(1). Retrieved 29 June 2009 from http://www.wce.wwu.edu/Resources/CEP/eJournal/v002n001/a004.shtml

Duncan, A. (2010a, December 7). Secretary Arne Duncan's remarks at OECD's release of the Program for International Student Assessment (PISA) 2009 results. Washington DC: U. S. Department of Education. Retrieved 10 January 2011 from http://www.ed.gov/news/speeches/secretary-arne-duncans-remarks-oecds-release-program-international-student-assessment

Duncan, A. (2010b, November 4). The vision of education reform in the United States: Secretary Arne Duncan's remarks to United Nations Educational, Scientific and Cultural Organization (UNESCO), Paris, France. Washington DC: U. S. Department of Education. Retrieved 10 February 2011 from http://www.ed.gov/news/speeches/vision-education-reform-united-states-secretary-arne-duncans-remarks-united-nations-ed

Duncan, A. (2010c, August 25). Secretary Arne Duncan's remarks at the Statehouse Convention Center in Little Rock, Arkansas. Washington DC: U. S. Department of Education. Retrieved 10 February 2011 from http://www.ed.gov/news/speeches/secretary-arne-duncans-remarks-statehouse-convention-center-little-rock-arkansas

Dutro, E. (2011). Review of "Waiting for Superman." Boulder, CO: National Education Policy Center. Retrieved 10 February 2011 from http://nepc.colorado.edu/think-tank/review-waiting-superman

Freire, P. (1998). *Pedagogy of freedom: Ethics, democracy, and civic courage.* Trans. P. Clarke. Lanham, MD: Rowman and Littlefield Publishers, Inc.

———. (1993). *Pedagogy of the oppressed.* Trans. M. B. Ramos. New York: Continuum.

Gorski, P. (2008, April). The myth of the "Culture of Poverty." *Educational Leadership, 65*(7), 32–36.

Hacker, H. K. (2009, August 9). Many Dallas–Fort Worth graduates struggle in college. *The Dallas Morning News.* Retrieved 10 August 2009 from http://www.dallasnews.com/sharedcontent/dws/dn/latestnews/stories/080909dnmetfroshgpa.3fc0ab4.html

Hirsch, D. (2007, September). Experiences of poverty and educational disadvantage. Joseph Rowntree Foundation. York, North Yorkshire, UK. Retrieved 27 December 2007 from http://www.jrf.org.uk/knowledge/findings/socialpolicy/2123.asp

Holton, G. (2003, April 25). An insider's view of "A Nation at Risk" and why it still matters. *The Chronicle Review, 49*(33), B13.

Hout, M., & Elliott, S. W. (2011). *Incentives and test-based accountability in education.* Washington, DC: The National Academies Press. Retrieved 23 June 2011 from http://www.nap.edu/catalog.php?record_id=12521

Kincheloe, J. L. (2005). *Critical pedagogy primer.* New York: Peter Lang.

Kincheloe, J. L, & Weil, D. (2001). *Standards and schooling in the United States,* vols. 1–3. Denver, CO: ABC CLIO.

King, Jr., M. L. (1967). Final words of advice. *Wealth and Want.* Retrieved 11 February 2011 from http://www.wealthandwant.com/docs/King_Where.htm

Klein, S. P., Hamilton, L. S., McCaffrey, D. F. & Stecher, B. M. (2000) What do test scores in Texas tell us? Issue Paper, Rand Education. Santa Monica, CA: Rand Corporation. Retrieved 20 August 2009 from http://www.rand.org/pubs/issue_papers/IP202/index.html

Kohn, A. (2010a, October 18). How to sell conservatism: Lesson 1—Pretend you're a reformer. *The Huffington Post.* Retrieved 8 February 2011 from http://www.huffingtonpost.com/alfie-kohn/how-to-sell-conservatism-_b_767040.html

Kohn, A. (2010b, January 14). Debunking the case for national standards: One-size-fits-all mandates and their dangers. *Education Week, 29*(17), 28, 30. Expanded version retrieved 7 February 2011 from http://www.alfiekohn.org/teaching/edweek/national.htm

Lyons, D. (2010, December, 20). Bill Gates and Randi Weingarten. *Newsweek.* Retrieved 11 January 2011 from http://www.newsweek.com/2010/12/20/gates-and-weingarten-fixing-our-nation-s-schools.html

Mathis, W. J. (2010). The "Common Core" Standards Initiative: An effective reform tool? Boulder and Tempe: Education and the Public Interest Center & Education Policy Research Unit. Retrieved 10 November 2010 from http://epicpolicy.org/publication/common-core-standards

Meier, D. (2011, January 6). Public education and fact vs. fiction. *Bridging Differences* [blog]. Retrieved 10 February 2011 from http://blogs.edweek.org/edweek/Bridging-Differences/2011/01/meier_blog_jan_6.html

Perrillo, J. (2010, October). Writing for the public: Teacher editorializing as a pathway to professional development. *English Education, 43*(1), 10–32.

Peske, H. G., & Haycock, K. (2006, June). Teaching inequality: How poor and minority students are shortchanged on teacher quality. Washington DC: The Education Trust, Inc. Retrieved 7 September 2009 from http://www2.edtrust.org/NR/rdonlyres/010DBD9F-CED8-4D2B-9E0D-91B446746ED3/0/TQReportJune2006.pdf

Peters, S. (2011, February 4). Why I am not a defender of the "status quo" in education—because the "status quo" is failed ed reforms. *Seattle Education 2010*. Retrieved 8 February 2011 from http://seattleeducation2010.wordpress.com/2011/02/04/why-i-am-not-a-defender-of-the-status-quo-in-education-because-the-status-quo-is-failed-ed-reforms/

Ravitch, D. (2010). *The death and life of the great American school system: How testing and choice are undermining education*. New York: Basic Books.

Report of the Committee of Ten on Secondary School Studies. (1894). National Education Association. Retrieved 25 September 2009 from http://www.archive.org/stream/reportofcomtens00natirich/reportofcomtens00natirich_djvu.txt

Riddile, M. (2010, December 15). PISA: It's poverty not stupid. *The Principal Difference* [blog]. Retrieved 11 January 2011 from http://nasspblogs.org/principaldifference/2010/12/pisa_its_poverty_not_stupid_1.html

Rothstein, R. (2010, October 14). How to fix our schools. Issue Brief 286. Washington DC: Economic Policy Institute. Retrieved 10 January 2011 from http://www.epi.org/publications/entry/ib286

Sirota, D. (2010, September 12). The neoliberal bait-and-switch—the Great Education Myth. *The Seattle Times*. Retrieved 10 February 2011 from http://seattletimes.nwsource.com/html/opinion/2012865372_sirota13.html

Thomas, P. L. (2004). *Numbers games: Measuring and mandating American education*. New York: Peter Lang.

———. (2010a, December 16). Finnish envy. *OpEdNews.com*. http://www.opednews.com/articles/Finnish-Envy-by-Paul-Thomas-101214–873.html

———. (2010b, October 24). The politicians who cried "crisis." *Truthout*. http://www.truth-out.org/the-politicians-who-cried-crisis64359

———. (2010c, August 17). Reconsidering education "miracles." *OpEdNews.com*. http://www.opednews.com/articles/Reconsidering-Education-M-by-P-L-Thomas-100816–438.html

———. (2011a, February 8). Lessons in education from South Carolina? *The Daily Censored*. http://dailycensored.com/2011/02/08/lessons-in-education-from-south-carolina/

———. (2011b, February 4). The agenda behind teacher union-bashing. *Guardian.co.uk*. http://www.guardian.co.uk/commentisfree/cifamerica/2011/feb/04/usdomesticpolicy-schools

———. (2011c, January 26). Belief culture: "We don't need no education." *Truthout*. http://www.truth-out.org/belief-culture-we-dont-need-no-education67154

———. (2011d, January 8). Defending the status quo?—False dichotomies and the education reform debate. *OpEdNews*. http://www.opednews.com/articles/Defending-the-Status-Quo—by-Paul-Thomas-110107–766.html

Zinn, H. (1994). *You can't be neutral on a moving train: A personal history of our times*. Boston: Beacon Press.

5. *Teaching* through *the Test: Building Life-Changing Academic Achievement and Critical Capacity*

Victor H. Diaz

Teachers who see themselves as allies of their working-class students see that literacy and school knowledge could be potent weapons in their struggle for a better deal by connecting school knowledge with the reality of working class lives… not just a bunch of sissy stuff for which they have no use—Patrick J. Finn (1999).

This chapter shares the work of secondary English/Language Arts teachers who have sought to turn Finn's vision into reality through our work in low-income communities. As a Program Director and Learning Team Leader in Teach For America (TFA), I have worked with many first- and second-year teachers on a concept I call "teaching through the test." People in Teach For America[1] tend to join the teaching profession with a motivation to offer poor and working-class youth an educational experience that will lead to increased life opportunities. We believe that all children should have the opportunity to attain an excellent education and we seek to close the achievement gap that exists between our students and their more privileged peers.

We also understand that academic achievement, in and of itself, will not ensure that our students will have the tools, resources, and support to participate meaningfully in a democracy. Good grades and high test scores may grant young people access to new spaces in schools, but more is needed to broker a better deal in the broader society. Thus, we try to offer our students an education that bridges the word and the world (Freire & Macedo, 1987) and aligns increased academic achievement to the development of a critical capacity that aids students in their struggle for liberation (Freire, 1998). We seek to make academic achievement life changing, a sword and a shield for students as they progress through a school system that has been historically structured to disadvantage them. To do this, we engage in a curriculum and pedagogy that "teaches through the test" en route to critical consciousness and participation in a democratic society.

To teach through the test, we create units in our English/Language Arts classes that are both relevant and rigorous. These units are aligned to state standards and high-stakes tests, while their content is grounded in critical pedagogy and our students' experiences growing up in poor and working-class communities. I first started planning and implementing such units as a high school English and English Language Development (ELD) teacher in the barrio of East San Jose[2], California, where I was placed as a corps member in TFA. After working in this predominately Latino and Vietnamese immigrant community for five years, I have worked in a variety of roles with TFA, supporting new teachers in both California and Arizona while also teaching middle-school language arts for the past four years. I work with middle and high school English/Language Arts teachers in metropolitan Phoenix to plan and implement the units described in this chapter. As participants in TFA, we all work in Title I schools with a history of underperformance on measures of academic achievement, located in working-class Latino communities.

In this chapter, I will share a framework for and some examples of this work. Although I am proud of what we've accomplished with our students, I will also share critical reflections, demonstrating the complexity of the tensions between critical pedagogy and increasingly stringent accountability measures placed on teachers and students.

Achievement by any measure necessary

Many social justice educators hold a "by any means necessary" disposition towards their work, no doubt inspired by Malcolm X's most famous quote. Yet, as they do so, many fail to demonstrate how their methods lead students to higher levels of critical awareness or actions related to social justice. Nor do they demonstrate correlation between their methods and increased academic achievement. This lack of evidence has contributed to a devaluation of social justice education in this time of testing and accountability.

In the real world, social justice educators cannot drop their weapons and pick up a standardized, scripted curriculum whose only goal is to prepare students for a test. Rather, they need to be equipped with tools that assist them in creating a curriculum that leads to achievement by any *measure* necessary, teaching through and beyond high-stakes tests. Achievement on these tests can serve as both a sword and a shield for social justice educators, who can use student achievement results to advocate for their pedagogical project as well as defend it against the attacks of those who seek to maintain the status quo of schools.

UbD and aligning instruction to assessments

State standards, performance objectives, and standardized assessments can and should be part of a strong social justice curriculum. While this may be a debatable assertion, tighter measures of accountability offer teachers little choice in teaching towards a test. There is a human cost to failure in schools, and the stakes around tests are often highest for minoritized students. Social justice educators must use methods that have been shown to work in increasing student achievement across many different demographics. One particular approach applies the work of Wiggins and McTighe (2005), who created the curriculum planning process titled "Understanding by Design" (UbD). While many educators work to align their instruction to standards, UbD provides a framework for aligning instruction to assessments, and the distinction is profound. While I can easily align reading Corky Gonzalez's poem "I Am Joaquin" to state standards by analyzing its use of figurative language or its theme, it is more difficult to ensure that my students' learning with this poem will appear on a standardized test that measures their reading skills using out-of-context and often irrelevant texts.

In order to align instruction to assessments, Wiggins and McTighe advocate for a process of deconstructing high-stakes assessments. Analyzing items on high-stakes tests provides teachers with an insight into the knowledge and skills needed to complete the item successfully, and a sequenced list of objectives. More important, these items provide question frames that teachers can use on diagnostic, formative, and summative assessments they create.

Consider the following example from Arizona's state standards for 6th grade reading. Standard 1.4.1. states that students must be able to determine the effect of affixes on root words. The following question from a sample AIMS[3] test posted on the Arizona Department of Education website is used to measure mastery of this standard:

21. Adding the prefix bi- to the word annual makes a new word that means:

    A.   Two times each year
    B.   More than two times
    C.   Three times each year
    D.   More than three years

Surely, not every AIMS test will have this same question, as any affix or any root word could be used to measure mastery. However the frame created by the question can be used to create similar items on assessments given to students throughout the year. Thus, teachers can use UbD to ensure the curriculum they plan is aligned not only to standards but also to high-stakes tests. The power of teaching through the test lies in using such question frames with texts that are grounded in students' critical understanding of the world around them.

The assessment item on the released AIMS test is connected to a letter that a student council has written to the school principal, proposing new activities for spirit week. During an expository text unit I conducted about the Development, Relief, and Education of Alien Minors (DREAM) Act[4], I used the same and similar assessment items after students read an op-ed from a local newspaper advocating for the passage of the DREAM Act. The article included the sentence, "Proponents of the DREAM Act hope to host a biannual conference aimed at providing information and support to undocumented students and their families." In reading this article, not only are students learning about the prefixes bi-, pro-, and un-, they are also learning about the DREAM Act and how they and others can advocate for this important legislation. Using the question frames, they are also practicing for the AIMS test they will take later in the year, which will be used by the state to assess their mastery of 6th grade content and our school's overall effectiveness. Later, students will have to pass this test in order to graduate from high school.

The cultural capital of academic achievement

Of course, there are critiques of this form of curriculum development, ranging from accusations of narrowing curriculum to disempowering other knowledge bases. A UbD-influenced curriculum surely runs the risk of promoting the status quo of schools in the hands of an uncritical educator who teaches to the test. Yet, social justice educators who see academic achievement infused with critical capacity as cultural and social capital can avoid such a pitfall.

Hong and Youngs (2008) argue that achievement on high-stakes tests can serve as both institutional and embodied cultural capital. Derived from Bourdieu's (1973, 1986) cultural capital theory, Olneck (2000) describes institutional capital as the markers provided by institutions of academic competence, including degrees, diplomas, and test scores. Alternatively, embodied capital is demonstrated by cultural behaviors and dispositions that reinforce dominant cultural knowledge. If schools are truly meritocratic institutions, achievement on high-stakes tests should foster the development of both institutional and embodied cultural capital that will serve poor and working class students as they progress through the educational system and engage in social systems. Although educational meritocracy has been debated by those who see it as the heart of the system (Ravitch, 1996; Hirsch, 1995), and those who see it as nothing more than a fantasy (Bowles & Gintis, 1976; Finn, 1999), the development of academic achievement by poor and working-class youth would force the hand of the public education system to either demonstrate how such academic achievement results in the development of cultural capital, or pull back the veil on the meritocratic promise of public education. In other words, academic achievement will allow poor and working-class communities to beat the public education system at its own game, or expose the game as nothing more than a hegemonic illusion.

Education for critical capacity

The example of using standard 1.4.1. and released AIMS items within an expository unit about the DREAM Act reflects both the academic side of "teaching through the test" as well as its more critical components. When teaching through the test, it is important to consider the world beyond assessments of student academic achievement. To this end, curriculum should not focus solely on outcomes like achievement on high-stakes tests, but rather the development of students' critical capacity for understanding what forces impact how their social world functions as well as the willingness and courage to take action to transform the structures causing oppressive situations (Freire, 1998). The group of students who engaged in the DREAM Act unit was predominately Latino, and most of the students were either undocumented or had family members who were. It was important for them to understand how immigration status affects educational opportunity, and more important, what could be done to change this relationship in order to broker a better deal for them in the broader society. This aligns to Freire's (1998) description of critical capacity: a relentless state of curiosity moving towards the revelation of hidden roots of oppressive situations. In addition, critical capacity includes one's willingness to take action and engage in risks that lead to the altering of an oppressive situation. Thus, critical capacity includes a cycle of praxis, where one's critical thinking and critical actions lead them to higher levels of critical consciousness and meaningful social action en route to less oppressive situations (Freire, 1973). In the English/Language Arts classroom, teachers can guide students through a curriculum that leads students towards critical consciousness and engaging in transformational resistance (Solorzano & Delgado-Bernal, 2001).

Critical consciousness

Freire (1973) describes critical consciousness as a consciousness that is integrated with reality, as people use empirical facts to understand causal and circumstantial relationships, particularly those that are at the root of oppressive situations. He differentiates between critical consciousness and other forms of consciousness that are created by and strengthen oppressive relationships. In a state of magic consciousness, people see facts as superior and arbitrary, and are thus controlled by them. Freire explains magic consciousness leads people to adapt to reality with a sense of fatalism and impossibility, in particular when considering their oppression. In between critical consciousness and magic consciousness is the state of naïve consciousness, where people find themselves superior or completely in control of facts, and thus superimpose themselves over reality. This limits people's ability to truly understand their oppression in a way that allows them to work towards their freedom, as naïve consciousness can lead a person to ignoring any set of facts, including the facts that describe their own oppression.

Too often, poor and working-class students resign themselves to magic and naïve consciousness. In their understanding of the relationship between immigration status and educational opportunity, many students see its oppressive nature, yet cannot conceive of how to take actions that will lead to any kind of meaningful transformation of the situation. This leads to feelings of helplessness for those students who are undocumented, as they cannot change their situation. It also leads to feelings of powerlessness for those who are citizens, including students and teachers, as they cannot help others who lack their own privileges. Ultimately, English/Language Arts curriculum must develop the critical consciousness of both students and teachers, as it furthers their critical capacity and ability to take part in transformative actions that will lead to the practice of education as freedom.

Transformational resistance

The realization of human agency, described by Solorzano and Solorzano (1995) as the possession of skills and confidence to act on one's own behalf, is an important outcome for any curriculum that seeks to develop critical capacity. When people realize their sense of human agency, they can begin to engage in acts of resistance. Giroux (1983a, 1983b) explains that resistance consists of the level of critique of social oppression as well as the level of motivation experienced from an interest in social justice. Using these dimensions, Solorzano and Delgado-Bernal (2001) explain that students who engage in transformational resistance have both a strong critique of social oppression and a strong interest in and motivation from social justice (see Figure 1). They argue that transformational resistance offers students the best chance at creating meaningful social change.

In the DREAM Act unit, students were not simply guided to increase their literacy skills with regard to expository text. Rather, they were led to use those skills in their engagement with transformational resistance, by learning more about the actions they could take to advocate and fight for the passage of the DREAM Act. Students wrote letters to friends and family that described the DREAM Act and encouraged others to become involved in advocating for it. They also wrote persuasive letters to elected leaders demanding support for the legislation. These letters were aligned to state standards as well as state writing assessments, and reflected the students' use of their academic achievement to struggle for liberation. It is not enough for students to merely achieve academic success. However, academic success is a vital part of the struggle for a better deal.

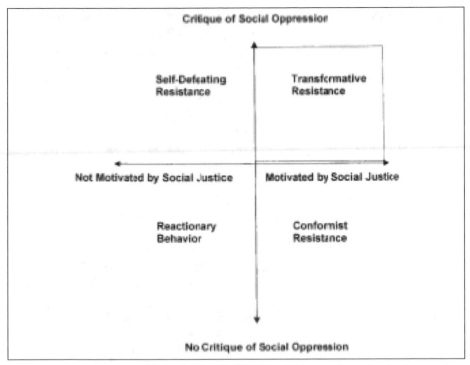

Figure 1. Solorzano and Delgado-Bernal's (2001) model for transformational resistance

Teaching through the test in practice

Academic achievement does not have to exist as precursor to the fostering of critical capacity and acts of transformational resistance. Both processes must occur simultaneously and are ultimately mutually constitutive. I will now turn our attention to sample units that engage in teaching through the test via their alignment to high-stakes tests and their explicit use of critical pedagogy. In our context in Arizona, where we teach in predominately Latino communities, issues related to labor, gangs, and immigration policies, the criminal justice system tend to occupy our students' worries as they represent just some of the forces that most deeply affect their lives and well-being (Syme, 2004).

Farm worker injustice

The same 6th graders who engaged in the DREAM Act unit took part in another unit that focused on both expository and literary text and an analysis of the injustices experienced historically and contemporarily by farm workers. Francisco Jimenez' (1997) memoir *The Circuit: Stories from the Life of a Migrant Child* inspired the farm worker injustice unit, which was organized around the following *essential questions*, another concept for planning curriculum outlined by UbD: (1) What are the current injustices farm workers face? (2) How do farm workers use the community to solve their problems? (3) How can we stand in solidarity with farm workers? (4) Who is the UFW and how do they fight injustice? This unit included reading "The Circuit" as well as a series of recent articles from periodicals found on the United Farm Workers' website that highlighted current injustices experienced by farm workers.

At the end of the unit, students wrote an expository essay describing how people can stand in solidarity with farm workers, which was used to create pamphlets intended to inform the public about injustices experienced by farm workers. The pamphlets were displayed at the school, and students had the option of distributing them in the community in whatever method they chose. Students also circulated an online petition organized by the UFW that pressured states to hold farm owners accountable in the deaths of workers. The students enthusiastically collected hundreds of signatures over the course of the four-week unit. Essays, pamphlets, and the petition all stand as examples of students taking acts of transformational resistance, armed with a critical consciousness about farm worker injustice.

Like the DREAM Act unit, this unit sought to develop literacy skills through reading and writing non-fiction text. In addition, the inclusion of Francisco Jimenez's memoir allowed the incorporation of literary analysis standards. As students read *The Circuit*, they learned and practiced the state standards for comprehending literary text. Students were instructed to describe the plot and characters of stories, identify the narrative point of view and theme, and analyze the setting, mood, and author's word choice: all in accordance to Arizona's 6th grade reading standards. Instruction and assessments were aligned to released AIMS items intended to measure mastery of these standards. Standards were spiraled throughout the unit, and progress towards them was measured on quizzes given at the end of each week.

At the end of the year, these students demonstrated incredible academic gains on the AIMS test when compared to their peers in the district. The students at this school passed the reading and writing AIMS tests at a higher rate than any other school in the district. The reliability of this demonstration of academic achievement will be discussed later in the chapter.

The history and effects of gangs

In his first year of teaching middle school language arts, Kurtis Indorf recognized his 8th graders' academic success was inhibited by a variety of social forces that made school seem unimportant, such as poverty, immigration reform, institutional racism, and a strong presence of gang activity in the community surrounding his school. Recognizing high levels of gang affiliation by students in his 8th grade classes, Mr. Indorf created a unit intended to study the history and effects of gangs. The unit used two essential questions: (1) Why were gangs created? and (2) What are gangs' effects on society? The unit's goals were to master writing logically organized expository essays and critically analyze the influences of gangs on their community.

Students analyzed several non-fiction texts, including informational articles on Prohibition-era gangs and contemporary gangs such as the Bloods, Crips, and Mexican Mafia. Students studied the connection between gangs and drugs, violence, and the victimization of community members. At the end of the unit, students considered how gangs could be good for a community, using a powerful editorial from the *Los Angeles Times* that explained how gangs give people a sense of community and identification that could be re-cast in a more positive way. Students engaged in the critical analysis of non-fiction text, developing standards-aligned skills like finding the main idea and summarizing the main points of the article, as well as broader notions of critical literacy such as understanding the power relationships and historical foundations of the topics of study. As students deconstructed the texts, they re-presented the information found in the articles by producing constructed responses. These responses demonstrated understanding of the text and explained their own reflections and ideas about gangs.

Mr. Indorf explains that the impact of this unit was seen in his students' sense of identity and belonging, which is an important part of critical consciousness. In his words, the unit led students to

> feeling not oppressed, marginalized and powerless. In the class culture, everyone felt like they belonged and the students knew where everyone was coming from. They all had hardships, they all endured a common struggle and they felt together. The gang unit brought the class together with a common understanding. They had a sense that they had all gone through a struggle together and all came through it successfully. (personal communication, March 30, 2011)

He explains that those students who had personally experienced the effects of gangs in their own lives felt this most poignantly. He says,

> There were students in class who joined gangs. Being able to name the psychology and the thinking behind that decision made everyone more understandable. They saw it was not really their fault, as there are huge structural and societal instances of violence. The understanding also made gangs less desirable. They connected gangs to social marginalization and poverty and the seeking of belonging. They grew in their understanding and analysis of society, and people became less attracted to it. They saw that joining a gang was less about an "I'm tough" mentality, but rather a feeling of "I don't belong." What they needed was a place where they belonged, and that is what the classroom became.

In addition, Mr. Indorf reports that his students' increased sense of belonging and critical consciousness, via this and other units that incorporated a similar pedagogy, led them to increased academic achievement. While he has no data to demonstrate the effectiveness of this unit in particular (an issue that will be discussed later), by the end of the year, he reports that his students grew an average of 2.78 years in reading, based on the Basic Reading Inventory (BRI) administered by his school throughout the year. He firmly believes that such an incredible growth in achievement would not be possible were it not for his students' engagement with a curriculum that was aimed at increasing their sense of belonging and critical consciousness.

The criminal justice system

The importance of teaching through the test and leading students to life-changing academic achievement is not lost on David Hall, a first-year high school teacher who works with students who are not on track to graduate. In Mr. Hall's English classes, these students are making up credits so that they earn enough to graduate, as they prepare to take the exit exam they have already failed, in the hopes that they will pass and complete that requirement for graduation. Yet, Mr. Hall recognizes that many of these students are not in his class just because they find reading and writing difficult. Rather, many of them are unmotivated by and disinvested in academic success and struggle to see the relevance and importance of school. With this in mind, Mr. Hall strives to create units that will prepare students for both the high school exit exam and the end of course exam, as well as help them to see the relevance of literacy in understanding and responding to the world around them, moving them away from magic and naïve consciousness and towards critical consciousness.

One of Mr. Hall's units is focused on the novel *Monster* by Walter Dean Myers (2001), a story about a 16-year-old young man who is being tried for murder. Mr. Hall has expanded the scope of the unit to consider the context of the criminal justice system, and its role in society. Students engage in understanding both the fictitious representation of crime and punishment in *Monster* as well as non-fiction case studies of recent high-profile murders in the Greater Phoenix area. In these case studies, students read articles and opinion pieces from the local newspaper about these crimes.

During this four-week unit, Mr. Hall leads his students in the consideration of "big questions" about crime and punishment: Why do people commit crimes and how does the criminal justice system operate? What role does racism play in the justice system? Is the prison system meant to punish or rehabilitate? Students engage in these questions with the literary and non-fiction texts provided by Mr. Hall, and are asked to reflect on these questions using examples of people from their own lives who have committed crimes and have been through the criminal justice system.

As students engage with texts, they are led through instruction and practice tied to the state standards in understanding both literary and non-fiction tests. At different points of the unit, students take standards-aligned and high-stakes assessment-aligned reading tests, and create timed essays that are scored on a writing rubric provided by the state. At the end of the unit, students write a persuasive essay, debating whether or not a society can exist without crime, using examples from *Monster*, the non-fiction case studies, and their own experiences.

At the culmination of the unit, Mr. Hall reported success in, using his words, both "student-focused," and "number-focused" terms. In describing student success, he writes in an e-mail:

> This was BY FAR the most engaging unit I had all year. Working in a largely Hispanic, low-income area where many students have relatives in prison (or in some cases been to prison themselves), this was about as applicable as books can get to their lives. Discussion was lively and students DIDN'T WANT TO PUT THE BOOK DOWN, a first in my classroom. Calls to stop for the day were often met with groans of 'Let us read more!'" (personal comunication, February 2, 2011)

In explaining numbers-oriented success, Mr. Hall reports that while only a third of students usually pass the end of unit tests needed for recovering credits, following this unit, more than two-thirds of students passed the assessment.

The MCSO's immigration enforcement policies

Ryan Booms teaches at a school in the Greater Phoenix area whose student population is 97% Latino, and where 94% of students qualify for free or reduced lunch. Among the most important issues this community faces is the ever-present threat of the Maricopa County Sherriff's Office (MCSO), which has increasingly exercised its right to enforce federal immigration laws throughout the county. Led by Sheriff Joe Arpaio, this unit's actions have been well documented in both the local and national media and have resulted in the arrest of more than 40,000 suspected undocumented immigrants over the past few years. Not surprisingly, Mr. Booms's students hold a well-founded anger and frustration towards the MCSO, as well as a sense of helplessness against the immigration policies of the law enforcement unit.

Knowing this, Mr. Booms has taught a four-week non-fiction text unit to his middle school students for the past two years that examines the issue of the MCSO's immigration enforcement policies. The unit is led by the following essential questions: What are the immigration enforcement policies of the MCSO? What are the effects of these policies? Are the policies of the MCSO good policies? In the unit, students read a variety of expository and persuasive articles from local newspapers, which they summarize and use for the culminating assignment of the unit: writing a letter to their local state senator stating their beliefs as to whether or not the MCSO should be allowed to enforce immigration policies. This letter stands as a powerful example of transformational resistance that deepens students' critical capacity.

Each day during this unit, students complete an exit ticket with two sentence frames: "I learned . . ." and "I will use this knowledge to . . . ." Not only are students learning academic literacy skills such as finding and restating the main idea and inferring the meaning of new vocabulary words, they are learning about the effects of the MCSO's policies detailed in the texts they read and comparing them to their own feelings and reflections about the MCSO. In a letter to her state senator, one student writes,

> My uncle was caught by Sherrif Arpaio. Joe's deputies arrested my uncle, and he was in jail for 6 months before he was sent back to Mexico. I felt like the world was going to end because he was a very good man. I hate to see other people suffer the way I did because their family or friends have been arrested or sent back to Mexico. (personal communication, April 6, 2011)

Mr. Booms reports dramatic gains in writing as a result of this unit. He explains,

> On our diagnostic [a recycled prompt from a released state test], only a handful of sixth graders wrote more than one paragraph for a persuasive essay. Very few used facts. Most just begged the reader with phrases like "pretty pretty pleeeeease." In their letters, nearly every student was able to write a well-organized five-paragraph essay that contained an introduction, three body paragraphs containing three distinct reasons, and a satisfying conclusion using a concession/rebuttal. Students were able to develop arguments based on facts from the articles rather than their personal opinions. (personal communication, April 6, 2011)

SB1070

In April 2010, the Support Our Law Enforcement and Safe Neighborhoods Act (SB1070) was signed into law in Arizona. Commonly recognized as the broadest and most strict anti-illegal immigration legislation in the United States, SB1070 makes it a crime for an immigrant to not carry their immigration documents at all times and expands the enforcement of immigration laws by state and local authorities. From the minute the bill was passed, significant demonstrations of opposition to the law were held across the nation. First-year teacher Regina Mills could see the force of the debate over SB1070 in her 9th and 10th grade English classes, and decided to use it to spearhead a unit on activism.

Over two weeks, her students read the law in its entirety, as well as articles discussing the court proceedings that followed constitutional challenges to it. Students also read commentaries in support of and in opposition to SB1070 in local and national newspapers. As students read these texts, they were instructed in finding the main idea and supporting details, and created summaries of the texts, which was particularly difficult with official legal documents. Students used these summaries to write a letter to a local leader of their choice, explaining their stance on SB1070.

As the students prepared their letter, they were instructed in using persuasive strategies in their writing, as well as properly formatting a business letter and an envelope, skills that Mrs. Mills was surprised her students did not have. They were also taught to use sources to defend their arguments, using the texts they read earlier in the unit. After the letters were completed, Mrs. Mills sent them in bundles to the local and state legislators and elected officials students had written to, in order to maximize the opportunity for students to receive a response from the leaders. As they awaited responses to their letters, students took a formative assessment on non-fiction reading standards, aligned to the AIMS test. On previous assessments, students had mastered a class average of 62% of the items related to finding the main idea of an article, while on this test (which featured out of context texts not related to SB1070), students mastered the objective at 82%. Similar growth was seen in distinguishing fact and opinion (74% to 85%), determining author's purpose (62% to 71%), and analyzing text features (68% to 81%)

In addition to the academic growth demonstrated at the end of the unit, several students received responses to their letter from, among others, Governor Jan Brewer, U.S. Representative Raul Grijalva, and County Sherriff Joe Arpaio. One student who received a reply from Sheriff Arpaio was surprised to see a letter from him, and reflected that the contents of the sheriff's reply only made the student less supportive of the sheriff. The student says,

> It was cool getting a letter from Sheriff Joe, though my mom almost smacked me when she saw my name and the Sheriff's address. Now that I have this mean-sounding letter from Sheriff Joe, I can show it to other people so they won't vote for him next time. (personal communication, April 7, 2011)

Another student says that receiving a reply from an elected leader has led to several conversations in her house about the current debate over immigration. She says,

> The biggest thing I remember about the SB1070 project was that my family and I discussed it a lot. We spent a lot of time focusing on the part of the Pledge of Allegiance, which said, "and liberty and justice or all." This means *everyone*, not just whites.

In both of these students' experiences, the demonstration of the power of academic achievement infused with critical capacity is profound. It is doubtful that students' letters would have been taken seriously, were they not well written. At the same time, it is doubtful that they would have been able to create such powerful letters and engage in such meaningful discussions were it not for an increased sense of critical capacity.

Reflections and recommendations

Teaching through the test and towards critical capacity can result in empowered students who conceive of themselves as active agents of change. Still, in teaching through the test, there are several issues that remain unresolved and need to be explored further. First, in this model, the role of assessments is critical, as they stand as the pivot between life-changing academic achievement and the development of critical capacity. Yet, creating assessments is an incredibly complex, time-consuming task that all of the teachers in this chapter struggle with. This includes both standards-aligned assessments as well as assessments of critical capacity. In order to improve our work, we recognize we must become better at understanding effective and efficient ways to create standards-aligned assessments, as well as ways to collect data that demonstrate the growth of students' critical capacity.

Given our challenges with assessments, it is important to note that the data collected from these units are only as good as the instruments used to collect them. The dramatic gains seen in these examples calls into questions the reliability of data gained from "official" assessments as well as teacher-created assessments. Such dramatic growth on measures such as AIMS and BRI suggests not only that students achieved at high levels after engaging in a pedagogy that teaches through the test, but also that they achieved at incredibly low levels before such an experience. If we look at the growth reported by Mr. Indorf, we need to ask ourselves if such dramatic growth (2.78 years of growth in one school year) is an effect of not just increased skills but increased motivation. For example, some of his students could have bombed the pre-test or previous year's test consciously by not trying or not caring about the assessment. Perhaps they were *always* capable of scoring at such a high level on the assessment, but chose not to put forth any effort in demonstrating this. Thus, the curriculum that teaches through the test may not lead students to anything they did not already possess in an academic sense, but rather made school seem more relevant and worthy of students' attention. While this calls into question claims of "growth" it still demonstrates the power of teaching through the test when, at the end of the day, increased achievement measured by official assessments allows students access to increased academic capital inside of school systems.

A second growth area in our teaching through the test is using student-generated topics for units. In the examples provided in this chapter, topics for study were generated by teachers' understandings of students and their social situations, as opposed to student understanding of their own social situations. While issues such as immigration reform and the criminal justice system are clearly important in the lives of the students described in this chapter, there are surely other social issues that students perceive to be important that are under-recognized by their teachers. Yet, allowing students to take more control and generate their own themes is challenging for several reasons. First, planning units such as these is a time-intensive task that is completed far in advance of the teaching of the units. Using student-generated topics to guide units would be very difficult in terms of the time required for designing units such as these. Also, teachers must work in a delicate balance of ensuring that students are engaged in understanding topics they find important while keeping track of all of the concepts students are required to learn and expected to understand in a given year.

In addition, the initiation of a pedagogical project which values critical capacity will always struggle with the need to measure critical capacity, and demonstrate correlation between increased levels of critical capacity and a given curricular intervention. Sadly, our project lacks this vital element, yet this speaks to the challenge of engaging in a curriculum that teaches through the test. When having to prioritize whether to focus on quantifiable outputs that measure academic achievement, or qualitative outputs that measure critical capacity, we have chosen to dedicate our limited time and resources to the former, given the consequences of such academic measures. If our students were able to demonstrate an increase in critical capacity and not increased academic achievement, the consequences within school systems would be far more drastic than the inverse. Yet, these measures are not mutually exclusive, and we must move towards incorporating more accurate and valid measures of student critical capacity.

Finally, more analysis must be made in understanding the privileges that are in play when a teacher finds that he or she is capable of creating such a curriculum. Not only can this be examined structurally (by looking at the differences between schools that use strict scripted curriculum versus schools that give teachers the ability to modify the curriculum), but this can also be viewed through a lens of race, class, and gender. It is important to recognize that most of the examples of teaching through the test in this chapter come from male teachers, something that was done neither unconsciously nor purposely. While I asked both male and female teachers to offer examples for this chapter, one of the females I asked declined to participate because she felt her work did not fit well within the framework I described to them, while another did not respond to the request. I feel very strongly that the examples discussed in this chapter best represent a framework of teaching through the test, yet it is important to consider how privilege may play a role in teachers' abilities to take such actions or be open to sharing their work with others.

Conclusion

Teaching through the test offers an example of how teachers can turn their critique of school systems and policies into a pedagogical project that seeks to address their analyses of the problem. Duncan-Andrade (2009) refers to this effort as an example of "critical hope," where teachers offer students the means with which to struggle for their liberation.

In the tension between critical pedagogy and the increasing presence of accountability measures centered on high-stakes and standardized assessments, three paths are commonly seen for social justice educators (Eversman & Diaz, 2010). They can abandon critical pedagogy and offer their students a curriculum devoid of critical capacity; they can shun accountability policies and risk losing their jobs to someone who will do what they are told; and they can leave teaching altogether due to their inability to navigate this tension. We must forge a fourth path, where the goals of critical pedagogy and accountability policies are not seen as a false binary, but rather a dialectic that offers hope and casts school success as a potent weapon in our students' struggle for liberation. Teaching through the test offers an example of such a path, which is increasingly needed as the accountability noose tightens on social justice educators worldwide.

Notes

1. Teach For America is a program for recent college graduates to commit two years to teaching in low-income rural and urban communities in an effort to close the achievement gap that exists between youth in low-income communities and their more affluent peers. Since its inception in 1990, the program has sparked controversy and heated debate over its role in education reform and teacher preparation, a full discussion of which lies outside the scope of this chapter. For additional discussion, see Labaree (2010) and Koerner, Lynch, and Martin (2008).
2. Attending workshops offered by the California State University Expository Reading and Writing Task Force was very influential in this work. These workshops are part of the CSU's efforts to professionally develop high school teachers in expository reading and writing instruction, grounded in critical literacy. My idea of "teaching through the test" is different from their work, mostly in its use of assessments, data collection, and unit topics.
3. Arizona's Instrument to Measure Standards, Arizona's testing system for accountability.
4. If passed, the DREAM Act would allow undocumented students under the age of 18 who have spent at least three years in the country and have graduated high school the opportunity to join the military and qualify for federal and state financial aid, rights that are currently restricted from them. It also includes a measure that would allow undocumented youth the opportunity to adjust their immigration status after completion of a higher education degree or military service.

References

Bourdieu, P. (1973). Cultural reproduction and social reproduction. In R. Brown (Ed.), *Knowledge, education and cultural change* (pp. 71–112). London: Tavistock.

Bourdieu, P. (1986). The forms of capital. In John Richardson (Ed.), *Handbook of theory and research for sociology of education* (pp. 241–258). New York: Greenwood Press.

Bowles, H., & Gintis, S. (1976). *Schooling in capitalist America: Economic reform and the contradictions of economic life.* New York: Basic Books.

Duncan-Andrade, J. (2009) Note to educators: Hope required when growing roses in concrete. *Harvard Education Review, 79*(2), 181–194.

Eversman, K. A., & Diaz, V. H. (2010). Navigating the tensions of globalization for social justice educators. *Journal of the International Society for Teacher Education, 14*(2), 59–65.

Finn, P. J. (1999). *Literacy with an attitude: Educating working-class children in their own self-interest.* New York: SUNY Press.

Freire, P. (1970). *Pedagogy of the oppressed.* New York: Continuum.

Freire, P. (1973). *Education for critical consciousness.* New York: Continuum.

Freire, P. (1998). *Pedagogy of freedom: Ethics, democracy, and civic courage* (P. Clarke, Trans.). New York: Rowman and Littlefield Publishers, Inc.

Freire, P., & Macedo, D. (1987). *Reading the word and the world.* South Hadley, MA: Bergin and Garvey.

Giroux, H. (1983a). Theories of reproduction and resistance in the new sociology of education: A critical analysis. *Harvard Educational Review, 55,* 257–293.

Giroux, H. (1983b). *Theories and resistance in education.* South Hadley, MA: Bergin and Garvey.

Hirsch, F. (1995) *Social limits to growth.* London: Routledge.

Hong, W. P., & Youngs, P. (2008). Does high-stakes testing increase cultural capital among low-income and racial minority students? *Education Policy Analysis Archives, 16*(6). Retrieved 1 Dec 2009 from http://epaa.asu.edu/epaa/v16n6/.

Jimenez, F. (1997). *The circuit: Stories from the life of a migrant child.* New York: Houghton Mifflin.

Koerner, M. Lynch, D., & Martin, S. (2008). Why we partner ith Teach for America: Changing the conversation. *Phi Delta Kappan, 89*(10), 726–729.

Larrabee, D. (2010). Teach for America and teacher ed: Heads they win, tails we lose. *Journal of Teacher Education, 61*(1–2), 48–55.

Myers, W. D. (2001). *Monster.* New York: Amistad.

Olneck, M. (2000). Can multicultural education change what counts as cultural capital? *American Educational Research Journal, 37*(2), 317–348.

Ravitch, Diane. (1996) *National standards in American education: A citizen's guide.* Washington: The Brookings Institution.

Solorzano, D., & Solorzano, R. (1995). The Chicano educational experience: A proposed framework for effective schools in Chicano communities. *Educational Policy, 9,* 293–314.

Solorzano, D., & Delgado-Bernal, D. (2001). Examining transformational resistance through a critical race and LatCrit theory framework: Chicana and Chicano students in an urban context. *Urban Education, 36*(3), 308–342.

Syme, S. L. (2004). "Social determinants of health: The community as empowered partner." *Preventing Chronic Disease: Public Health Research, Practice, and Policy, 1*(1), 1–4.

Wiggins, G. P., & McTighe, J. (2005) *Understanding by design.* Alexandria, VA: ASCD.

SECTION 2.

De-standardizing Teachers and Learning

6. *Just What Is Response to Intervention and What's It Doing in a Nice Field Like Education? A Critical Race Theory Examination of Response to Intervention*

Nicholas Daniel Hartlep & Antonio L. Ellis

In her (1998) *Qualitative Studies in Education* article, "Just What Is Critical Race Theory and What's It Doing in a Nice Field Like Education?" critical race theorist elder stateswoman Gloria Ladson-Billings writes that "[a]dopting and adapting CRT [critical race theory] as a framework for educational equity means that we will have to expose racism in education *and* propose radical solutions for addressing it. We will have to take bold and sometimes unpopular positions" (p. 22, italics in original). Inspired by her article, this chapter, "Just What Is Critical Race Theory and What's It Doing in a Nice Field Like Education?" is our attempt to use critical race theory as an analytical lens to examine response-to-intervention's (RTI) (in)ability to reduce disproportionality in special education, hence the chapter's subtitle "A Critical Race Theory Examination of Response to Intervention."

Disproportionality and overrepresentation

According to Blanchett (2006), "Disproportionality exists when students' representation in special education programs or specific special education categories exceeds their proportional enrollment in a school's general population" (p. 24). And overrepresentation, according to Artiles and Trent (2000), occurs when there are "unequal proportions of culturally diverse students in special education programs" (p. 514). Artiles and Trent explicate that there are two patterns associated with disproportionately, namely over- and underrepresentation.

This chapter uses the terms "disproportionality" and "overrepresentation" interchangeably since both cover students who are placed in special education who do not need to be and, likewise, students who are not placed in special education who do need to be. In either situation, students' educational needs are not being met; this is a problem. RTI's interest in the No Child Left Behind Act (NCLB) and disproportionality are topical concerns for students of color. Artiles, Bal, and King Thorius (2010, p. 252) remind us that:

> Diverse learners' inappropriate placement in special education prevents these students from access to high-status resources such as programs and curricula in general education and narrows their chances for future learning opportunities because disability identification is associated with higher school dropout rates and reduced access to higher education programs.

Response to intervention's interest in standards and No Child Left Behind

An examination of RTI is important in the context of standards based reform efforts because RTI supports the NCLB push for academic accountability (A. Artiles, personal communication, June 27, 2011; Kauffman, 2004). Kavale and Spaulding (2008) indicate that RTI serves an accountability function, and is promoted not because it reduces disproportionality, but rather because NCLB promotes its use (A. Artiles, personal communication, June 27, 2011). Accordingly, Kavale and Spaulding assert, "The NCLB foundation provides the reason for general education embracing RTI when historically many special education initiatives (e.g., inclusion) have not been so readily embraced" (p. 138). Others besides Kavale (A. Artiles, personal communication, June 27, 2011; Kauffman, 2004; Kavale & Spaulding, 2008) believe that the objectives of RTI are aligned with NCLB.

Purpose of chapter

This chapter analyzes six consecutive years of state-level data (all 50 states plus the District of Columbia). The analysis examines RTI's (in)ability to reduce disproportionate representation of minorities—African American, Hispanic, Asian/Pacific Islander, American Indian—in special education. It begins with a brief background of the RTI model compared to the ability-achievement discrepancy model (Braden, 1987; Cone & Wilson, 1981; Evans, 1992; Finlan, 1992; Payette, Clarizio, Phillips, & Bennett, 1995; Vaughn, Wanzek, Woodruff, & Linan-Thompson, 2007). Critical race theory is then briefly referenced, outlining theories and critical concepts that can help the reader better understand why RTI is so popular (special theme issue of *Theory into Practice*, 2010) and why it may not be achieving desired results. This is followed by an outline of the data and methodologies used when examining RTI. The penultimate section of the chapter is the study's findings, followed by the provision of four policy recommendations that can help reduce overrepresentation in special education.

Background

In order for students to qualify for, and to be *labeled* in need of special education, they must first be identified. The RTI model is an alternative to the ability-achievement discrepancy model (Braden, 1987; Cone & Wilson, 1981; Evans, 1992; Finlan, 1992; Payette, Clarizio, Phillips, & Bennett, 1995) to identify learning disabilities. The latter requires children to exhibit a severe discrepancy between their IQ and academic achievement as measured by standardized tests (Mercer, Jordan, Allsop, & Mercer, 1996), while the former requires children to fail to respond to interventions. One report, *A New Era: Revitalizing Special Education for Children and Their Families* discusses why RTI is a better model than the discrepancy model (President's Commission on Excellence in Special Education, 2002). The commission's report says,

> Eliminating IQ tests [or discrepancy models] from the identification process would help shift the emphasis in special education away from the current focus, which is on determining whether students are eligible for services, *towards providing students the interventions* they need to successfully learn. (p. 25, italics added)

The popularity of RTI stems from the notion that providing early intervention for students is better than waiting to see if there is a discrepancy between achievement and what would be expected given a student's IQ. According to the National Center on Response to Intervention (NCRTI) (2010a), "A goal of RTI is to minimize the risk for long-term negative learning outcomes by responding quickly and efficiently to documented learning or behavioral problems and ensuring appropriate identification of students with disabilities" (p. 4), and, most importantly that "RTI implementation should improve academic performance and behavior, simultaneously *reducing the likelihood that students are wrongly identified as having a disability*" (p. 5, italics added).

The ability-achievement discrepancy model has severe limitations for culturally and linguistically diverse (CLD) students, and has been questioned for years (Fletcher, Coutler, Reschly, & Vaughn, 2004; Fletcher, Francis, Rourke, Shaywitz, & Shaywitz, 1992; Siegel, 1992; Stuebing et al., 2002; Vellutino, Scanlon, & Lyon, 2000). One reason is that culturally biased standardized tests, as well as low teacher expectations, create conditions of "double jeopardy" for CLD students. In California, the *Larry P.* v. *Riles* case established the legal precedent that tests administered to minority children must have been validated for use with that population (C. Ajirotutu, personal communication, January 28, 2011; see also Vallas, 2009). The case provided the legal precedent against cultural bias in testing.

But we ask, what happens if programs that are created to reduce over-representation (programs which are seemingly well intentioned) nevertheless retain cultural biases? As Gerber (2005) mentions, bias is unavoidable; teachers can differ significantly despite their professional development and training. "Teachers are the test" then, not RTI (Gerber, 2005). Would we expect CLD students to respond to interventions positively if their teacher had a deficit view of their educability? Does RTI assist in reducing disproportionality in special education? Bouman (2010) found that the California school districts that he investigated that had implemented RTI did not have significantly lower placement rates than non-RTI districts. In fact, according to his analysis of five years of data from 2002 to 2007, African American students' disproportionality in special education significantly increased.

Response to intervention models compared to discrepancy models

Putatively, RTI reduces disproportionality by matching student needs with appropriate services (Barnes & Harlacher, 2008). RTI is a multi-tiered approach that aims to intervene and to measure student *responses to* teacher led *interventions*—hence its name (Barnes & Harlacher, 2008). Despite the fact that Fuchs and Fuchs (2005) advocate for a two-tiered approach, and Ikeda et al. (2002) advocate for a four-tiered approach, this chapter (consistent with the common description as seen in Diagram 2 below), operationalizes RTI as a three-tiered approach (Vaughn, Wanzek, Woodruff, & Linan-Thompson, 2007). Tier one consists of instruction with screening three times a year for all students. "Progress monitoring" occurs for students who are considered at risk (Vaughn & Fuchs, 2003). And while Tier two consists of intervention and progress monitoring for students who are struggling academically, "Tier three includes intensive interventions for students for whom the Tier two intervention was insufficient" (Vaughn, Wanzek, Woodruff, & Linan-Thompson, 2007, p. 19).

RTI is different from a discrepancy model since RTI continually monitors students' (in)abilities, while a discrepancy model simply waits for students to fall far enough behind so that they can qualify for special education services (Barnes & Harlacher, 2008). This is the reason that the ability-achievement discrepancy model has been labeled by some the "wait-to-fail" model, since once a student falls behind, s/he has a low likelihood of ever catching up. Given that RTI is perceived to be proactive and that the multiple tiers of instruction "provide increasing levels of support based on the student's need" (Barnes & Harlacher, 2008, p. 422), it is gaining popularity. However, the actual implementation of RTI by educators can be biased (Gerber, 2005).

Definition of Response to Intervention

The NCRTI (2010b) officially defines RTI as the following:

> Response to intervention integrates assessment and intervention within a multi-level prevention system to maximize student achievement and to reduce behavior problems. With RTI, schools identify students at risk for poor learning outcomes, monitor student progress, provide evidence-based interventions and adjust the intensity and nature of those interventions depending on a student's responsiveness, and identify students with learning disabilities.

RTI is the most recent recommended educational initiative by the U.S. Department of Education regarding the identification, treatment, and referral of students with special needs.

It is important, then, that special education students are properly identified, since inaccurate identification for special education has negative life consequences for students. Being placed into special education when a student does not need services can lead students to (a) being stereotyped and stigmatized by their peers; (b) having a low self-esteem; and (c) receiving an inadequate education, which will have cascading, educational, occupational, and economical repercussions.

This is why some have considered the problem of overrepresentation in special education to be like the "miner's canary"—a forewarning of something that threatens us all (Waitoller, Artiles, & Cheney, 2010, p. 29). The problem of overrepresentation cannot be "examined by focusing solely on the canary but on a situated relationship between the canary and the coal mine (i.e., the educational system and its attendant policies and practices that afford and constrain opportunities)" (Waitoller, Artiles, & Cheney, 2010, p. 29). This is why we feel that we must examine RTI and its outcomes critically.

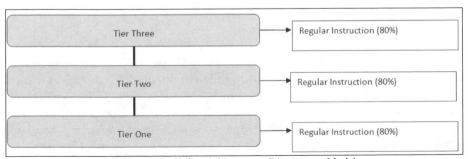

Diagram 1. Ability-Achievement Discrepancy Model

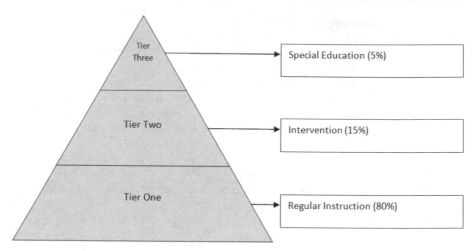

Diagram 2. Response to Intervention Model

The discrepancy model (see Diagram 1) is rectangular shaped. There is no perceived reduction in the number of students that are labeled in need of special education as students move through the model. The reason is because in this model there is no narrowing in the number of students at its base (who may receive special education services) compared to the top. Compare this to the RTI model.

The RTI model (see Diagram 2), however, is pyramid shaped. Presumably, there will be a reduction in the number of students who are labeled for special education since there is a narrowing as students move from the base to the apex of the model. The RTI model is logically constructed, and leads onlookers to believe that a reduction in the number of students that are labeled special education should follow. But does a reduction occur when RTI approaches are implemented (e.g., see Conclusion below)?

Critical race theory

In this section, we will discuss how critical race theory (CRT) is a popular theoretical/analytical model to employ in the field of (special) education studies in order to advocate for equity and justice in education (e.g., see Taylor, Gillborn, & Ladson-Billings, 2009). Drawing on three interpretations, concepts, and theories—Bell's (1980) theory of interest convergence, Swartz's (1992) concept of master scripting, and Stephan and Stephan's (2004) interpretation of "aversive racism"—this study questions the widespread belief that RTI is an effective program that is logically constructed to "ensure proper identification of students with disabilities" (NCRTI, 2010a, 2010b).

Although on the surface RTI appears to have the potential to reduce the number of students in special education, a CRT approach seeks to examine whether RTI may be simply "tinkering around the edges." RTI does not ask critical questions such as, *Why are minority children overrepresented?* and *How does the current educational structure—including standardization—feed into this overrepresentation?* Neither does RTI question itself. For instance, RTI fails to ask how can interventions work for nonwhite students when the (largely white) teachers who are the interventionists may question the educability of the intervened (nonwhite students)? RTI, in essence, could be labeled as merely an extension of an already Eurocentric and culturally biased battery of education processes and practices.

CRT would disbelieve RTI helps minority students as it is structured currently, because it is a "medical model." While the ability-achievement model (read: the "wait-to-fail" model) is a "social model" (Vallas, 2009)—incidentally a deficit model—RTI believes that it can fix the student's disability (or inability to learn at the rate and fluency we want) with a certain type of program, strategy, or intervention. RTI contends that the "disability," whatever it may be, is an abnormality of the student, rather than a characteristic that may be related to the learning environment—specifically at the culture or climate that we create as school leaders—or at the culturally biased instructional strategies that many teachers use (A. Renteria, personal communication, January 28, 2011). It also fails to look at factors outside the school that position students to have a "disability." The dominant culture assumes that there is something wrong with the student, rather than with the educational establishment, which is causing him/her not to learn. This is precisely why the "medical model" paradigm proliferates and speaks to the popularity of RTI and intervention programs. Intervention programs exonerate Eurocentric biases' culpability, and maintain the *modus operandi*—which results in overrepresentation.

For these aforesaid reasons, CRT questions the integrity of the interventions and the intention of RTI interventionists. According to Ladson-Billings (1998), "Critical race theory sees the official school curriculum as a culturally specific artifact designed to maintain a White supremacist master script" (p. 18). RTI fulfills the *master script* since it requires (minority) students to undergo interventions that legitimize dominant culture (White male) as the standards of knowledge. Swartz (1992) posits that master scripting silences multiple student voices and perspectives while legitimizing the dominant culture.

Interest convergence and master scripting

Bell's (1980) theory of interest convergence is also clearly at play since the advent of No Child Left Behind (NCLB) requires transparency and monitoring of disproportionality. RTI thus morphs into a veiled and paper attempt at reducing overrepresentation. As Kavale and Spaulding (2008) indicate, RTI has less to do with ridding special education of disproportionality, and more to do with NCLB focus on standards-based education. Research indicates that NCLB serves students unequally: white middle-class students well, minority and poor students not so well (Darling-Hammond, 2007). RTI is attractive from afar, but only because the policy is window-dressed (Kavale and Spaulding, 2008). In October 2001, George W. Bush commissioned a Presidents Commission on Excellence in Special Education (PCESE) report titled, *A New Era: Revitalizing Special Education for Children and Their Families* (Kauffman, 2004). Like RTI, the report pushed for "a culture of compliance to a culture of accountability" (PCESE, 2002, p. 4). The PCESE (2002) later reemphasizes the need to "insist on high academic standards and excellence" (p. 8), and "focuses on the importance of *expanding standards-based reforms*" (p. 35, italics added).

Aversive racism

Stephan and Stephan (2004) state that aversive racism is when people experience negative attitudes and beliefs toward a minority group, but avoid having outward behavioral or racist manifestations since they hold egalitarian values. These aversive racists regard themselves as non-prejudiced. CRT believes that culturally biased instructional strategies are not perceived to be biased by aversive racists. Therefore, when instructional problems emerge, aversive racists assume that something is wrong with the student, not the educational system, and especially not with the teacher. The cause (read: need for special education), then, is an individual (his/her family, culture, etc.) issue, not a deficiency of the school; the symptom is not caused by "unconscious bias" (Arnold & Lassmann, 2003), racist curriculum, instruction, and teachers' judgments (Gerber, 2005; Neal, McCray, Webb-Johnson, & Bridgest, 2003). Neal et al. (2003) studied 136 middle school teachers who viewed a videotape and completed a questionnaire. These researchers found that the teachers perceived students with African American culture–related movement styles as lower in achievement, higher in aggression, and more likely to need special education services than students with standard movement styles.

Following this study's findings, this chapter proposes four (possibly unpopular) policy recommendations that can lead to the reduction of special education disproportionality. These recommendations are, in essence, a response to Ladson-Billings's (1998) challenge that "we will have to expose racism in education *and* propose radical solutions for addressing it. We [social justice educators] will have to take bold and sometimes unpopular positions" (p. 22, italics in original).

Data and Methodology

The data come from the National Center for Culturally Responsive Educational Systems' (NCCRESt) (available online at http://www.nccrest.org) national data maps. Our analysis is based on data from 2000 through 2006 containing national statistics on disproportionality by race and disability. The original data from the NCCRESt database were imported, re-configured in Excel, and analyzed using SPSS Statistics *v. 17.0* and SAS software. Stat/Transfer was utilized to move SPSS data to SAS.

Methods for determining disproportionality

There are five main methodological approaches to determine disproportionality in special education: (1) "best judgment" (Dunn, 1968), (2) composition index (MacMillan & Reschly, 1998; Reschly, 1997), (3) risk index (Reschly, 1997), (4) odds ratio (Finn, 1982; Lipsey & Wilson, 2000), and (5) relative risk.

Dunn (1968) employed a "best judgment" methodology, which was deduced from his years of experience and observation. Meanwhile, MacMillan and Reschly (1998) and Reschly (1997) used a percent of category or placement by group (composition index) methodology whereby comparisons of the percentage of students from different racial groups within a certain category are made. Composition is useful when discussing the racial/ethnic makeup of a disability or educational environment category.

Composition, however, varies directly with the racial/ethnic demographics of the state or district for which it is calculated. With composition, the size of the racial/ethnic group's percentage of the disability or educational environment category is directly related to the size of that racial/ethnic group's percentage of the total student enrollment. Caution must be used when using composition in states or districts that have extremely homogeneous racial/ethnic distributions. When a state's or district's student enrollment is composed almost entirely of one racial/ethnic group, it can become impossible to demonstrate racial/ethnic disproportionality using composition. Thus, composition should not be used under these circumstances.

Reschly (1997) used a percentage of group in a category or placement (also referred to as a risk index) methodology, whereby the number of students in a racial category (e.g., African American, Hispanic, etc.) that are also in a certain category (e.g., LD, Disabled, etc.) are divided by the total number of students in that group.

Finn (1982) calculated the odds of a student of a certain racial group (e.g., African American, Hispanic, etc.) being placed in a certain category (e.g., MMR, special education, etc.). Finn's (1982) methodology was a form of an odds ratio (Finn, 1982; Lipsey & Wilson, 2000). Unlike composition, the size of the risk ratio for a particular racial/ethnic group does not depend on that racial/ethnic group's percentage of the state's or district's enrollment. Furthermore, unlike risk, the size of a racial/ethnic group's risk ratio does not depend on differences in overall special education identification rates because the risks for the racial/ethnic group and for the comparison group both come from the same state or district. Therefore, we feel that the risk ratio is the *single* best method to measure disproportionality.

The risk for each racial/ethnic group, however, is directly related to overall special education identification rates. In other words, the size of a racial/ethnic group's risk for receiving special education and related services either for a particular disability or in a particular educational environment is directly related to the size of the overall risk for special education in the state or district.

Relative risk compares the risk index for one group to the risk index of another group. This methodology has been used as an antidote to the odds ratio's major shortfall—that it provides only a binary comparison of one group (i.e,. special education vs. non-special education). We used risk index (Reschly, 1997), odds ratio (Finn, 1982; Lipsey & Wilson, 2000), and relative risk in our analysis.

Research questions

Our research questions were, "By giving the option to use RTI for fulfilling criteria requirements for specific learning disabilities (SLD), what is the effect on disproportionality in special education? Is there a difference in the percentage/ratio of minority students in traditionally defined special education programs (pre-RTI and post-RTI moments)?"

Analysis and results

We used six time points in order to assess change(s) in states' percentages of students disabled by race: (1) 2000–01; (2) 2001–02; (3) 2002–03; (4) 2003–04; (5) 2004–05; and (6) 2005–06. Although NCCRESt provided nine school years of data (1998–99 thru 2006–07), these nine years were intentionally winnowed down to six school years.

These six school years were selected because: (a) it was decided in order to best answer the research question that the year 2003–04 be considered the starting point of RTI, when it was an option for fulfilling criteria requirements for specific learning disabilities (SLD) (Fuchs & Fuchs, 2005); (b) the 2006–07 data set did not provide the total number of students for each state and each race; therefore, percentages were could not be calculated; and (c) since statistics were going to be used, it was decided that in order to keep a *balanced design* the two school years (1998–99 and 1999–00) would not be used.

Table 1 illustrates national percentage of students considered disabled by race and by year(s) (Pre-RTI and RTI). Since RTI was introduced as an option for fulfilling criteria requirements for specific learning disabilities (SLD) in 2004, the three school years from 2000 to 2003 are considered to be pre-

RTI (2000–2001; 2001–2002; and 2002–2003). The three school years from 2003 to 2006 are considered to be RTI (2003–2004; 2004–2005; and 2005–2006).

As one can deduce from the information presented in tabular form (see Table 1), the racial groups analyzed were categorized into the following groups: (a) African American, (b) Hispanic, (c) Asian/Pacific Islander, (d) American Indian, and (e) White. It is important to note that the U.S. Census only began separating Asian and Pacific Islander data in 2000. Notwithstanding, many education sources still conflate and combine Asians and Pacific Islanders into one category (Diaz, 2004). For this reason, unless otherwise noted, whenever "Asian," "Asian American," or "Asian American student" is used in this chapter, the statistic is for the category "Asians *and* Pacific Islanders."

TABLE 1. National Percentage of Students Considered Disabled by Race, Year (Pre-RTI and RTI)

Year	AA	H	A/P	Am Ind	W
2000–01[a]	14.4%	10.4%	5.6%	13.3%	12.4%
2001–02[a]	14.7%	10.4%	5.5%	13.6%	12.5%
2002–03[a]	14.7%	10.4%	5.6%	13.5%	12.6%
2003–04[b]	15.0%	10.5%	5.7%	13.9%	12.7%
2004–05[b]	15.1%	10.7%	5.8%	14.4%	13.0%
2005–06[b]	14.8%	10.4%	5.8%	14.2%	12.8%

Note. AA = African American; H = Hispanic; A/P = Asian/Pacific Islander; Am Ind = American Indian; W = White
[a]Percentage of students considered disabled by race Pre-RTI
[b]Percentage of students considered disabled by race RTI

Table 2 illustrates the risk ratio, also called relative risk—the risk of being labeled disabled in comparison to being White. A risk ratio of 1.00 indicates that a student of a particular minority group has the same probability of being labeled disabled.

TABLE 2. Risk Ratios (95% Confidence Intervals/Limits) Minority vs. White Students Labeled Disabled

Year	AA	H	A/P	Am Ind
2000–01	1.16 (1.1652, 1.1697)	0.84 (0.8419, 0.8458)	0.45 (0.4482, 0.4535)	1.07 (1.0725, 1.0872)
2001–02	1.18 (1.1730, 1.1775)	0.83 (0.8338, 0.8375)	0.44 (0.4350, 0.4401)	1.09 (1.0841, 1.0986)
2002–03	1.17 (1.1624, 1.1668)	0.83 (0.8272, 0.8308)	0.44 (0.4402, 0.4452)	1.07 (1.0658, 1.0799)
2003–04	1.18 (1.1766, 1.1811)	0.83 (0.8266, 0.8301)	0.45 (0.4457, 0.4507)	1.09 (1.0849, 1.0990)
2004–05	1.16 (1.1650, 1.1694)	0.82 (0.8230, 0.8265)	0.45 (0.4494, 0.4543)	1.11 (1.1058, 1.1200)
2005–06	1.16 (1.1589, 1.1633)	0.81 (0.8144, 0.8178)	0.45 (0.4475, 0.4524)	1.11 (1.1015, 1.1155)

Note. AA = African American; H = Hispanic; A/P = Asian/Pacific Islander; Am Ind = American Indian; W = White
The model used to find the risk ratio was: RR = RiskMinority (non-White race)/RiskWhite (Referent Group).

Where (1) RR is the risk ratio—the risk of a particular student being labeled disabled; (2) $Risk_{Minority \ (non\text{-}White \ race)}$ is the risk ratio—the risk of a minority student (either African American, Hispanic, Asian/Pacific Islander, or American Indian) being labeled disabled; and (3) $Risk_{White \ (Referent \ Group)}$ is the risk ratio—the risk of a white student being labeled disabled. The referent group was a consistent group for comparison (White students) and was the denominator in the equation.

Various research designs—e.g., case-control design—do not allow researchers to compute a relative risk since they oftentimes require selecting research participants on the basis of an outcome measure rather than based upon exposure. The present study operates under the assumption that RTI, or minimal RTI, was beginning to be used in 2003–04 since it was an option for fulfilling criteria requirements for specific learning disabilities (SLD). Of course, some states/schools may have already been using RTI, which one would hope would improve in effectiveness, still leading to a reduction in disproportionality.

The 95% confidence intervals/limits (CIs) were found by using SAS. The CIs refer to the risk ratio of minority to White for being labeled disabled. Stated otherwise, for a given predictor (non-White race) with a level of 95% confidence, we can say that we are 95% confident that the "true" population relative risk ratio comparing overrepresentation to the referent group (Whites) lies between the lower and upper limits of the interval. The advantage of using a CI is that it is illustrative, since it provides a range where the "true" relative risk ratio may fall.

For example, as shown by Table 2, the risk of being labeled disabled if you are an African American student is 1.16 times higher than if you are White.

Although this number may not appear extraordinary in isolation, if applied to an aggregation of 1 million students (approximately 1 out of every 50 U.S. students), 160,000 more African American students than White students are expected to be labeled disabled and in special education. Therefore a 1.16 is a meaningful statistic.

Overall, it appears there is not a change in the pattern of relative risk across time. Table 3 below provides additional descriptive information on the states with the highest five percentages of students (by race) labeled disabled by school year (authors' note: tables available upon request).

The risk ratios presented in this study are at times slightly lower than previous studies. Such an example is the risk ratio of American Indian students. According to our analyses, American Indians during the 2005–06 school year had a risk ratio of 1.11 percent. The U.S. Department of Education (2006) states that Native American/Alaska Native children are more likely to receive special education services than the general population with a risk ratio of 1.35 percent. Notwithstanding this difference, we believe that our findings support previous research.

Compared with Whites, for instance, the risk ratio for being labeled disabled among African Americans was 1.18 (95% confidence interval (CI): 1.1730, 1.1775) in 2001–02 and 1.18 (95% CI: 1.1766, 1.1811) in 2003–04. Of the four non-White racial groups, African American students appeared to be at most risk of being labeled disabled. Following African American students were American Indian students, then Hispanic students, and last were Asian/Pacific Islander students with the least risk. This confirms previous research indicating that Asian Americans are underrepresented in special education (e.g., see Hartlep, 2010).

For purposes of description and pattern analysis, Table 3 and Table 4 articulate the five states with the highest percentage of students labeled disabled. Each of the five races is presented. State 1 refers to the state with the highest percentage of students labeled disabled whereas State 5 would be the state with the fifth-highest percentage. We believe that it is important to see which states have perennially high cohorts of disabled (special education) students for each of the five races. Most salient is the relationship between these top five states and each individual state's percentage of that race.

For example, in 2000–01, Iowa had the highest *state percentage* of African American students labeled disabled. However, what is most problematic is that Iowa in 2000–01 had a *disproportionate rate* of African Americans labeled disabled. This disproportionality is found using the following information: in Iowa in 2000–01 approximately 20.4% of African American students were labeled disabled (see Table 3); however, this is a markedly higher percentage than what would be expected since African Americans only represented approximately 4.0% of Iowa's population in 2000–01.

TABLE 3. Highest 5 States with Percentage Labeled Disabled by Race and by Year (Pre-RTI)

	Race	State 1 (Highest)	State 2	State 3	State 4	State 5
	African American	Iowa (20.41%)	New Mexico (20.24%)	New Jersey (18.72%)	Montana (18.24%)	Massachusetts (18.21%)
	Hispanic	Massachusetts (15.82%)	North Dakota (15.41%)	New Mexico (15.23%)	New Jersey (14.72%)	Rhode Island (14.65%)
2000–01	Asian/Pacific Islander	Oklahoma (17.34%)	Michigan (13.87%)	Hawaii (12.36%)	Nebraska (7.80%)	Montana (7.60%)
	American Indian	District of Columbia (22.50%)	Nebraska (19.89%)	Rhode Island (19.60%)	Minnesota (18.88%)	South Dakota (18.47%)
	White	Rhode Island (19.27%)	New Jersey (16.01%)	West Virginia (15.66%)	Maine (15.42%)	Massachusetts (15.34%)
	African American	Iowa (21.37%)	New Mexico (20.12%)	New Jersey (19.14%)	Massachusetts (19.01%)	District of Columbia (18.91%)
	Hispanic	Massachusetts (16.84%)	Rhode Island (15.18%)	New Mexico (15.04%)	New Jersey (14.77%)	North Dakota (14.47%)
2001–02	Asian/Pacific Islander	Oklahoma (18.05%)	Hawaii (11.79%)	North Dakota (8.60%)	South Dakota (8.52%)	Nebraska (7.89%)
	American Indian	Rhode Island (22.30%)	Nebraska (21.52%)	Vermont (19.60%)	Minnesota (19.25%)	South Dakota (19.10%)
	White	Rhode Island (20.00%)	New Jersey (16.24%)	Maine (15.89%)	West Virginia (15.86%)	Indiana (14.81%)
	African American	Iowa (22.26%)	New Mexico (20.20%)	New Jersey (19.37%)	Massachusetts (19.19%)	Oklahoma (17.63%)
	Hispanic	Massachusetts (17.22%)	North Dakota (16.58%)	Rhode Island (15.22%)	New Jersey (14.80%)	New Mexico (14.72%)
2002–03	Asian/Pacific Islander	Hawaii (12.25%)	Nebraska (8.64%)	Oklahoma (8.63%)	South Dakota (8.48%)	Montana (8.31%)
	American Indian	Rhode Island (28.39%)	Nebraska (21.51%)	Minnesota (19.51%)	Idaho (18.97%)	South Dakota (18.65%)
	White	Rhode Island (20.44%)	New Jersey (16.42%)	Maine (16.15%)	West Virginia (16.04%)	Indiana (15.29%)

Note. The % inside ( ) refers to the percentage labeled disabled in that year and race.

TABLE 4. Highest 5 states with Percentage Labeled Disabled by Race and by Year (Post-RTI)

	African American	Iowa (23.04%)	New Mexico (19.56%)	Massachusetts (19.42%)	New Jersey (19.36%)	Wisconsin (17.86%)
	Hispanic	Nebraska (23.81%)	Massachusetts (17.86%)	North Dakota (15.86%)	Rhode Island (15.35%)	New Jersey (14.79%)
2003– 04	Asian/Pacific Islander	Hawaii (12.03%)	South Dakota (9.39%)	Oklahoma (8.68%)	Nebraska (8.59%)	Montana (8.53%)
	American Indian	New Jersey (30.63%)	Rhode Island (27.42%)	Maine (23.57%)	Nebraska (22.93%)	South Dakota (19.61%)
	White	Rhode Island (20.05%)	New Jersey (16.76%)	Maine (16.57%)	West Virginia (16.06%)	Indiana (15.53%)
	African American	Iowa (23.19%)	New Jersey (19.71%)	Massachusetts (19.56%)	Wisconsin (19.00%)	New Mexico (18.61%)
	Hispanic	Massachusetts (18.40%)	Rhode Island (15.91%)	New Jersey (14.95%)	Maine (14.75%)	Wyoming (14.49%)
2004– 05	Asian/Pacific Islander	Hawaii (11.70%)	South Dakota (9.82%)	Oklahoma (8.68%)	Nebraska (8.64%)	Montana (8.53%)
	American Indian	Rhode Island (25.54%)	Maine (22.69%)	Nebraska (21.72%)	Wisconsin (20.224%)	South Dakota (20.220%)
	White	Rhode Island (19.48%)	New Jersey (16.95%)	Maine (16.66%)	West Virginia (15.96%)	Indiana (15.64%)
	African American	Iowa (22.62%)	New Jersey (19.99%)	Massachusetts (19.95%)	Wisconsin (19.41%)	Rhode Island (17.78%)
	Hispanic	Massachusetts (18.22%)	Rhode Island (16.98%)	North Dakota (16.10%)	Maine (15.87%)	New Jersey (15.40%)
2005– 06	Asian/Pacific Islander	Hawaii (11.27%)	South Dakota (9.70%)	Michigan (9.11%)	Nebraska (8.96%)	Wyoming (8.86%)
	American Indian	Maine (27.34%)	Rhode Island (23.63%)	Nebraska (20.84%)	Minnesota (20.49%)	Wisconsin (20.45%)
	White	Rhode Island (18.87%)	New Jersey (17.15%)	Maine (16.57%)	Indiana (15.72%)	West Virginia (15.64%)

Note. The % inside ( ) refers to the percentage labeled disabled in that year and race.

Instances of overrepresentation appeared quite often in our analyses. In fact, the national frequency of overrepresentation of students labeled disabled by race was analyzed for all states (and the District of Columbia) for all six years of data. The 50 states + District of Columbia yielded 51 observations, multiplied by a factor of 6 (for each year) = 306 opportunities. Frequency tables (see Appendix) were then created in order to interpret which racial group was more overrepresented in special education than others in terms of each state (and District of Columbia). A state (or the District of Columbia) would be classified as being overrepresented for a particular year if the percentage of a racial group that was labeled disabled was higher than the actual percentage of that racial group in that state (or the District of Columbia) in that year. A state (or the District of Columbia) would be classified as being normal (normally expected) or underrepresented for a particular year if the percentage of a racial group that was labeled disabled was proportionately equal to or lower than the actual percentage of that racial group in that state (or the District of Columbia) in that year.

Examination reveals that American Indian students are overrepresented 287/306 (93.8%), Asian/Pacific Islander students 260/306 (85%), Hispanic students 206/306 (67.3%), African American students 181/306 (59.2%), and White students 5/306 (1.6%). Through interpretation, it is understood that White students are the most underrepresented racial group in special education.

Conclusion

The empirical results support several conclusions. *First, giving the option to use RTI for fulfilling criteria requirements for specific learning disabilities (SLD) has not really reduced the likelihood that students are wrongly identified as having a disability.* This may be due to the fact that some states have not adopted RTI programs and some states may be reluctant to do so. As Waitoller, Artiles, and Cheney (2010) state, "states can define disproportionality in their own terms, making disproportionality comparisons between states a challenging endeavor" (p. 31).

Second, Asian Americans remain underrepresented in special education in relation to all other races examined in this study. Although this study analyzes state-level data for all states (plus the District of Columbia), we still do not know what Asian subgroups are/aren't being serviced in special education classrooms. Artiles and Trent (2000) define disproportionality as "unequal proportions of culturally diverse students in special education programs. Two patterns are associated with disproportionality, namely over- and underrepresentation" (p. 514). Therefore, while overrepresentation is an issue of concern, underrepresentation is equally threatening to us all. Underrepresented minorities may in fact need special education services that they are not currently receiving.

Third, African American students remain the most at risk of being labeled special education. American Indians follow African Americans in terms of the most risk of being labeled special education. Asian American students are the most underrepresented group in special education. The option to use RTI for fulfilling criteria requirements for specific learning disabilities (SLD) has not led to substantial improvements in risk for all nonwhites analyzed in this study. Risk ratios for the pre-RTI years and post-RTI years hold steady.

Four policy recommendations

Recommendation number one: Ethnic disaggregation. The No Child Left Behind Act (NCLB) of 2001 requires that student data be disaggregated by race, and does not require data be disaggregated by ethnicity. By not disaggregating ethnicity, academic achievement gaps and disproportionality in special education are masked, impacting the learning experiences of many subgroups of students. If states provide data on all of their students (in racial and ethnic format), nothing will be hidden from researchers, and most importantly information will be readily available to the community at large.

Nowhere is this more apparent than in regard to the special education needs of Asian Americans (Donovan & Cross, 2002; Hartlep, 2010). According to Hartlep (2010), Asian Americans continue to be underrepresented in special education. This may be attributable to the "model minority" stereotype that envelops certain Asian American students. Ethnic disaggregation would be helpful since Asian Americans are a bimodal distribution, not the homogenous high achievers many make them out to be (Woo, 2000). It would also raise the question of why there are disparities in terms of certain student populations that are under- or over-represented in special education. The results of this study reveal that the acronym NCLB may truly stand for "No Caucasian Left Behind."

Recommendation number two: Utilize a framework for culturally and linguistically responsive design of a response to intervention model. García and Ortiz's (2008) systems framework for culturally and linguistically responsive implementation of RTI, which takes into account the sociopolitical, cultural, and linguistic contexts of schooling, is one possible alternative approach to administering interventions to students. This aligns with NCCRESt (2005), which "promotes a system approach to reform that entails looking across multiple layers of the home, community, school, and society-at-large" (p. 3). According to García and Ortiz (2008), it is unlikely RTI will reduce disproportionate representation of CLD children and youth in special education unless it is "ensure[d] that RTI models are culturally and linguistically responsive" (p. 38). Therefore, schools and teachers should utilize a framework for culturally and linguistically responsive design of a response to intervention model.

Recommendation number three: Utilize culturally responsive interventions. The National Center for Culturally Responsive Educational Systems (2005) maintains that culture must be considered when carrying out interventions as well as when developing interventionist programs. In their position statement, NCCRESt (2005) had this to say about culture and RTI:

We at NCCRESt are encouraged by the potential of RTI models to improve educationalopportunities for culturally and linguistically diverse students and to reduce their disproportionate representation in special education. At the same time, *we are concerned that if we do not engage in dialogue about how culture mediates learning, RTI models will simply be like old wine in a new bottle, in other words, another deficit-based approach to sorting children, particularly children from marginalized communities.* (p. 1, italics added)

Therefore, recommendation three is that RTI develop culturally responsive interventions that work across and within cultures, interventions that are not Eurocentric in nature.

Recommendation number four: Utilize equity audits on special education data. Equity audits are attempts to use data to uncover and erase systemic inequities (Scheurich & Skrla, 2003). According to Scheurich and Skrla (2003), *systemic inequities* are internal inequities that are built in to processes and procedures. When patterns of inequity are made visible—a goal of equity audits—proper decisions can be made in order to stop the spread of over-assigning and under-assigning students of color into special education. Equity audits need not supplant a culturally and linguistically responsive design of RTI; rather, they should accompany it.

While these recommendations may be unpopular, their intentions are consistent with the goal of social justice in, and through, educational endeavors.

Acknowledgments

We would like to thank the following who read various sections/iterations of this manuscript and for their feedback and suggestions: Drs. Alfredo Artiles, Alba Ortiz, Russell Skiba, and Donna Ford.

Appendix

National frequency of Overrepresentation of labeled disabled by race

African American

	Frequency	Percent	Cumulative Percent
Overrepresented	181	59.2	59.8
Expected or Underrepresented	123	40.2	100
Total	306	100.0	

Hispanic

	Frequency	Percent	Cumulative Percent
Overrepresented	206	67.3	68.0
Expected or Underrepresented	98	32.0	100
Total	306	100.0	

Asian/Pacific Islander

	Frequency	Percent	Cumulative Percent
Overrepresented	260	85.0	85.6
Expected or Underrepresented	44	14.4	100
Total	306	100.0	

American Indian

	Frequency	Percent	Cumulative Percent
Overrepresented	287	93.8	94.4
Expected or Underrepresented	17	5.6	100
Total	306	100.0	

White

	Frequency	Percent	Cumulative Percent
Overrepresented	5	1.6	2.3
Expected or Underrepresented	299	97.7	100
Total	306	100.0	

References

Arnold, M., & Lassmann, M. E. (2003). Overrepresentation of minority students in special education. *Education, 124*(2), 230–236.

Artiles, A. J., Bal, A., & King Thorius, K. A. (2010). Back to the future: A critique of response to intervention's social justice views. *Theory into Practice, 49*(4), 250–257.

Artiles, A. J., & Trent, S. (2000). Representation of culturally/linguistically diverse students. In C. R. Reynolds & E. Fletcher-Jantzen (Eds.), *Encyclopedia of special education* (Vol. 1, 2nd ed., pp. 513–517). New York: Wiley.

Barnes, A. C., & Harlacher, J. E. (2008). Clearing the confusion: Response-to-intervention as a set of principles. *Education and Treatment of Children, 31*(3), 417–431.

Bell, D. A. (1980). *Brown v. Board of Education* and the interest convergence dilemma. *Harvard Law Review, 93,* 518.

Blanchett, W. J. (2006). Disproportionate representation of African American students in special education: Acknowledging the role of white privilege and racism. *Educational Researcher, 35*(6), 24–28.

Bouman, S. H. (2010). *Response-to-intervention in California public schools: Has it helped address disproportional placement rates for students with learning disabilities?* (Unpublished doctoral dissertation). Retrieved from Dissertations and Theses (ProQuest). (ProQuest document ID: 2076080451)

Braden, J. P. (1987). A comparison of regression and standard score discrepancy methods for learning disabilities identification: Effects on racial representation. *Journal of School Psychology, 25,* 23–29.

Cone, T. E., & Wilson, L. R. (1981). Quantifying a severe discrepancy: A critical analysis. *Learning Disability Quarterly, 4,* 359–371.

Darling-Hammond, L. (2007). Race, inequality and educational accountability: The irony of No Child Left Behind. *Race Ethnicity and Education, 10*(3), 245–260.

Diaz, V. M. (2004). "To 'P' or Not to 'P'?": Marking the territory between Pacific Islander and Asian American Studies. *Journal of Asian American Studies, 7*(3), 183–208.

Donovan, M. S., & Cross, C. T. (2002). *Minority students in special and gifted education.* Washington, DC: National Academy Press.

Dunn, L. M. (1968). Special Education for the mildly retarded: Is much of it justifiable? *Exceptional Children, 35,* 5–22.

Evans, L. D. (1992). Severe does not always imply significant: Bias of a regression discrepancy model. *The Journal of Special Education, 26,* 57–67.

Finlan, T. G. (1992). Do state methods of quantifying a severe discrepancy result in fewer students with learning disabilities? *Learning Disability Quarterly, 15,* 129–134.

Finn, J. D. (1982). Patterns in special education placement as revealed by the OCR survey. In K. A. Heller, W. Holtzman, & S. Messick (Ed.), *Placing children in special education: A strategy for equity* (pp. 322–381). Washington, DC: National Academy Press.

Fletcher, J. M., Coutler, W. A., Reshly, D. J., & Vaughn, S. (2004). Alternative approaches to the definition and identification of learning disabilities: Some questions and answers. *Annals of Dyslexia, 54*(2), 304–331.

Fletcher, J. M., Francis, D. J., Rourke, B. P., Shaywitz, S. E., & Shaywitz, B. A. (1992). The validity of the discrepancy-based definitions of learning disabilities. *Journal of Learning Disabilities, 25*(9), 555–561.

Fuchs, D., & Fuchs, L. S. (2005, Sept/Oct). Responsiveness-to-intervention: A blueprint for practitioners, policymakers, and parents. *Teaching Exceptional Children, 38,* 57–61.

García, S. B., & Ortiz, A. A. (2008). A framework for culturally and linguistically responsive design of response-to-intervention models. *Multiple Voices for Ethnically Diverse Exceptional Learners, 11*(1), 24–41.

Gerber, M. M. (2005). Teachers are still the test: Limitations of response to instruction strategies for identifying children with learning disabilities. *Journal of Learning Disabilities, 38*(6), 516–524.

Hartlep, N. D. (2010). *Going Public: Critical race theory and issues of social justice.* Mustang, OK: Tate.

Ikeda, M. J., Grimes, J., Tilly III, W. D., Allison, R., Kurns, S., & Stumme, J. (2002). Implementing an intervention-based approach to service delivery: A case example. In M. R. Shinn, H. M. Walker, & G. Stoner (Eds.), *Interventions for academic and behavior problems II: Preventative and remedial approaches* (pp. 53–69). Bethesda, MD: National Association of School Psychologists.

Kauffman, J. M. (2004). The president's commission and the devaluation of special education. *Education and the Treatment of Children, 27*(4), 307–324.

Kavale, K. A. and Spaulding, L. S. (2008). Is response-to-intervention good policy for specific learning disability? *Faculty Publications and Presentations.* Paper 119. Retrieved on June 21, 2011 from http://digitalcommons.liberty.edu/educ_fac_pubs/119

Ladson-Billings, G. (1998). Just what is critical race theory and what's it doing in a nice field like education? *Qualitative Studies in Education, 11*(1), 7–24.

Lipsey, M. W., & Wilson, D. B. (2000). *Practical meta-analysis.* Thousand Oaks, CA: Sage.

MacMillan, D. L., & Reschly, D. J. (1998). Overrepresentation of minority students: The case for greater specificity of the variables examined. *The Journal of Special Education, 32,* 15–24.

Mercer, C. D., Jordan, L., Allsop, D. H., & Mercer, A. R. (1996). Learning disabilities definitions and criteria used by state education departments. *Learning Disability Quarterly, 19,* 217–232.

National Center for Culturally Responsive Educational Systems (NCCRESt). (2005, Fall). *Cultural considerations and challenges in response-to-intervention models: An NCCRESt position statement.* Retrieved on January 29, 2011 from http://www.nccrest.org/PDFs/rti.pdf?v_document_name=Culturally%20Responsive%20RTI

National Center on Response to Intervention. (2010a, March). *Essential components of RTI–A closer look at response to intervention.* Washington, DC: U.S. Department of Education, Office of Special Education Programs, National Center on Response to Intervention.

National Center on Response to Intervention. (2010b). *Definition.* [On-line]. Available: www.rti4success.org

Neal, L. I., McCray, A. D., Webb-Johnson, G., & Bridgest, S. T. (2003). The effects of African American movement styles on teachers' perceptions and reactions. *The Journal of Special Education, 37,* 49–57.

Payette, K. A., Clarizio, H. F., Phillips, S. E., & Bennett, D. E. (1995). Effects of simple and regressed discrepancy models and cutoffs on severe discrepancy determination. *Psychology in the Schools, 32,* 93–102.

President's Commission on Excellence in Special Education (PCESE). (2002). *A new era: Revitalizing special education for children and their families.* Washington, DC: U.S. Department of Education. Retrieved on June 20, 2011 from http://www2.ed.gov/inits/commissionsboards/whspecialeducation/reports/images/Pres_Rep.pdf

Reschly, D. J. (1997). *Disproportionate minority representation in general and special education: Patterns, issues, and alternatives.* Des Moines: Iowa Department of Education.

Scheurich, J. J., & Skrla, L. (2003). *Leadership for equity and excellence: Creating high-achievement classrooms, schools, and districts.* Thousand Oaks, CA: Corwin Press.

Siegel, L. S. (1992). An evaluation of the discrepancy definition of dyslexia. *Journal of Learning Disabilities, 25*(10), 618–629.

Stephan, W. G., & Stephan, C. W. (2004). Intergroup relations in multicultural education programs. In J. A. Banks, & C. A. Banks (Eds.), *Handbook of research on multicultural education* (2nd ed., pp. 782–798). San Francisco: Jossey-Bass.

Stuebing, K. K., Fletcher, J. M., LeDoux, J. M., Lyon, G. R., Shaywitz, S. E., & Shaywitz, B. A. (2002). Validity of IQ-discrepancy classifications of reading difficulties: A meta-analysis. *American Educational Research Journal, 39*(2), 469–518.

Swartz, E. (1992). Emancipatory narratives: Rewriting the master script in the school curriculum. *Journal of Negro Education, 61,* 341–355.

Taylor, E., Gillborn, D., & Ladson-Billings, G. (Eds.). (2009). *Foundations of critical race theory in education*. New York: Routledge.

Vallas, R. (2009). The disproportionality problem: The overrepresentation of black students in special education and recommendations for reform. *Virginia Journal of Social Policy & the Law, 17*(1), 181–208.

Vaughn, S., & Fuchs, L. S. (2003). Redefining learning disabilities as inadequate response to instruction: The promise and potential problems. *Learning Disabilities Research and Practice, 18*(3), 137–146.

Vaughn, S., Wanzek, J., Woodruff, A. L., & Linan-Thompson, S. (2007). Prevention and early identification of students with reading disabilities. In D. Haager, J. Klinger, & S. Vaughn (Eds.), *Evidence-based reading practices for response to intervention* (pp. 11–27). Baltimore, MD: Paul H. Brookes Publishing.

Vellutino, F. R., Scanlon, D. M., & Lyon, G. R. (2000). Differentiating between difficult-to-remediate and readily remediated poor readers: More evidence against the IQ—achievement discrepancy definition of reading disability. *Journal of Learning Disabilities, 33*(3), 223–238.

Waitoller, F. R., Artiles, A. J., & Cheney, D. A. (2010). The miner's canary: A review of overrepresentation research and explanations. *The Journal of Special Education, 44*(1), 29–49.

Woo, D. (2000). *Glass ceilings and Asian Americans: The new face of workplace barriers*. Walnut Creek, CA: AltaMira Press.

7. *The Yoga in Schools Movement: Using Standards for Educating the Whole Child and Making Space for Teacher Self-Care*

ANDREA HYDE

> *These great aims are meant to guide our instructional decisions. They are meant to broaden our thinking—to remind us to ask why we have chosen certain curriculums, pedagogical methods, classroom arrangements, and learning objectives. They remind us, too, that students are whole persons—not mere collections of attributes, some to be addressed in one place and others to be addressed elsewhere.*
> —NEL NODDINGS (2005, P. 10)

Part of the national education agenda

In *The Learning Compact Redefined: A Call to Action*, the Association for Supervision and Curriculum Development's Commission on the Whole Child (ASCD, 2007) frames education "within the context of the personalized engagement and nurturing of the whole child" (p. 2). Whole children are intellectually active; physically, verbally, socially, and academically competent; empathetic, kind, caring, and fair; creative and curious; disciplined, self-directed, and goal oriented; free; critical thinkers; confident; and cared for and valued (p. 10). The report positions student success as positive "social, emotional, physical, ethical, civic, creative, and cognitive development." (p.10). The new learning compact is meant to replace the "one-size-fits-all," high stakes accountability, standards-driven reform that is currently upon us, and which the commission finds to be doing harm to our children.

This renewed interest in educating the whole child appears as a stated purpose of public education policy and curriculum practice (AAHE, 2007; NASPE, 2004) and has found expression in several federally endorsed school and community programs in the U.S., such as "Let's Move" (HHS et al., 2010) and the "NFL Play 60" Campaign (NFL, 2009). Attention to the health and wellness of public school students corresponds to widespread concern, bolstered by media attention, about the increase of U.S. citizens who are overweight and obese. Anyone who consumes dominant media forms could tell you that childhood obesity is on the rise. Positioned to take advantage of this "crisis" discourse is the yoga in schools movement (hereafter referred to as the YIS movement) (Berliner & Biddle, 1995).

The movement to include yoga and meditation in schools contributes to a revised discourse on the goals of public education, one that attends to the health and wellness needs of "the whole child." Here is a phrase just as politically invulnerable to criticism launched by progressive educators as "no child left behind." In this case, however, this discourse allows, rather than blocks, social justice educators and advocates to take part in the national conversation on accountability. Furthermore, this "crisis" discourse positions educators and scholars within the YIS movement to hijack the conservative neoliberal agenda, so as to make transformative practices of self-care and empowerment available to all students. This holds special relevance for students in what are now called "challenge" schools, in the language of the latest proposal for reauthorizing the Elementary and Secondary Education Act/NCLB, called *A Blueprint for Reform* (USDOE, 2010). These are the same schools that were labeled "failing" under NCLB.

In this chapter, through specific examples of how yoga programs are impacting students, teachers, and communities in K–12 schools across the U.S., I will illustrate the potential to exploit the official and ideological power of the health crisis discourse, state social-emotional learning standards, and state and national Health and Physical Education standards for spreading a socially transformative agenda.[1] Next, I will capture some of the key aims behind the yoga movement in order to illustrate how it offers schools a socially transgressive pedagogy, which has the potency to improve students' and educators' individual well-being as well as to eradicate systemic barriers and forces causing oppression in schools and in the wider society. Finally, I will conclude by arguing that social advocates and critical pedagogues must take the yoga movement seriously because it has the potential to change the purpose and structure of the unjust institutions in the U.S. from within, making use of whatever resources are currently available and working within and through whatever conditions are at hand.

Post-NCLB possibilities

Blueprint calls for supporting "successful, safe and healthy students" (p. 31) by moving toward a model of full-service community schools. Building on the American Recovery and Reinvestment Act goals and funding, competitive grants are available to fund before- and after-school and summer programs with priority given to those projects that will serve challenge schools. Most of the concern is for students to have "safe, healthy, and drug-free environments" and grant RFP's (requests for proposals) state a preference for programs that "take a comprehensive approach to meeting student needs, drawing on the contributions of community-based organizations, [and] local agencies" (p. 32). Here is an opportunity for community organizations offering yoga and meditation to received federal and state dollars, access to school buildings, and to support school-based programs.

Though we are far from free of the core ideological assumptions of NCLB and the threat of extreme negative sanction remains for the most vulnerable schools in each state, President Obama's latest reauthorization proposal does acknowledge the considerable influence of "out of schools factors" (Berliner, 2009) on in-school achievement. Most interesting for the YIS movement, *Blueprint* supports a vision of public schools as "full-service community schools" that would provide "enrichment activities, which may include activities that improve mental and physical health" (p. 32).

Much has already been said to criticize *Blueprint* as being far too punitive in pushing accountability and not nearly different enough from NCLB as to actually represent educational change for the better. Heavy emphasis on standardized test scores and a preoccupation with raising such scores remain. Furthermore, the Obama/Duncan policy proposal champions competition for funds and prefers a vision of charter school proliferation, despite a lack of evidence showing that charter schools do more than public schools in supporting student success by any measure (Mathis & Welner, 2010; Noguera, 2010). I am not advocating for the creation of yoga charter schools. My present interest is in how the introduction of yoga into public schools as a "movement approach to educational reform" (Palmer, 1992) can change the purpose and structure of the institution from within.

Education reformers critical of the Obama/Duncan plan may wince at the ASCD report's suggestion that schools and communities should "lay aside perennial battles for resources and instead align those resources in support of the whole child" (p. 8). However, the much-admired teacher and education scholar Noguera, who delivers one of the most comprehensive critiques of *Blueprint,* was a commission member (Noguera, 2010). The report provides examples of public school–community partnerships and lauds state and district programs that express their vision of developing whole children. This spotlights schools that are doing well according to data from multiple measures, in contrast to reports that reinforce an ideology of crisis and failure. It is a hopeful document; it is designed to alter hegemonic philosophy of education in the U.S., which is to prepare children to become mindless, obedient consumers, dutiful workers, and passive citizens.

Grant magnets

Offering customized yoga programming for students, and trainings or group workshops for teachers, reflects a belief that partnering with schools should be an empowering, locally relevant, and highly personalized process. In most cases, programs are designed to meet the needs of teachers, counselors, administrators, and students alike. In some cases, the needs of the community drive the long-term goals of the programs. Services range from yoga instruction for students, yoga curriculum instruction for Physical Education teachers, yoga techniques for classroom teachers, and yoga for self-care for teachers and other staff.

Some yoga program providers have been successful in securing competitive public and private grants to fund their programs. This is due, in part, to the hard work and social advocacy-identity of so many yoga educators; however, a major aspect of crafting a winning grant request involves co-opting the language of several school "crises": children's heath/stress/obesity, school safety, teacher burnout, and the overall failure of U.S. public schools. Smaller nonprofit organizations that teach yoga and meditation to students and teachers in public schools have won competitive grants usually by working with larger NPOs and private foundations, some of which critical educators might readily disapprove. For example, New Visions for Public Schools is a privately funded nonprofit and the largest education reform organization in New York City. After September 11, 2001, New Visions asked the nonprofit yoga education organization Bent on Learning to coordinate a yoga program to help children to heal and to manage the symptoms of post-traumatic stress disorder. Bent on Learning now serves more than 20 school and approximately 1,000 students each week. New Visions may appear suspicious to critical educators for its association with large financial corporations, and its mission to expand charter schools. But they received 26 million in federal stimulus money under the Investing in Innovation Fund (i3) grants.[2] Critical educators might consider whether it might make sense for some of the resources to be spent on critical-transformative change projects.

Yoga programs like the one at Jefferson Elementary School in Berwyn, IL, could be funded with stimulus money. Quoting the 2009 ASCD report "Using Stimulus Dollars for Lasting Impact," Principal Violet Tantillo said "[our school yoga program] is a 'sustainable' school improvement and 'capacity-building professional development' that 'guarantees lasting effect of the education reforms funded by the stimulus dollars, which translates into long-term benefits for our students.'" The added benefit in the eyes of the ASCD would be the program's focus on the whole child. The program, called "Student Wellness in 8–10 Minutes Each Day" ("Mindful Practices," 2011) takes very little time out of the day and costs nothing to use. Jefferson serves a high "at-risk" population of K–5 students. Before implementing this program, Principal Tantillo was beset with a long line of daily behavior referrals for incidents such as hitting and pushing. Now, "[i]ncidents of inappropriate behavior have dropped over 50%. Aggressive behavior, bullying, trash-talking, etc. has significantly decreased" (Tantillo, 2009, personal communication).

The Wellness Initiative (TWI), which brings yoga to low-income students from more than 20 schools in Adams, Boulder, Arapahoe, and Denver Counties in Colorado, is supported by a host of private foundations, corporations, and government agencies. The Colorado Health Foundation recently recognized TWI with a $40,000 Healthy Living program grant for teaching lifestyle skills that will help to decrease the growing obesity rates in Colorado. TWI uses the Yoga Ed™ ("Yoga Ed," 2011) curriculum in their "secular yoga-based wellness programs" including yoga classes for students (before or after school, or during the day as part of PE), a Tools for Teachers workshop (meant to demonstrate yoga-based techniques that teachers can use in their classrooms), and yoga classes for teachers and other school staff (The Wellness Initiative, 2010).

Wielding policy language in service of transformative projects

The International Association for Human Values, an NGO dedicated to serving communities affected by trauma and stress, has developed a youth program called Youth Empowerment Seminar for Schools! (YES!). The YES! Program fits neatly into state mandated Service Learning, School Safety, and Social Emotional Learning Programs and can be aligned with state and national standards in Health and Physical Education. As of this writing, 40 schools in the United States are using the program. Because the program incorporates a medically proven breathing and relaxation technique (Brown & Gerberg, 2005),[3] it reduces stress and increases self-control and focused attention. As these have been positively linked with a reduction in violence and increased academic performance, schools should be able to argue effectively for using YES!

ChildLight Yoga, in Dover, NH, will help schools write grants to pay for their modestly priced training for schools to implement the Yoga 4 Classrooms™ curriculum, which is aligned with the National Association for Sport and Physical Education (NASPE) standards and the CDC's National Health Education Standards (NHES). This organization acknowledges the goals and purposes of No Child Left Behind: "to expand local control and flexibility of education, to do what works based on scientific research, to have accountability for results, and to have more options for parents" ("Yoga 4 Classrooms," 2011). The point to be taken is that ChildLight helps schools to accomplish these goals; it does not represent efforts *in addition* to these goals. This is a major rhetorical success for school yoga programs and the specific point at which academics can help the movement. University faculty who partner with non-profit organizations and local yoga teachers can use their facility with the discourse of educational research and policy and their knowledge of where to find and how to use research to support their assertions. For instance, when a harried district principal was concerned that continuing yoga programming would take away from time that the school needed to focus on "improving teacher effectiveness" as a condition of receiving an award from a powerful private foundation, I was able to help draft a letter explaining that the current yoga program and curriculum *was consistent with* increasing teacher effectiveness.

Research-based practice

For those who value or, as is often the case, need it to gain approval to implement yoga programs in their educational communities, "scientifically based" research abounds to support what practitioners know experientially to be true. Clinical or controlled studies that use sophisticated statistical analysis support the positive effects for children of mindfulness (yoga and meditation, in particular) on stress reduction (Benson et al., 2000; Berger et al., 2009; Galantino et al., 2008; Khalsa et al., 2011; Vempati, 2002), depression (Bennett et al., 2008; Gates & Wolverton, 2007; Woolery et al., 2004), ADHD (Jensen, 2004; Treuting & Hinshaw, 2001), and autism (Kenny, 2002). Studies have also connected stress reduction to an increase in desirable behaviors for children and to academic achievement. Because of the value placed on making a more direct connection between yoga programs and academic achievement, work here is ongoing and promising (Cohen, n.d.; Jennings et al., 2001; Mendelson et al., 2010; Slovacek et al., 2003; Stewart Stanec et al., 2010). Specifically, yoga and meditation have been found to decrease school behavior referrals (Marie et al., 2008; Walker et al., 2004), increase "time-on-task" (Peck et al., 2005), and improve academic performance by reducing stress (Beets & Mitchell, 2010; Kauts & Sharma, 2009). School psychologists use yoga as an alternative or complement to behavioral and medical interventions for children with attentions problems (Peck et al., 2005) and other social, emotional, behavioral, and academic difficulties (Nardo & Reynolds, 2002). University of Pennsylvania researchers have found yoga to be beneficial to teachers working in "high-risk," urban settings (Jennings et al., 2011). Researchers are investigating other mind-body practices, in particular Tai Chi Chuan, Qi Gong, and Transcendental Meditation. However, it is easiest for public schools to incorporate a generic, infinitely adaptable style of yoga, which is not nearly as strict—nor as pure—in its disciplinary requirements as these.

And for those of us who are qualitatively minded, observation and self-report surveys, participant feedback, program evaluations, and self-studies reveal a consensus of firsthand experience bearing witness to the positive effects of yoga on themselves and others. These informants often include teachers, principals, and students (Lamb, 2006).

Almost all of the studies, stories, and reports recognize that evidence linking yoga and meditation to increases in academic achievement would be the surest way to implement additional yoga programs in schools. While funding may not be the problem (since yoga programs often come at very little to no cost to schools), time certainly is, and time in schools is mandated by the states, in part, responding to federal mandates that they show progress toward raising test scores and increasing graduation rates. Clearly, many factors contribute to test performance that lie outside the control of the school environment, including student motivation and physical, psychological and emotional health. Using test scores as a proxy for learning assumes that the tests actually measure "achievement"; that recall or sight identification of the right answers counts as achievement; and that this achievement is valuable (Thomas, 2004). One of the chief complaints of NCLB is that the law relies on one measure of academic success, when many parents, educators, cognitive scientists, and other researchers argue that learning involves much more than, and perhaps something entirely different from, the ability to score well on a standardized test (AFT, 2004; Apple, 2007; Bloomfield & Cooper, 2003; Fusarelli, 2004; Hill & Barth, 2004, Kumashiro, 2003; Meier & Wood, 2004; NEA, 2007; Ohanian, 2007; Sunderman et al., 2005; Thomas, 2004; Valencia et al., 2001). Still, since high-stakes testing increases stress for the whole school community (Kruger et al., 2007), stress-reduction programs that do not interfere with test preparation and which may even reduce test anxiety are an easy sell to those who have control over resources earmarked toward schools. Foucault (1979/1995) would say that yoga educators and teachers are using disciplinary power *productively* when they secure resources to promote their transformative agendas in K–12 schools. Unlike some progressive educators, they are not letting the discursive and material constraints of high-stakes testing block them from challenging the status quo.

Yoga educators, like most teachers, are interested in individual harmony in the community, personal growth, and happiness. We want academic success for our students, but we also want to have our field theories about what "successful" children need, about what "successful" teachers need to be validated by research, but even more so, by those that we immediately serve *in practice*. Teachers want their students to be cared for, to be healthy, and to enjoy themselves and learning. Yoga programs adapt to teachers' practice, based on local wisdom and what works best in each school and in each classroom.

Furthermore, yoga and mindfulness are always practiced at each individual's pace. Participants are encouraged to listen to their own bodies; to let go of expectations, competition, and judgment; and to act compassionately toward themselves. Cueing for poses or breathing always involves affirmation and reminders to relax, be still, slow down, and enjoy. This alone contradicts the prevailing message of many public schools in the U.S.: hurry, do as much as possible, don't waste time just sitting there, and try your hardest to be the best. In a way, school yoga is the antithesis of (external) *accountability* and an exemplar of (personal) *responsibility* (Biesta, 2004).

The school yoga movement

The core aims of yoga are increased strength, flexibility, and balance for the body and the mind. Unlike other sports and fitness systems that do, of course, also improve mental health, yoga is a gentle, noncompetitive self-care practice of physical, emotional, and psychological wellness. As a complete philosophical system, yoga can be traced to practices arising in India more than 5,000 years ago. Yoga, as it is most often practiced in the United States, is a system of mind-body techniques that includes physical postures (asanas or body positions), conscious breathing, and deep relaxation. Yoga poses are more closely related to early 20th-century European gymnastics than to any religious practice of Hinduism or Buddhism (Singleton, 2010). They are infinitely adaptable; there are many traditions to choose from but in the United States, the tendency to invent a personal practice is arguably more popular than any of those specific practices brought over from India and the Far East. Studies also show that children and adults can experience the breathing exercises and postures of yoga and meditation as therapeutic interventions without adopting any particular philosophical or spiritual aspects of ancient tradition (Khalsa, 2006).

Yoga as multicultural education

Yoga is not a religion; therefore, including yoga and meditation in public schools as part of the regular school day, or as a before- or afterschool program, does not constitute an establishment of religion. However, yoga postures, breathing, and meditation can be used as spiritual technologies akin to prayer. Spirituality as an experience of aliveness of mind and body as a unity (Capra, 2002) holds appeal and benefits for the religious and nonreligious alike. And yoga expressed by individual students as a personal spiritual practice cannot and should not be prohibited in public schools. Learning about yoga can also be a way to explore cultural beliefs and secular, spiritual or religious tenets. In this way, yoga can be seen as inclusive multicultural education. Using yoga as a curricular theme, history, philosophy, geography as well as psychology and physiology can be explored cross-culturally, comparative, and internationally. Even the pockets of controversy over including yoga in public schools provide opportunities for critical, democratic conversations about democratic schooling in a culturally pluralistic society (Douglass, 2010).

Ameliorating the effects of poverty

And yoga may be a good resource for children living in disadvantaged communities associated with significant stressors because it helps to reduce stress and negative behavior in response to stress. The minimal cost and ability for participation after being exposed to yoga is another benefit for these populations (Berger et al., 2009). Yoga can benefit urban youth, in particular, as it reduces the stress associated with poverty and with living in neighborhoods with high incidence of violence (Mendelson et al., 2010).

   Obesity has become a social marker, so closely is it correlated with poverty and therefore race and ethnicity. Writing for the *Atlantic*, politics editor Marc Ambinder (2010) says that stigmatizing individuals—making obesity a failure of will—is immoral and racist. Reporting on the American obesity epidemic, Ambinder found that obesity rates are above average for African American women, Mexican American boys, and twice the national average for young Native Americans. "Obesity researchers increasingly believe that material disadvantages best explains the spread of obesity among poor people" (p. 76). As medical scientists and public health professionals agree, the target of our prevention and treatment should be children (Walsh, 2008). This means that state and local boards of education must be included in making policy changes that will go far beyond education campaigns. School health policy must include wellness activities and nutritious food during every school day.

The anti-obesity campaign dominating school health policy discourse is problematic when students' bodies are made another target of surveillance and shame. Describing the CA state mandate that students submit to body mass index testing, VanderSchee writes that the CA State Department of Education chose to penalize students with extra PE classes in order to motivate them to be fit (VanderSchee, 2009, p. 140). Additionally,

> It is not enough to criticize, explain or understand [health discourse]. We have to engage with the paradox of wanting to reject utterly the performative values that are driving social change while at least considering that there might also be an immediate problem to deal with in the form of poor diet, too few opportunities for play and exercise, and ill health, and their origins in the social conditions of people's lives in the context of global capitalism. (Evans et al., 2008, p. 149)

Yoga is a positive and affirming approach to health that offers an alternative to the "commonsense" notion that weight loss equals health. Yoga supports an integrated approach to weight management. It brings mindfulness to habitual behaviors, including eating and exercise, or lack thereof. Vigorous practice (power yoga) can serve double duty as a moving meditation and workout, but the real advantage of yoga is that "[t]he combined effects of self-acceptance, increased body awareness, and inward reflection that are natural byproducts of a regular yoga practice can increase your ability to achieve and maintain a healthy weight, and can have a positive impact" on body image (Sparrowe, 2010, p. 74). Vigorous yoga practice can be an effective way to lose or maintain weight, with the added benefit of increasing self-esteem (Benavides & Caballero, 2009; Kristal et al., 2005).

Yoga and social justice (education)

School yoga, as critical-emancipatory pedagogy, effectively uses the legitimizing power of standards—national standards for physical education; the PA Academic Standards for Health, Safety and Physical Education; and the current IL statewide, and proposed national, Social/Emotional Learning standards (SEL)—to provide self-care knowledge and skills to students and teachers. This is done without adopting the alienating technologies of standardization and while attempting to interrupt the "prison pipeline" operating in some inner-city schools. According to the SEL standards, by late high school, IL students should be able to "[e]valuate how advocacy for the rights of others contributes to the common good" (ISBE, 2003) (2B.5b). A social justice educator could make use of yoga tools to prepare students toward this end. Specifically, the Yoga Ed High School Curriculum has as some of its outcomes "awareness and understanding of feelings" (emotional fitness), "tolerance and respect" (mental fitness), and "understanding of one's impact and contributions" (social fitness) (Yoga Ed, 2007).

To this end, the urban-focused nonprofit organization Y.O.G.A. for Youth serves mostly African American students in the South Central Los Angeles area, including the Watts Learning Center. In 1993, Krishna Kaur,brought yoga directly to students at "Fremont, Locke, Crenshaw and Jordan High Schools, as well as…teachers, seniors, pregnant mothers, inmates, drug rehabilitation clients and 'at-risk' youth" with a dedicated mission "to break the cycle of incarceration in our inner cities" ("Yoga for Youth," 2011). The Y.O.G.A. for Youth curriculum is being used "in juvenile detention facilities, prisons and after school programs and shared with pregnant and parenting teens throughout Southern California with satellite programs in New York, Minneapolis, Seattle, Chicago and Mexico"("Yoga for Youth," 2011).

Social justice, according to Connie North's excellent mapping (North, 2008), involves recognizing "cultural groups' claims for respect and dignity," and a "more equitable sharing of wealth and power," also called redistribution (p. 1185). In education, knowledge of both oppression and agency, what used to be called consciousness-raising (Nixon, 1999), is sometimes placed in opposition to student and teacher action, where one is figured as more important, relevant, or proper for schools to pass along to youth. But, in general, a social justice perspective is one that views the purpose of education as social transformation and the primary job of education as liberation (Freire, 1973/2000). The social element of a justice-oriented belief system holds that relieving the suffering and oppression of some members of a society is the only way to ensure the overall well-being or happiness for all members. From a social justice perspective then, yoga education and practice represent both knowledge and action taken for liberation (of others) and transformation (of self). Yoga is something shared by those who have experience with those who seek it. Yet it is ever afterward something that people can do for themselves and adapt to their own interests, needs, and beliefs. There are no tests and no competition. It is free to practice and even learn. You can do it alone or with others; there is no specific equipment required and you can practice anywhere with very little space. There is no prerequisite physical form or level of ability, beyond the ability to breathe. Yoga is for *every* body. Aside from using the practice for physical fitness, people use yoga stretching, breathing, and meditation to prevent or combat poor self-esteem, depression, attention problems, anger, anxiety, and stress. Yoga has also been used to increase focus, awareness, happiness, connectedness, and confidence.

The Niroga Institute, located in the San Francisco Bay area, is engaged in community outreach, education, and research on the preventative, therapeutic, and rehabilitative effects of yoga for hard-to-serve populations including children with special needs, "at-risk" teens, incarcerated persons, and the elderly. Their Transformative Life Skills (TLS) Program consists of 15 minutes of yoga exercise, breathing, and meditation. A report on the success of the TLS program at Alameda County Juvenile Justice Center "suggests that the delivery of a TLS program within Juvenile Hall among predominantly African American males and females, between the ages of 12 and 17…leads to a significant decrease in perceived stress, and a significant increase in self control" (Matthew, 2010, p. 2). After conducting a controlled test of the TLS program at El Cerrito High School, where students practiced TLS at least once a week for 18 weeks, researchers found that students who received the training reported feelings of greater self-control and less stress, with males perceiving a greater increase in self-control and a greater reduction in stress than females. Teachers reported that the student did seem more focused and relaxed and found the program to be very easily adapted to regular classroom instruction (Matthew, 2008).

This is particularly exciting since Duckworth and Seligman (2005) found self control to be a greater predictor than IQ of academic achievement and grade improvement (GPA not standardized test scores) among eighth graders. So any program that demonstrably increases self-control should be desirable where academic improvement, not simply an increase in test scores, is the goal. Perhaps the most significant impact that Niroga will have on their community is in training a new generation of urban, minority youth to be yoga teachers. Creating instructors with language and culture skills to match vulnerable target populations achieves one of the major social justice goals of the yoga community, democratizing and equitably distributing the practice. Other programs that are working to interrupt the school-to-prison pipeline in urban areas are Street Yoga in Portland, OR, and The Lineage Project in New York City.

(Self) transformation, rather than emancipation

In the broadest and most basic sense, critical theories criticize functionalist explanations of systems and relationships and usually involve some observations of domination and oppression. Change is usually reproductive of the status quo and freedom from this cycle of reproduction is called *emancipation.* Postcritical theories make use of the critical lens but go further; they also call out the limitations of critical theories, recognize fluctuations in relations of power, and most importantl, they also acknowledge agency. Change can be reproductive and/or emancipatory, but in situations where there may be no extraction from relations of power (for Foucault, this is every situation), postcritical scholars may speak of freedom as *transformation* rather than emancipation.

Meanwhile, mindfulness practice is transformative, in the Foucauldian sense, in that it reveals the various ways that power normalizes teachers and students according to dominant constitutions of "good teachers" as obedient technicians (Hyde, 2007) and "good students" as compliant competitors. Focused awareness and attention to each moment, especially in stressful environments, reveal the ways in which the rules of the system operate—in discursive (dominant educational ideology and agenda) and nondiscursive (institutional polices) ways so that individuals might develop strategies of resistance.

Considering the prevalence of teacher deskilling and deprofessionalization via standardization, curriculum restriction, and the current punitive accountability environment (Gunzenhauser, 2006a; Schultz, 2005; Sirotnik, 2004; Ingersoll, 2003), I see much more possibility and action in practices of teacher self-care and teacher and student self-transformation. Yoga is a practice that allows participants access to all of the domains of work upon the self, recognized in transformative education: knowing the self, controlling the self, caring for the self (paying attention to oneself, self-compassion), and (re)creating the self (Tennant, 2005).

Professional ~~development~~ "empowerment"

Within the dominant discourse of accountability, programs to "empower" teachers are often structured to examine and improve teachers so that they have more flexibility to be able to raise student test scores by whatever means necessary. But the language is a kind of doublespeak: the "empowerment" training aims to insure that teacher, know exactly how to conform to the mandates of standards. This kind of professional development is really a normalization process (Foucault, 1979/1995). In contrast, professional development that gives teachers the knowledge and skills that they want, in the way that they want it, and shows them how to take care of (change) themselves as well as their students is truly *empowering*; it treats teachers as ends in themselves.

The nonprofit organization for which I consult, Yoga in Schools, provides yoga programming and teacher training to a dozen districts in the Greater Pittsburgh area. As the director, Joanne Spence's personal mission is to empower people to sustain their own healing networks; her service approach has always been to identify the people inside of an organization, such as Physical Education and Health teachers, who will do the work of sustaining a yoga program. We are just now finishing a two-year project working with the Physical Education and Health teachers from the largest district, Pittsburgh Public Schools. Final self-reports, as well as field observations of the teachers by the instructional team, suggested that *participants experienced both personal change and change to their professional practice* as a result of participating in the yoga training program. The participants' responses revealed that *these teach-*

ers learned that making time to take care of themselves has a direct benefit to their students and their teaching practice. They felt that the training gave them new techniques to relax, stay fit, and relieve anxiety. Some reported being reminded of the reasons that they entered into Health and Physical Education teaching in the first place. They were called to reexamine how well they were living their values of personal wellness. Some resumed balanced diet and exercise routines for themselves; others made the healthy changes for their households.

Yoga as critical pedagogy: Freirean conscientization and praxis

School yoga curriculum and instruction represent mindfulness pedagogies that are critical in the Freirean sense of involving *conscientization*—social consciousness-raising starting with liberating the self from oppressive beliefs; and *praxis*—reflection and action upon the world in order to transform it. For thousands of years, people have approached yoga as a path to enlightenment. And those who come to yoga as a mean for stress reduction or physical conditioning will typically still notice the transpersonal or transcendent qualities. But what does this mean? In Freiean terms, yoga raises consciousness of one's personal and social position and puts one in touch with the world as it really is. Freire assumed that people who are oppressed are under a false consciousness or even unconscious. This is a result of being uneducated or miseducated to believe that things are as they must or should be; they are unaware of the benefit to the oppressor of their complicity and ignorance. Plainly speaking, most Western educators will tell you that education is power, a way out of poverty, and the means to personal happiness and material success. What is often missing from this "awareness" is a critique of schooling as a place of banking education—where instead of being empowered, students are actually prevented from realizing their ability to choose what they learn, what they want to know, and how to participate in making changes in the world. Every individual already has valuable knowledge. But the status quo system of education controls and legitimates official knowledge, mandates that all must learn it, and then evaluates teachers and students on how well they can demonstrate that they have learned it. But there are others things—such as knowledge of the self—that are worth knowing. Students need to be alerted to this fact through problem-posing education.

Those who take up the mission of bringing yoga into public schools will typically have a personal transformation back story. Yoga changed something in their lives and left them feeling such gratitude and hope that they were compelled to share it with others who were suffering. This is especially the case for those working in urban environments. Yoga curricula are different from classical or even contemporary (popular culture-based) student empowerment programs based on critical pedagogies. Yoga emphasizes a light touch on others and the world. What this means is that instead of rallying students against an organized oppressive force or group, yoga identifies the oppressor within. The battle then is against irresponsible and self-damaging behaviors. The emphasis is on taking care of the self, paying attention, being patient, and making incremental internal changes toward refinement.

That is not to say that yoga curricula ignore social conditions such as poverty, violence, and school failure. Taking local social action is compatible with practicing yoga. Contributing to the community could be a form of service yoga. Students may feel motivated to be positively involved because they feel better, and are more compassionate and loving as a result of doing yoga. They may feel more connected to other people and more aware of their capacity for helping.

For teachers, leading students in yoga practice in the classroom and being more mindful in their teaching and in their relationships with their students are expressions of praxis: reflection and action. It is a living through of integrity. Yoga requires personal reflection simultaneous with movement/action-posing or breathing, stilling the mind, or expanding the consciousness.

The social movement model of school reform

The popularity and success of yoga in schools illustrates what Parker Palmer (1992) calls a "movement approach to educational reform," one that can change the purpose and structure of institutions from within, making use of whatever resources are currently available and working within and through whatever conditions are at hand.

> By giving public voice to alternative values we can create something more funda-
> mental than political change. We can create cultural change. When we secure a place
> in public discourse for ideas and images like [yoga education] we are following those
> reformers who minted phrases like "affirmative action" and made them the coin
> of the realm. When the language of change becomes available in the common cul-
> ture, people are better able to name their yearnings for change, to explore them
> with others, to claim membership in a great movement—and to overcome the dis-
> abling effects of feeling isolated and half-mad. (Palmer, 1992, pp. 14–15)

Teachers deserve to be happy and fulfilled on the job and off. They are not just a means to student achievement, nor the only barriers to it. Too often, teachers are positioned as instruments, some good or bad, for taking action on students: getting them to learn, perform, behave, make good choices, and now be healthy and well. It is rare to see professional development programs that take teacher well-being into consideration unless it is proven to directly impact student achievement (performance). It is as if nothing else matters. Teacher turnover is notoriously high in poor neighborhoods and teacher burnout is figured as just part of the job, now, in all schools. Why must this be? Why must teaching be so difficult, stressful, all consuming? Why is good teaching such hard work? If we treat teachers as valuable and lovable people, if we care for them, teach them to care for themselves and their students, won't this positively affect the school climate? But none of this matters unless it is also associated with increases in academic performance.

There is no reason to accept this ideology in order to take advantage of the benefits to all of practicing yoga in schools. Yoga programming does not uncritically accept teachers or students as problems that need to be fixed in order than students get better scores on tests. I don't know any program or yoga educator that takes raising test scores as a prime objective, even when they promote their programs as something that may do that very thing. Yoga programs do not ignore the devastating effects of poverty and racism, the systemic and structural explanations for the achievement gap. A focus on internal change does not negate efforts toward social change. It does not excuse or ignore the out of school factors that affect school performance. As Parker Palmer (1992) advises, we can begin to create change in large organizations through self-change, person-to-person relationships, and the networks of like-minded people as they grow organically from them. Actually, no social movement has ever developed by any other means.

Notes

1. Based, in part, on a paper presented at the 2010 AESA annual conference.
2. The i3 fund, which is part of the historic $10 billion investment in school reform in the American Recovery and Reinvestment Act (ARRA), will support local efforts to start or expand research-based innovative programs that help close the achievement gap and improve outcomes for high-need students. The competition was open to school districts as well as nonprofit organizations and institutions of higher education working in partnership with public schools. See http://www2.ed.gov/programs/innovation/index.html.
3. Sudarshan Kriya Yogic breathing (SKY).

References

AAHE. (2007). *The national health education standards: Achieving excellence.* Second edition. Reston, VA: American Association for Health Education.

AFT. (2004). NCLB: Let's get it right. From http://www.aft.org/topics/nclb/index.htm.

Ambinder, M. (2010). Beating obesity. *Atlantic* (May, 2010), 72–83.

Apple, M. W. (2007). Ideological success, educational failure? *Journal of Teacher Education, 58*(2), 108–116.

Beets, M. W., & Mitchell, E. (2010). Effects of yoga on stress, depression, and health-related quality of life in a nonclinical, bi-ethnic sample of adolescents: A pilot study. *Hispanic Health Care International, 8,* 47.

Benavides, S., & Caballero, J. (2009). Ashtanga yoga for children and adolescents for weight management and psychological well being: An uncontrolled open pilot study. *Complementary Therapies in Clinical Practice, 15*(2), 110–114.

Bennett, S., Weintraub, A., & Khalsa, S. (2008). Initial evaluation of the lifeforce yoga program as a therapeutic intervention for depression. *International Journal of Yoga Therapy, 18,* 49–57.

Benson, H., Wilcher, M., Greenberg, B., Huggins, E., Ennis, M., Zuttermeister, P. C., et al. (2000). Academic performance among middle school students after exposure to a relaxation response curriculum. *Journal of Research and Development in Education, 33*(3), 156–165.

Berger, D. L., Silver, E. J., & Stein, R. E. K. (2009). Effects of yoga on inner-city children's well-being: A pilot study. *Alternative Therapies in Health and Medicine, 15*(5), 36–42.

Berliner, D. (2009). Poverty and potential: Out-of-school factors and school success. Retrieved April 19, 2010, from http://epicpolicy.org/publication/poverty-and-potential

Berliner, D., & Biddle, B. (1995). *The manufactured crisis: Myths, fraud, and the attack on America's public schools.* New York: Perseus.

Biesta, G. J. (2004). Education, accountability, and the ethical demand: Can the democratic potential of accountability be regained? *Educational Theory, 54*(3), 233–250.

Bloomfield, D. C., & Cooper, B. S. (2003). NCLB: A new role for the federal government: An overview of the most sweeping federal education law since 1965. *THE Journal (Technological Horizons in Education), 30*(10), p. 6.

Brown, R., & Gerbarg, P. (2005). Sudarshan kriya yogic breathing in the treatment of stress, anxiety, and depression: Part i-neurophysiologic model. *Journal of Alternative and Complementary Medicine, 11*(2), 383–384.

Capra, F. (2002). *The hidden connections: Integrating the biological, cognitive and social dimensions of life into a science of sustainability.* New York: Doubleday.

Cohen, D. (n.d.). Mindfulness in school curricula. Cambridge, MA.

Douglass, L. (2010). Yoga in the public schools: Diversity, democracy and the use of critical thinking in educational debates. *Religion and Education, 37*(2), 162–174.

Duckworth, A. L., & Seligman, M. E. P. (2005). Self-discipline outdoes IQ in predicting academic performance of adolescents. *Psychological Science, 16*(12), 939–944.

Evans, J., Rich, E., Davies, B., & Allwood, R. (2008). *Education, disordered eating and obesity discourses: Fat fabrications.* London: Routledge.

Foucault, M. (1979/1995). *Discipline and punish: The birth of the prison.* New York: Vintage Books.

Freire, P. (1973/2000). *Pedagogy of the oppressed* (30th Anniversary edition). New York: Continuum International Publishing Group.

Fusarelli, L. D. (2004). The potential impact of the No Child Left Behind act on equity and diversity in American education. *Educational Policy, 18*(1), 71–94.

Galantino, M. L., Galbavy, R., & Quinn, L. (2008). Therapeutic effects of yoga for children: A systematic review of the literature. *Pediatric Physical Therapy, 20*(1), 66–80.

Gates, G., & Wolverton, M. (Eds.). (2007). *Emerging thought and research on student, teacher, and administrator stress and coping.* Incorporated, CT: Information Age Publishing.

Gunzenhauser, M. G. (2006a, September 29, 2006). *Resistance as a component of educator professionalism.* Paper presented at the Ohio Valley Philosophy of Education Society, Dayton, OH.

HHS, USDA, & DOE. (2010). Let's move: Healthier schools. Retrieved April 18, 2010, from http://www.letsmove.gov/index.html

Hill, D. M., & Barth, M. (2004). NCLB and teacher retention: Who will turn out the lights? *Education and the Law, 16*(2–3), 173–181.

Hyde, A. (2007). *Self-constitution as resistance to normalization: Agency and resistance in the era of accountability.* Unpublished Dissertation, University of Pittsburgh, Pittsburgh.

Ingersoll, R. M. (2003). *Who controls teachers' work? Power and accountability in America's schools.* Cambridge, MA: Harvard University Press.

ISBE. (2003). Social/emotional learning (SEL): Illinois State Board of Education.

Jennings, P., Snowberg, K., Coccia, M., & Greenberg, M. (2001). Improving classroom learning environments by cultivating awareness and resilience in education (care): Results of two pilot studies. *Journal of Classroom Interactions, 46*(1), 37–48.

Jensen, P. (2004). The effects of yoga on the attention and behavior of boys with attention deficit/hyperactivity disorder (ADHD). *The Journal of Attention Disorders, 7*(4), 205–216.

Kauts, A., & Sharma, N. (2009). *Effect of yoga on academic performance in relation to stress, 2*(1), 39–43.

Kenny, M. (2002). Integrated movement therapy™: Yoga-based therapy as a viable and effective intervention for autism spectrum and related disorders. *International Journal of Yoga Therapy, 12*(1), 71–79.

Khalsa, S. B. S., Hickey-Schultz, L., Cohen, D., Steiner, N., & Cope, S. (2011). Evaluation of the mental health benefits of yoga in a secondary school: A preliminary randomized controlled trial. *Journal of Behavioral Health Services & Research, 38*, 1–11. From http://www.springerlink.com/content/427p456821974064/

Khalsa, S. B. (2006). A perennial debate. *International Journal of Yoga Therapy, 16*(1), 5–6.

Kristal, A. R., Littman, A. J., Benitez, D., & White, E. (2005). Yoga practice is associated with attenuated weight gain in healthy, middle-aged men and women. *Alternative Therapies in Health and Medicine, 11*(4), 28–33.

Kruger, L. J., Wandle, C., & Struzziero, J. (2007). Coping with the stress of high stakes testing. In L. J. K. D. Shriberg (Ed.), *High stakes testing: New challenges and opportunities for school psychologists.* Binghamton, NY: Haworth Press.

Kumashiro, K. (2003, October 19). Leaving good teachers behind. *Tallahassee Democrat.*

Lamb, T. (2006). Yoga and education (grades K–12). From http://www.zenergyyoga.net/content/media/education.pdf.

Marie, D., Wyshak, G., & Wyshak, G. H. (2008). Yoga prevents bullying in schools. NEED PUB INFO

Matthew, R. (2008). *Executive summary: El Cerrito High School transformative life skills program.* Oakland: Niroga Institute.

Matthew, R. (2010). *Unit 6 transformative life skills (TLS) program at the Alameda County Juvenile Justice Center.* Oakland: Niroga Institute.

Mathis, W. J., & Welner, K. G. (Eds.). (2010). The Obama education blueprint: Researchers examine the evidence. Charlotte, NC: Information Age Publishing.

Meier, D., & Wood, G. H. (2004). *Many children left behind: How the No Child Left Behind Act is damaging our children and our schools.* Boston: Beacon Press.

Mendelson, T., Greenberg, M. T., Dariotis, J. K., Gould, L. F., Rhoades, B. L., & Leaf, P. J. (2010). Feasibility and preliminary outcomes of a school-based mindfulness intervention for urban youth. *Journal of Abnormal Child Psychology, 38*, 985–994.

Mindful practices. (2011). From http://www.mindfulpracticesyoga.com/index.html.

Nardo, A. C., & Reynolds, C. (2002, February). *Social, emotional, behavioral, and cognitive benefits of yoga for children: A nontraditional role for school psychologists to consider.* Paper presented at the annual meeting of the National Association of School Psychologists, Chicago, IL.

NASPE. (2004). Moving into the future: National standards for physical education, Second edition. New York: McGraw-Hill. NEA. (2007). *NCLB/ESEA it's time for a change: Voices from America's classrooms.* Washington, DC: National Education Association.

NFL (2009). NFL play 60. The National Football League. From http://www.nflrush.com/play60/

Nixon, G. (1999). Whatever happened to "heightened consciousness"? *Journal of Curriculum Theorizing, 31*(6), 625–633.

Noddings, N. (2005). What does it Mean to Educate the Whole Child? *Educational Leadership, 63*(1): 8–13.

Noguera, P. (2010). A new vision of school reform, *The Nation,* June 14, 2010.

North, C. E. (2008). What is all this talk about "social justice"? Mapping the terrain of education's latest catchphrase. *Teachers College Record, 110*(6), 1182–1206.

Ohanian, S. (2007, 2007–01–23 11:59:35). Before the fall: Or how I see NCLB impacting me. From http://www.susanohanian.org/show_sarahsnotes.php?id=21

Palmer, P. J. (1992). Divided no more: A movement approach to educational reform. *Change Magazine, 24*(2), 10–17.

Peck, H., Kehle, T., Bray, M., & Theodore, L. (2005). Yoga as an intervention for children with attention problems. *School Psychology Review, 34*(3), 415–424.

Schultz, B. C. (2005, October, 29 2005). *Teachers' perspectives of how high-stakes testing influences instructional decisions and professionalism.* Paper presented at the Council of Professors of Instructional Supervision (COPIS) Annual Conference, Athens, GA.

Singleton, M. (2010). Yoga's greatest truth. *Yoga Journal* (November), 66–69; 106–107.

Sirotnik, K. A. (2004). *Holding accountability accountable: What ought to matter in public education*. New York; London: Teachers College Press.

Slovacek, S. P., Tucker, S. A., & Pantoja, L. (2003). *A study of the yoga ed program at the accelerated school*. Los Angeles, CA: Program Evaluation and Research Collaboration (PERC).

Sparrowe, L. (2010). Inner light: For a radically different approach to weight loss, start not with diet and exercise, but with connecting to yourself. *Yoga Journal* (February), 72–79.

Stewart Stanec, A. D., Forneris, T., & Theuerkauf, B. (2010). Yoga in school communities. *Strategies: A Journal for Physical and Sport Educators, 23*(3), 1–40.

Sunderman, G. L., Kim, J. S., & Orfield, G. (2005). *NCLB meets school realities: Lessons from the field*. Thousand Oaks, CA: Corwin Press.

Tennant, M. (2005). Transforming selves. *Journal of Transformative Education, 3*(2), 102–115.

Thomas, P. L. (2004). *Numbers games: Measuring and mandating American education*. New York, NY: P. Lang.

Treuting, J., & Hinshaw, S. P. (2001). Depression and self-esteem in boys with attention-deficit/hyperactivity disorder: Associations with comorbid aggression and explanatory attributional mechanisms. *Journal of Abnormal Child Psychology, 29*(1), 23–39.

Valencia, R. R., Valenzuela, A., Sloan, K., & Foley, D. E. (2001). Let's treat the cause, not the symptoms: Equity and accountability in Texas revisited. *Phi Delta Kappan, 83*(4), 318–326.

VanderSchee, C. (2009). (Re)considering the neutrality of care: The case of body mass indexing in schools. *Philosophical Studies in Education, 40*, 138–152.

Vempati, R. P. (2002). Yoga-based guided relaxation reduces sympathetic activity judged from baseline levels. *Psychological Reports, 90*(2), 487–494.

Walker, H. M., Ramsey, E., & Gresham, F. M. (2004). Heading off disruptive behavior: How early intervention can reduce defiant behavior-and win back teaching time. Washington D.C: American Federation of Teachers.

Walsh, B. (2008, June 12). It's not just genetics. *Time*.

The wellness initiative. (2010). From http://www.wellnessinitiative.org/.

Woolery, A., Myers, H., Sternlieb, B., & Zeltzer, L. (2004). A yoga intervention for young adults with elevated symptoms of depression. *Alternative Therapies in Health and Medicine, 10*, 60–64.

Yoga 4 Classrooms. (2011). From http://www.yoga4classrooms.com/about-yoga-4-classrooms.

Yoga Ed. (2011). From http://www.yogaed.org/.

Yoga Ed. (2007). Yoga ed high school curriculum overview 9–12: Yoga Ed. From http://www.yogaed.com/instructors.html

Yoga for Youth. (2011). From http://www.yogaforyouth.org/

8. Students with Learning Disabilities Writing in an Inclusion Classroom

Patricia Jacobs & Danling Fu

Writing is difficult for all students, but poses special challenges for students with learning disabilities (Harris, Graham, & Mason, 2006). These students have historically been marginalized (Berry, 2006; McPhail & Freeman, 2005) through education in classroom settings away from most of the peers their age. In resource rooms, students diagnosed as language impaired or emotionally disturbed are grouped for instruction, where they often work on isolated skills and do not gain a broader picture of the complexities of writing (Graham, Harris, Fink-Chorzempa, & MacArthur, 2003; Rhodes & Dudley-Marling, 1996). Year by year, these students continue to fall behind their peers in regular classrooms (Smith & Luckasson, 1995). These kinds of homogeneous grouping practices have been challenged because students with learning disabilities are separated from mainstream education, limiting interaction with their mainstream peers and often receiving inferior instruction. Research has indicated that students with learning disabilities (LD) benefit from learning in an environment that engages them in peer-interaction and authentic literacy learning activities (Jenkins et al., 1994).

To provide students with LD equal learning opportunities and effective learning environments, an inclusion model has been recommended by researchers (McLeskey & Waldron, 2000; Vaughn, 1995) since the late 1990s. The inclusion model came about as a result of the Individuals with Disabilities Education Act (IDEA) that was passed in 1997. It mandated that students with disabilities be educated along with their peers in an integrated educational system where services are provided for students with special needs. Students with mild learning disabilities who have the opportunity to participate fully in the least restrictive environment (LRE) have been found to benefit academically, socially, and emotionally (Ferretti, MacArthur, & Okolo, 2001; Madden & Slavin, 1983; Waldron & McLeskey, 1998).

This chapter presents a case study of the writing experiences of students with learning disabilities in an inclusion model classroom. Two children with learning disabilities were chosen as the study focus to highlight how an inclusion model setting helped them to progress as writers despite two significant obstacles: an environment pressured by standards and test preparation and their classification as "learning disabled." Eleven children in the class were identified as having special needs and accommodations. Four of these children were diagnosed with specific learning disabilities (SLD) and language impairment; of this group, two students, Julia and Tyrone (pseudonyms),[1] were chosen for this study. Both of them had repeated a grade because of their academic struggles and were a year older than their peers.

The research setting

This research took place in a K–4 school, Millhopper Elementary, located in a small rural town in north-central Florida. The school enrolled approximately 500 students, 49% of whom received free or reduced lunch. Millhopper Elementary was an "A" school. In the state of Florida standardized test scores in reading and math are assigned percentage points and then converted into a school grade. In spite of its top score, the school failed to meet Adequate Yearly Progress (AYP)[2] and received state and federal funds to purchase reading, math, and science materials to supplement before and after school tutoring and to provide extra training for staff through professional development. This school converted to a full inclusion model in 2007. This research was conducted in Mrs. Lane's fourth grade inclusion model class. In Florida, all fourth graders are required to take a writing test named Florida Writes. Our research explored how the students identified as LD were guided to progress as writers in a high-stakes test environment. As we illustrate below, this was a challenging situation for both learners and teachers.

The participant teacher and her fourth grade class

Mrs. Lane was certified in special education with ten years of teaching experience. She had taught in self-contained classrooms for most of her career and had started to teach an inclusion class two years ago. This year, her fourth grade class had 23 students, 11 of whom were provided with accommodations for special needs in math, reading, and writing. A full-time aide was employed on a daily basis and a special education teacher was assigned to the class four afternoons a week for 90 minutes to help students who needed one-on-one assistance.

Most of the writing children do in school today is driven by the demands of high-stakes testing (Higgins, Miller, & Wegmann, 2006) and Mrs. Lane's classroom was no exception. Writing for test preparation began the first week of school. Fourth grade teachers in the county were required to use a test preparation writing curriculum to prepare students for expository and narrative prompt writing. Writing instruction occurred from 8:00 to 9:00 am on a daily basis. Lessons designed to help students to learn the test format included coding the prompt, using a graphic organizer to plan writing, writing interesting sentences and paragraphs, and elaborating with details.

Rather than being restricted by test-preparation requirements, Mrs. Lane brought her personal passion for writing, and her belief in writing as a powerful communication tool, to her class. She had previously taken a course in writing children's books and had participated in a school-wide writing group that focused on using writing process methods guided by *The Art of Teaching Writing* by Lucy Calkins (1994). Her beliefs about and passion for writing impacted her writing instruction and the children in her class. Instead of drilling her students relentlessly, Mrs. Lane alleviated the stress of the test by helping the children connect writing with their life experiences, and empowered them to find their own voices while learning to be skilled and competent writers.

The LD students chosen as case studies

Four students in Mrs. Lane's class were diagnosed as learning disabled. Two of them, Julia and Tyrone, were selected as the study focus based on similarities in their struggles with language processing and learning. Julia had long black hair parted in the middle. She had been removed from her home and lived with her grandparents because her mother had problems with substance abuse. Julia attended church on the weekends, was active in the youth group, and sang in the choir. She was very social and enjoyed friendships with several girls in the class. Julia had an Individual Education Plan (IEP) for specific learning disabilities (SLD) and language impairment. Her educational priority, as stated in her IEP, was to increase her language skills in order to be able to participate more fully in school and gain access to the curriculum.

Tyrone was an 11-year-old boy, small in size, and very quiet in class. He interacted easily with his peers and was a friend to all, but often preferred working alone because he found it difficult to concentrate in a noisy atmosphere. Tyrone lived with his mother, 9-year-old brother, and 16-year-old half brother. He had come to Millhopper Elementary in third grade after attending two other elementary schools. Tyrone had an Individual Education Plan (IEP) for specific learning disabilities (SLD) and language impairment. He struggled with language fluency and questions that involved higher order comprehension. A speech language pathologist worked with Tyrone twice a week on language development. His Exceptional Student Education (ESE) teacher came to the class daily during the afternoon to monitor his progress and assist him with his classroom work.

Learning disabilities and school writing

Students with learning disabilities face greater challenges than their regular education peers when learning how to write. Writing is a complex process that requires the integration of many cognitive and social processes and comprehensive language skills. Students with learning difficulties struggle with generating topics, planning and organizing, editing, revising, monitoring the writing process, and transcribing words (Patel & Laud, 2007; Troia, 2006). They have fewer strategies for writing, less knowledge about writing, and behavior and motivational factors that impede success as school writers (MacArthur, 2009). Scholars who study effective techniques for teaching and learning have found considerable evidence that a process approach to writing, combined with direct strategic instruction, has been beneficial in improving writing skills of children with learning disabilities (Danoff, Harris, & Graham, 1993; MacArthur, Schwartz, & Graham, 1991).

Although faced with standardized test demands and the diverse needs of her students, Mrs. Lane integrated approaches that took into consideration the children's individual learning styles, the curriculum, and the school culture to create a writing curriculum that gave all her students space to grow as writers. While many teachers struggle with keeping students engaged during test preparation, Mrs. Lane succeeded in helping her students to learn to become effective writers. She focused extensively on writing for meaningful expression. Mrs. Lane "understood the cultural boundaries separating her from her students" (North, 2009, p. 39), built on their prior knowledge and stretched their abilities beyond what was familiar (Routman, 2004).

She guided her students to revise their work on multiple drafts and nudged them to try newly learned skills from draft to draft. Frequently, she discussed the importance of adding actions and feelings, similes and metaphors, and using active verbs and precise nouns to engage the reader with vivid description. On several occasions, she came out of the classroom closet with a funny mask or wig and asked the children to use their imaginations to write for a few minutes. While preparing for the test through constant practice with prompts for expository and narrative essays, Mrs. Lane focused on best writing practices to move her diverse students forward. Along with their peers, Julia and Tyrone worked hard, and made steady progress with their writing throughout the school year.

Julia's progress as a writer

Julia was not afraid to ask for help with her writing. She had the ability to work alone to get started on planning or writing a first paragraph, but inevitably she raised her hand for Mrs. Lane. After talking through her areas of trouble and getting some direct help from the teacher, she would go back to work. That was her typical writing pattern. One day in October, the class was given the following prompt:

> *Everyone has a favorite holiday. Think about your favorite holiday and explain how you celebrate it.*

Julia wrote:

> Everybody has a favorite holiday. Mine is easter. I like to paint the eggs. I like to find the egg's to. that's what I like about easter.
> I like to paint the eggs different colors you can paint difernt pictures on them to. Once I painted A egg orange and blue whitch is the gator colors. then I painted A gator on the front.
> I like to Hunt for eggs. Sometimes when I find an egg I find a couple of dollars in there. I get a lot of candy on easter. In 2003 I found a big red egg whith 20 dollars inside it. That was my favorite easter ever.

For a student who had barely written anything in her previous school years, this was a big improvement. Despite many errors in conventions, her teacher pointed out the positive aspects of her work: she stayed on the topic with egg hunting and painting and included good details. Through daily practice, encouragement, and direct guidance from her teacher, and surrounded by her peer writers, Julia worked diligently on one piece after another and made visible progress month by month as a writer. In January, for this prompt:

> *Everyone has someone who is very special to him/her. Before you begin writing, think about someone who means the world to you. Explain to the reader of your paper what makes that person so special to you.*

Julia wrote the following, the longest piece she ever wrote for school:

> Everybody has someone that's special in there life time. My mom is special in my life time. My brother Joseph and I got serperated from our mom. My brother and I got adapted by our grandma. so really only what my brother Joseph and I have is each other. I pray almost every night to ask God to help my mom were she can get better, and for Joseph and I go live whith her. My mom had No choice she had to give Joseph and me up. Joseph and I cryed 24–7 each day thinking that will Never see our mom again. but stuff changed we got to see her. My mom broke Josephs and my heart all the time by not going to our birthday. Joseph and I would always be looking on the road hoping she would come,

but she never did, but she turned everything around she did started coming to mine and Joseph's birthday! My mom fixed everything and tried not let the Devil to force her to go get alcahall and drugs in my opinion I think she's doing a great Job at that. Now you pretty much see why my grama had to adapt my brother and me.

Now my mom would start to come over to our house like on the weekends and stay the night and go to church whith us. I love my mother whith all my heart and soul. but I hate my guts because Every time my mom came over I would always be a hog and I would not let my brother talk to her one bit and that's why I hate my guts. Now you pretty much know a lot of stuff about my mom, my brother, and me.

In this piece we can see and feel Julia with her passionate voice, true emotion, and honest wishes, prayers, and reflection. Julia loved her mom regardless of her faults. Despite mechanical errors, this piece flowed well, and was filled with strong emotion. It was a moving story and showed the tremendous growth that Julia had experienced as a writer who was learning to use language for true expression. Even though Julia continued to say writing was hard, she was rapidly advancing with her writing skills, which enabled her to pass the state writing test.

Tyrone's growth as a writer

In contrast to Julia, Tyrone did not like to ask for help during writing time. Whenever asked how his writing was going he would respond, "Great." In spite of his struggles with language, he was able to maintain a good attitude. Tyrone started fourth grade with very weak writing skills; he was clearly at risk of failing the state test. He repeatedly received failing grades on his responses to prompts during the beginning months of the year. Early in the school year, the class was presented with the prompt:

> *Everyone looked forward to having a day off from school. Think about what you do on a day off from school. Now, write a story about a time when you had a day off from school.*

He had a hard time writing a cohesive story:

I would read a book. play vido games with my brother. I would play football with my friends. Then I will watch a movie with my mom and brother. Me my mom and brother will go to The pool because it's always hot outside but sometime we go to the pool on Sundays. Me and the whole family went on a vacation we went to Daytonna.

We went to are hotel it was cool inside The hotel. We went to are room and it had a desk, tv, bed, and window view we can see the beach from up thierd. We got out the hotel and went to The beach we was having fun. We made sand catles and we wnet ot the water. We pack are things and went back home.

Mrs. Lane was not pleased with this piece and commented: "This writing lacks focus and is fragmented." She knew she needed to give more attention to help Tyrone gain the skills he needed to become a competent writer. Tyrone showed quiet determination and worked steadily on his writing, making small gains over time. Mrs. Lane praised him for every gain he made. She always found time to help him one on one, and worked with him piece by piece on strategies such as using a graphic organizer, adding details, and using a variety of words and sentence structures. Slowly, Tyrone was able to add creativity, interesting language, and feeling to his writing. He imitated examples that were provided, worked with a friend in class, and made progress from one prompt to another. He benefited from learning alongside his peers and receiving the same quality instruction to help prepare him for the upcoming test. By January, Tyrone had made so much progress that he received an "A" on the following prompt, a grade he had rarely received in his school career:

> *Everyone has someone who is very special to him/her. Before you begin writing, think about someone who means the world to you. Now explain to the reader of your paper what makes that person so special to you.*

Tyrone wrote:

> Do you have a person that's special i do it's my grandma. I have a few thing why i think she special. Grandma is funny she tells me and my brother jokes she have good jokes too she told me this good joke too I laugh so hard I could stop laughing my brother stop laughing neither sometime she do some action that's very funny. Grandma bring us to the park every Monday to feed the ducks she always watching me doing flips she push my brother on the swings she watch my brother on the monkey bars.
>
> Granma favorite subject is fish we love fishing to but its not my favorite subject. Grandma love catching fish she like catching a catfish that's her favorite thing to catch she is good catching fishes I cot a mudfish we didn't like mud fishes so we throw it back in fishing is fun when your with grandma. The final thing about grandma is she make sure if were hungry she like cooking some ribs on the grill sometimes she cook chilly I love grandma's cooking your taste bus will call out more! More! That's all the thing why I think grandma is special I love Grandma joyce because she's there for me.

Like Julia's piece on a special person, this piece revealed the joy and love Tyrone had for his grandma. When he writes, "I love grandma's cooking your taste bu(d)s will call out more! More!" we shared the feeling! Tyrone was able to extend his writing and describe his grandma's sense of humor, going to the park and cookin' on the grill with her. Tyrone's early writing had been weak in terms of organization, elaboration, and personal engagement. In this piece, Tyrone led readers to know his grandmother as a lovely, warm, and funny lady through vivid language and examples. He was beaming at his success and gained confidence in writing.

By working on writing every day along with their peers in a writers' community, Julia and Tyrone made progress as writers in many significant aspects of the writing process: planning, organization, adding details, learning to revise, writing from their hearts and personal experience, and working with their peers. With daily practice in writing, Mrs. Lane's one-on-one guidance, constant encouragement, and their peers' direct and indirect influence, Julia and Tyrone were gradually gaining self-confidence and skills as writers.

Digital storytelling

In order to diversify her students' writing experiences, Mrs. Lane decided to bring digital storytelling into her classroom as she continued to get her students ready for the high-stakes test. Digital storytelling combines narration, visuals, and sound through technology. After students go through the rigors of drafting, revising, and editing written scripts, the final publication is a digital media production such as an iMovie, MovieMaker, or PhotoStory. Students often discover personal power and creativity in writing stories and using digital tools to present their voices to a larger audience. They use visual and digital technologies in which they are often proficient in their out-of-school literacy practices (Kadjer, 2006) and feel a sense of competence working out difficulties they may encounter. Using visual materials may help students, especially the students identified as LD, to elicit language and find new ways of representation for their thoughts and words (Rose & Meyer, 2002). When students with learning disabilities write for digital stories they not only build upon and extend skills in literacy learning, they also develop skills that help them to be successful in today's Information Age. This type of activity creates space and opportunity for transforming writing experiences, while at the same time, meeting the state standards for technology integration in the curriculum (Routman, 2004).

While learning to navigate the complexities of print, visual, and sound texts, students drew on personal experience to create stories in a digital domain and developed skills that could be used both inside and outside of school. Mrs. Lane used the writing and technology standards as an opportunity for intensive and varied writing instruction. She taught her students how to be authors using best writing practices, without neglecting test demands.

Tall tales for digital stories

In February, a month before the test time, the students in Mrs. Lane's class were learning to write tall tales and create iMovies (short digital stories of their tales), while preparing to write to meet the test requirements (such as writing to the prompts with a limited time frame). Tall tales are stories that are often humorous with exaggerated or mythical events. They are fictional in nature. After reading *The Tale of Pecos Bill* as a model text, the class worked for three weeks writing scripts for their tall tales, then created narration and visuals to complete their iMovies. Every afternoon when Mrs. Lane announced it was time to work on tall tales, the excitement in the classroom was apparent. Children rushed from their seats to get a laptop and find a place to sit with a friend and work—a contrast to the serious atmosphere of test preparation time where everyone worked quietly and individually. In this learning community, Julia and Tyrone, like all their peers, wrote tall tales by drawing on their personal knowledge: Julia wrote about her church choir and her love of music and Tyrone created a character named Rockin' B Road who liked adventures. This writing activity engaged students' creativity, imagination, and passion using language, conventions and organizational skills in the context of meaningful writing.

Julia's tall tale: **All in All, Open the Eyes in My Heart Lord**

Drawing on her church experiences and her participation in the youth choir, Julia worked with enthusiasm and ease to write her tall tale. She found freedom in moving to a new genre of writing where she could choose her own topic. Julia took pleasure and pride in her writing and stopped complaining as she had before. She added details, gave specific examples, and worked hard to create a picture in the reader's mind, using her knowledge of what it took to be a good writer. In one section she wrote:

> My brother Joseph and I jumped out of the car ran inside I grabbed my guitar Joseph grabbed his guitar and we ran back outside. I stand by our youth leader Joel. Joseph stand in front of me. We are playing fore songs Halliaugh, how great is our god, All in All, open the eyes in my heart Lord, And last but Not least Im singing by myself playing the guitar at the sam time is Jesus take the weel. So we practice two hours later we did the real round in front of hundreds and hundreds of people.

Julia's story continues with an exaggeration—her youth leader's hands suddenly start playing the guitar extremely fast! Once Julia's story was written, she was enthusiastic to learn Garage Band software to record her story and to work with friends on recording the narration and drawing the visuals. During the publishing process, she worked with her friend Anna to revise words in her story and find the right voice and tone for recording. Julia was well aware that her iMovie would be shared with others in her class and she worked hard to perfect her story for her audience. What was most evident during this time was that Julia exchanged expertise and information with her friends and peers. In front of the computer, she was an expert who could sing, practice reading her work with expressions, and navigate computer applications. Julia's struggles with literacy seemed to melt away. She benefited from collaborating with others about her writing and from the digital tools she would use to present her story. Julia was plugged in—socially, academically, and technologically—to this writing community.

Tyrone's tall tale: **Rockin' B Road**

Tyrone took time to plan out his tall tale and created the following list:

> *Rockin' b Road*
>
> *He's funny*
>
> *He have big smile*
>
> *He's fast*
>
> *Green hair*
>
> *Tall*
>
> *Thin*
>
> *He's tall as a pole*
>
> *He likes adventures*

Tyrone had no trouble getting down to the task of writing and expressed that writing a tall tale for a digital story was exciting because "you get to draw pictures and add your own voice." His character, Rockin' B Road, drew on Tyrone's interest in popular culture. Tyrone clearly used his imagination to create his character in this piece:

> My character play's Gutiar he is good a Gutier Because he's in the Band. My character is tall, fast, funny, green spike hair. He have a big smile. He likes Adventures. He live in New York. He travel around concers. My characters name is Rockin'B road. He is rockin' it out to night. He is loud he dream to be a rockin'roll kind of person.

To represent his story visually, Tyrone created unique cartoon-like drawings with captions. Tyrone loved technology. He had a Facebook page, played the Xbox, Wii, and Playstation, and had a DS and a cell phone. He loved to tell people what he could do with his digital toys. His confidence with using technology enabled him to become immersed in the process of creating his tall tale: he enjoyed practicing his recording and took great pleasure in creating the visuals. The chance to use digital technologies during a school project connected to Tyrone's love of, and expertise in, multiple technologies that he used at home. He felt like an expert in this writing community and was extremely proud of his accomplishments as a writer among his peers.

Tyrone and Julia made further progress as writers during the digital story-telling unit. Independently they were able to draw on their knowledge of how to organize, plan, revise, provide details, and express feelings in their stories. They no longer felt they were disabled learners, but were able to work well to capture their ideas using personal experience and their imaginations in their digital story writing. During digital production, they continued to revise and make improvements, striving to find a voice to convey their thoughts and emotions. Julia delighted in working with her close friend and adding popular music to her presentation, while Tyrone discovered that he was talented at drawing visuals and captions. In this inclusion class, these two students were *enabled* users of 21st-century literacies that combined print, visuals, and sound—rather than disabled learners who struggled with language and learning.

Conclusion

Students with learning disabilities benefit from the inclusion model classroom where they learn alongside their regular education peers. In this setting, they have a chance to reach their full potential in an instructional model that is inclusive and geared to support and challenge students with and without identified disabilities (Waldron & McLeskey, 1998). Children with learning disabilities need the same high-level instruction that is offered to their peers and need practice to work out the difficulties of writing with direct and explicit instruction in writing strategies (Dudley-Marling & Paugh, 2009). Focusing on students' strengths and teaching writing as a process can give children with learning disabilities confidence to work through their struggles with writing and find success as authors.

The stress of standardized test preparation is alleviated when instruction focuses on best writing practices such as revising, encouraging creativity, learning conventions of writing, and working on a variety of genres (Higgins et al., 2006). Mrs. Lane gave her students intensive daily practice and exposure to multiple genres of writing throughout the school year. Julia and Tyrone benefited by receiving this writing instruction and grew as writers in their inclusion class. Writing digital stories gave Julia and Tyrone the chance to draw on out-of-school multiple literacy practices, giving them confidence and allowing them to build their writing and technology skills (Kadjer, 2006) while working with digital texts that they had expertise in. The digital story writing went beyond the mandated curriculum by supporting writing skills that were broader in scope and gave students strategies that were more applicable to a larger variety of school and real-life situations. Both students were becoming competent as writers with tools of technology, an aspect of literacy they need to be successful in the world today and tomorrow. The children felt their contribution was valued, regardless of what kind of learners they had been diagnosed as by the education system. Rather than feeling undermined and alienated, they experienced connection to their peers and were able to connect their school knowledge to their lives (McLaren, 1994).

Success in a writing curriculum comes from focusing on best writing practices, not test taking. Good writing instruction focuses on learners, and enables all learners despite their learning abilities and styles to make steady progress. To support the growth and creativity of students, to help them find their voice as authors, and to foster the critical process of independent thinking, educators must take caution in how they interpret standardization. Required pedagogy must be implemented in a way that benefits students rather than hampers and confines them through narrowly defined instruction and goals. Julia and Tyrone left their fourth grade class with advancement in literacy skills that helped to empower them as individuals, enable them as learners, and position them as equals among their classmates (Freire, 1970; Macedo, 2006; Shor, 1996).

Notes

1. Pseudonyms are used for all participants, as well as the study site.
2. Adequate Yearly Progress (AYP) is a system used in the state of Florida that measures student achievement based on results on the Florida Comprehensive Assessment Test (FCAT) as well as several other indicators. Achievement is broken down by racial groups, students with disabilities, English Language Learners, and economically disadvantaged. Groups must reach their goal for the school year to make AYP.

References

Berry, R. A. W. (2006). Creating a better classroom environment for students with learning disabilities. *Learning Disability Quarterly, 32*(3), 123–141.

Calkins, L. (1994). *The art of teaching writing.* Portsmouth, NH. Heinemann.

Danoff, B., Harris, K., & Graham, S. (1993). Incorporating strategy instruction into the school curriculum: Effects on children's writing. *Journal of Reading Behavior, 25,* 295–322.

Dudley-Marling, C., & Paugh, P. (2009). *A classroom teacher's guide to struggling writers.* Portsmouth, NH: Heinemann.

Ferretti, R., MacArthur, C., & Okolo, C. (2001). Teaching for historical understanding in inclusive classrooms. *Learning Disabilities Quarterly, 24,* 59–71.

Freire, P. (1970). *Pedagogy of the oppressed.* New York: Continuum.

Graham, S., Harris, K., Fink-Chorzempa, B., & MacArthur, B. (2003). Primary grade teachers' instructional adaptations for struggling writers: A national survey. *Journal of Educational Psychology, 95,* 279–292.

Harris, K., Graham, S., & Mason, L. (2006). Improving the writing, knowledge, and motivation of struggling young writers: Effects of self-regulated strategy development with and without peer support. *American Educational Research Journal, 43,* 295–340.

Higgins, B., Miller, M., & Wegmann, S. (2006). Teaching to the test...Not! Balancing best practice and testing requirements in writing." *International Reading Association, 60*(4), 310–319.

Jenkins, J.R., Jewell, M., Leicester, N., O'Conner, R.E., Jenkins, L. M., & Troutner, M. N. (1994). Accommodations for individual differences without classroom ability groups: An experiment in school restructuring. *Exceptional Children, 60,* 344–368.

Kadjer, S. (2006). *Bringing the outside in: Visual ways to engage reluctant readers.* Portland, ME. Stenhouse Publishers.

MacArthur, C. (2009). Reflections on research on writing and technology for struggling writers. *Learning Disabilities Research and Practice, 24*(2), 93–103.

MacArthur, C. , Schwartz, S., & Graham, S. (1991). Effects of a reciprocal peer revision strategy in special education classrooms. *Learning Disabilities Research and Practice, 6,* 201–210.

Macedo, D. (2006). *Literacies of power.* Cambridge, MA: Westview.

Madden, N.A., & Slavin, R. (1983). Mainstreaming students with mild handicaps: Academic and social outcomes. *Review of Educational Research, 53,* 519–569.

McLaren, P. (1994). *Life in schools: An introduction to critical pedagogy in the foundations of education.* New York: Longman.

McLeskey, J., & Waldron, N. L. (2000). *Inclusive schools in action: Making differences ordinary.* Alexandria, VA: ASCD.

McPhail, .C., & Freeman, J. G. (2005). Beyond prejudice: Thinking towards genuine inclusion. *Learning Disabilities Research and Practice, 20*(4), 254–267.

North, C. (2009). *Teaching for social justice? Voices from the front lines.* Boulder, CO: Paradigm Publishers.

Patel, P., & Laud, L. (2007). Integrating a story writing strategy into a resource curriculum. *Teaching Exceptional Children, 39,* 34–41.

Rhodes, L., & Dudley-Marling, C. (1996). *Readers and writers with a difference.* (2nd ed.). Portsmouth, NH: Heinemann.

Rose, D., & Meyer, A. (2002). *Teaching every student in the digital age. Universal design for learning.* Alexandria, VA: ASCD.

Routman, R. (2004). *Writing essentials: Raising expectations and results while simplifying teaching.* Portsmouth, NH: Heinemann.

Shor, I. (1996). *When students have power: Negotiating authority in a critical pedagogy.* Chicago, IL: University of Chicago Press.

Smith, D., & Luckasson, R. (1995). *Introduction to special education: Teaching in the age of challenge.* Needham Heights, MA: Allyn & Bacon.

Troia, G. A. (2006). Writing instruction for students with learning disabilities. In C. A. MacArthur, S. Graham, & J. Fitzgerald (Eds.), *Handbook of writing research* (pp. 324–336). New York: Guilford Press.

Vaughn, S. (1995). Responsible inclusion for students with learning disabilities. *Journal of Learning Disabilities 28*(5), 264–270.

Waldron, N., & McLeskey, J. (1998). The effects of an inclusive school program on students with mild and severe disabilities. *Exceptional Children, 64,* 395–505.

9. *"Standardized" Play and Creativity for Young Children? The Climate of Increased Standardization and Accountability in Early Childhood Classrooms*

Lindsey Russo

Sometimes the more measurable drives out the more important.
—Rene Dubos (as cited in Peshkin, 1993, p. 23)

Quality early childhood experiences have long-term academic benefits for children and lay the foundation for lifelong learning (Bergen, 2002). Young children learn best when they are active as opposed to passive, when their social skills are being utilized, and when opportunities for learning are presented in playful and meaningful ways (Walsh & Gardner, 2005).

Play itself mediates the learning of children and fosters and supports all aspects of a child's development (Vygotsky, 1978). It encourages the use of imagination and creativity, and generates opportunities for intellectual development. Play allows a child to function above the zone of proximal development—the gap between what the learner has already mastered, the actual level of development, and what he/she can achieve when provided with support from peers and adults.

Early learning cannot be separated into the areas of cognitive, social/emotional, and physical development. These domains are integrated and interdependent. Many early childhood educators support this understanding through the whole child approach to teaching and learning. This approach is grounded in the belief that balanced learning is achieved for young children through creative, interactive play that supports and scaffolds all developmental areas (Steinhauer, 2005). While the whole child approach recognizes the importance of reading, writing, and numeracy skills being stressed in today's early childhood curriculum, it identifies these skills as being only *one aspect* of learning, or one part of a complex and interconnected developmental system. Ironically, due to the synergistic relationship between and among the developmental domains, the current shift to academic learning and standardized testing adversely affects the acquisition of the academic skills being highlighted in today's early childhood curricula (Raver & Zigler, 2004; Zigler & Bishop-Josef, 2006).

Despite supportive theory, research, and practice, we are experiencing the disappearance of play from the early childhood classroom and curriculum. The case for exposure to academics is one of the most controversial topics in the field of early childhood education today (Elkind, 2001). School in the early childhood years used to be filled with opportunities to play. Today we view early childhood education from a very different perspective from that of Frederick Froebel (1898), who created the first kindergarten and introduced the idea that play was a child's natural way of learning and self-expression. Even though the concept of "play" is supported by research in the field of early childhood education, the activities associated with it are often viewed by some policy makers, administrators, educators, and parents as "just play." Play, therefore, is seen as having few redeeming qualities because it is not aligned with the current view of academic learning, i.e., the acquisition of information to assure that students can be successful on standardized tests.

Alternatively, many early childhood educators and theorists stand firm in the belief that an increased emphasis on academics must not overshadow opportunities for children to develop social, emotional, and cognitive skills while naturally engaged in play (Bodrova & Leong, 2005; Paley, 2004; Zigler, 1987).

The purpose of this chapter is twofold. First, it will pinpoint how the standards and accountability movement has had a deleterious effect on early childhood education in the United States over the past decade by the obviation of important pedagogical dimensions and instructional activities from the classroom, including the elimination of play. It will conclude by illustrating how some schools have successfully responded to the pressures associated with standards-based assessment and accountability policies, maintaining their philosophies, missions, and values. In these academic communities, play is a vital pedagogical element serving to foster students' intellectual growth.

Assessment for young children and the current educational climate

The current climate in early childhood education has become one of standardization and accountability. This has forced early childhood administrators, teachers, and parents to become more focused on academic learning and school readiness (Miller & Almon, 2009). The 2001 No Child Left Behind

Act (NCLB) provided direct federal support for this standardization and accountability movement and was closely followed by the release of the Good Start, Grow Smart (GSGS, 2001) initiative. This initiative calls for improved performance and increased accountability in early childhood programs. The aim of GSGS is to ensure that every child begins school "with an equal chance at achievement" so that "no child is left behind."

The GSGS initiative also acknowledges that the first five years of a child's life are a time of enormous physical, emotional, social, and cognitive growth; it also highlights the importance of developing students' cognitive skills through formal academic domains and instructional strategies, such as pre-reading, language, vocabulary, and numeracy. Moreover, the Early Reading First program (ERF), established by NCLB, provides competitive grants to school districts and preschools to fund the development of model programs that support school "readiness," with a focus on low-income families (Russo, 2009). The concept of readiness is a significant issue for educational reform as pressures mount to improve student performance (Mashburn & Henry, 2004). This concept, as defined by many researchers, policy makers, and educators, suggests that most 5-year-olds have achieved a developmental level that enables them to adapt to the challenges of kindergarten (Ladd, Herald, & Kochel, 2006). The term "readiness" may be one of the most frequently used terms in discussions about early childhood education (La Paro & Pianta, 2000). While there are many definitions of readiness, it is almost always viewed through the prism of children's academic or pre-academic skills, rather than social skills. In an attempt to hold schools accountable for the achievement of young children, there is an increased focus upon the assessment of "pre-academic skills including motoric, cognitive, perceptual, sensory, and social behaviors" (La Paro & Pianta, 2000, p. 444). Children who fail these assessments are then viewed as being "not ready" and face the very real possibility of being placed in transition classes or waiting another year before beginning formal schooling and kindergarten (Bredekamp, 2004).

Since young children are now under pressure to meet inappropriate expectations, including academic standards that until recently were reserved for older children, many of them are now being exposed to debilitating forms of pedagogies. For instance, on any given day, it is possible to enter a classroom in New York City and be unable to recognize whether you are in a kindergarten or a first grade classroom. I have experienced classroom environments where 5-year-old children are sitting in rows completing worksheets while their teacher models handwriting skills on an overhead projector. There is no sign of a rug or dramatic play area, both of which were staples of the kindergarten classroom. In contemporary scripted classrooms, children must follow a highly regimented routine where lessons are linked to standardized tests designed to measure children's progress in learning discrete facts and skills.

When assessing young children, we need to take into consideration that development across domains is highly variable from child to child. If the assessment is to be trustworthy and valid, it needs to be authentic. Authenticity means reflective of the skill being assessed—and occurring within a safe, nurturing environment where children interact with familiar adults within a familiar environment (Almy & Genishi, 1979). Authentic assessment must also be linked to social and emotional development, a domain that is especially variable in young children (Allen & Marotz, 2010). To obtain a complete picture of the child's learning, multiple methods of assessment need to be used. These include observations, anecdotal notes, running records, audio tapes, videotapes, photographs, work samples, check lists, grading scales, time and event sampling, and interviews.

What does standardization mean for play?

With the push from policy makers and administrators to standardize teaching and learning as well as implement accountability schemes in early childhood education, some teachers have failed to identify the difference between the imitative, repetitive play frequently seen in today's classrooms, and the more elaborative and creative play that supports learning. Teachers have different understandings of why and how to incorporate play into the early childhood curriculum (DeVries, 2001). As a result, the classroom environment, culture and curriculum vary widely from one classroom to another. Teachers' views of play determine children's classroom experiences (Ranz-Smith, 2007). The way play is integrated into the curriculum depends upon the teachers' beliefs, philosophy, and perceptions, as well as the motivation to make these visible. When faced with the academic expectations for school readiness and the curricular and pedagogical dilemmas that accompany them, teachers tend to move away from a play-based curriculum. This often results in a form of cognitive dissonance—with teachers' beliefs at odds with the actual role they adopt in the classroom (Russo, 2009). Their role tends to shift to that of *instructor rather than facilitator* as they attempt to reconcile their pedagogical beliefs with increasing academic expectations. Teacher-directed activities, especially instruction in literacy and mathematics, are taking up the majority of the time in many early childhood classrooms. Additionally, standardized testing and preparation for those tests are now a daily activity in many early childhood classrooms.

According to Gmitrova and Gmoitirov (2002), children think more, learn more, remember more, spend more time on task, and are more productive in well-implemented cooperative groups, rather than when engaged in structured, teacher-directed and -organized play. Direct instruction, by nature, inhibits the possibility of cooperative grouping, learning, and play. By placing unrealistic demands upon children who are not developmentally ready, we are asking teachers to spend most of their time attempting to push children in ways that may set them up to fail.

Helm and Gronlund (2000) believe that the pressure of taking a standardized test can inhibit thinking and, therefore, decrease the accuracy of the assessment. Traditional methods of assessments, such as multiple choice questions, the recall of facts, written question and answer formats, and other written or oral tests, may be considered appropriate for the evaluation of (skills such as) sight words and number or color recognition. For the majority of assessment purposes in early childhood education, however, they are not viewed as authentic or developmentally appropriate and are insufficiently sensitive to the ways young learners demonstrate their competencies.

Assessment needs to be immediate in the early childhood classroom since curriculum is constantly being developed "in the moment" (Helm & Gronlund, 2000). If standardized assessments require computerized grading and statistical analysis, then the results will not be immediately available to teachers and, therefore, cannot be used for the modification of learning experiences for the children. Effective early childhood teachers systematically collect information about each child's learning. This documentation is then tied to the benchmarks/standards enabling the teacher to evaluate the child's progress and make decisions about curriculum, classroom materials, and personal interactions. This helps move the child to a greater level of competency.

Play facilitates socialization in children, reduces stress, and improves memory, executive functions, and self-regulation. This means that children exhibit better behavior, are better prepared, and, ultimately, are more able to engage in academics if they are allowed to play regularly. By de-emphasizing play and over-emphasizing academics, we may be inhibiting their development. Kohn (2000) questions what it means to be smart, asking whether it is a race to see who can memorize the most or about developing capabilities to deal with a complex world.

Also, play is a valuable authentic assessment tool. By observing a single play episode lasting no more than five minutes, a teacher can assess a child's fine and gross motor skills, social competence in a wide range of areas, the level of expressive and receptive language skills, vocabulary strengths and weaknesses, and the ability to count, estimate, and predict. This is impressive when compared with a standardized test that would assess only one of these areas, and take considerably longer to score and analyze.

Both research and practice identify the importance of integrated, play-based, and creative curricula used in conjunction with authentic and developmentally appropriate assessments. *If we identify the importance of these practices, how do we meet the educational needs of young children within an environment of standardization and accountability?* In the face of these pressures, many schools are holding on to their philosophies, missions, and values in ways that are realistic for them and their unique situations. They are constantly juggling the needs of the children and families with the pressures of accountability (Feldman, 2000). Below are examples.

The Blue School

One New York City private school, founded by an internationally recognized entertainment group, has taken an "if you can't beat them, join them" approach in responding to the question posed above. Since the founding of the Blue School community in 2004, teams of educators, in collaboration with the founders, have worked together to develop an educational environment where play, creativity, social/emotional learning, and authentic assessment are core elements of the curriculum. This philosophical stance is reflected in developmentally appropriate benchmarks, scope and sequence, and assessment tools aligned with the mission and values of the school. It is antithetical to a prescribed curriculum. The Blue School staff values the intellectual and philosophical freedom to assess curriculum and learning as it unfolds in each classroom. This provides them with opportunities to design (and redesign) curriculum in response to the individual needs of their students, supporting their desire to avoid the pressures associated with "teaching to the test." In short, effective early learning environments encompass a diverse array of cultures and approaches to teaching and learning.

The Blue School began as a small playgroup in 2004. A group of parents, unable to find a preschool with an acceptable educational environment for their 2- and 3-year-olds, decided to develop their own. Seven years later, in September 2011, the Blue School has become a vibrant learning community of children, teachers, administrators, parents, and educational specialists. It will accommodate 200 students ranging from 2-year-olds through second grade. The intention is to expand one grade each year until they reach fifth grade in the 2013–2014 academic year. Most of the families and children who were part of the original playgroup are still enrolled in the lead grade and the parents remain an integral component of the school community. The Blue School is founded on the belief that

> our most exuberant creativity and fruitful learning spring from a place of emotional and physical well-being and a deep connection to a caring community. We celebrate intellectual risk-taking, collaboration, authenticity and empathy, and consider these qualities to be as important as the conventional measures of academic achievement. (Blue School Curriculum Guide, 2010, p. 4)

The Blue School classrooms are identified as dynamic and engaging spaces that facilitate exploration, personal expression, group collaboration, open communication, wonder, and active play. The children are encouraged to shape and transform their environment by experimenting with both familiar and unique materials. They are encouraged to learn from the world outside their class-rooms and to take advantage of New York's cultural landscape. The chil-dren's work is prominently displayed throughout the school, making the experience of learning visible and further reflecting respect for children's nat-ural ability to create and develop ideas.

Co-constructivist theory and the Reggio Emilia approach inspire the Blue School's curriculum. Co-constructivists view learning as an active process in which learners construct their own understanding and knowledge of the world through action and reflection. Knowledge is socially constructed. It is a social process involving interactions and experiences with others and with the environment. Children learn by doing rather than by absorbing information. Consequently, they bring prior knowledge to the learning situation. Co-con-structivism utilizes peer and adult feedback as a way of reaching a new level of understanding. The Reggio Emilia approach originated in the municipal pre-primary schools in the town of Reggio Emilia, Italy. Its focus is upon the child's development and how it connects with and supports learning. The curriculum is child centered and child directed, meaning that the child's point of view is respected. Every child is encouraged and supported as they follow their own educational path and development. Learning is focused upon children's sym-bolic representations through multiple media such as oral language, painting, drawing, sculpture, poetry, descriptive writing, drama, puppetry, etc., and identified as "The Hundred Languages of Children" (Edwards, Gandini, & Forman, 1998).

The learning process takes place within long term projects that are at the heart of the curriculum and the children's progress is assessed and docu-mented through the use of portfolios. Parents and the Reggio Emilia com-munity are extremely involved in the school and are integral contributors to the learning that takes place. In fact, within the spirit of co-constructivism, the whole community of Reggio Emilia is viewed as a "community of learners."

As a result of in-depth research and thoughtful, reflective practice, rele-vant resources such as the New York State Early Learning Standards, the Collaborative for Academics, Social and Emotional Learning (CASEL), Arizona State Early Learning Standards, and the International Baccalaureate (IB) model were identified to support the development and implementation of the integrated curriculum strands, benchmarks, and scope and sequence that form the framework of the Blue School's curriculum. Play, though not the sole pedagogical strategy, is absolutely essential to balancing children's development and their readiness for school and life experiences. At the Blue School, it is used to encourage and support the use of imagination, creativity, and planning skills while generating opportunities for intellectual development. By practicing skills or trying out ideas within a play situation, children become better able to handle real situations (Russo, 2009). The belief is that the opportunities for problem solving, reasoning, conversing, exploring language, using numeracy skills, predicting, and observing are endless within play episodes. The curriculum encourages complex forms of play, which research shows help children develop language skills as well as empathy.

So, as stated, the Blue School's approach is aligned with constructivist theory and based upon the belief that children learn best by "constructing" their own knowledge in a playful and intellectually rich social environment. Through the use of an inquiry-based teaching method, the school is committed to supporting the needs and learning style of the whole child. Students are taught to reflect upon their own experiences as well as those of others so that they can gain the combination of self-awareness and social insight that will empower them to engage in the world with confidence and compassion and meet the challenges of the 21st century.

Blue School teachers implement an integrated, child-centered curriculum where the content is both integrated and interdependent. An example of this model was visible recently in one of the kindergarten rooms where the children were engaged in the construction of a "marble run." When they needed to document the way they solved the problem of getting a marble to "run" uphill, they identified "learning letters" as a thread of inquiry. First, the teachers determined what the children already knew about letters; then, they determined what more the children wanted (and needed) to learn. The next step was to develop a web of inquiry with the children and set goals for the inquiry. The teacher's role was to develop multiple media through which the children could explore and discover the answers to their questions and to integrate the content areas of the curriculum and address appropriate benchmarks. Within the area of Language Arts, the children made letter books and a collection of clay marbles labeled with different letters. For mathematics they studied the different geometric shapes that are found in the letters and they explored how those shapes could fit together to form a letter. They practiced their social skills by working together on different projects in small and large groups. In response to the expressive arts component of the curriculum, they illustrated their letter books and developed different movements and sounds to symbolize different letters. As part of the physical awareness thread of the curriculum, they practiced moving their bodies into different shapes to represent different letters. This integrated approach motivates children with different learning styles and provides opportunities for success.

The Blue School's policies and practices aim to provide a strong social/emotional foundation for learning, encourage process over just product, and allow children to be free to be themselves while exploring and connecting with subject matter in a way that motivates them and utilizes their own learning styles. By connecting many ways of working with content areas, skills, and social and emotional processes, The Blue School hopes to create prepared, capable, and flexible learners. The educational framework developed by the school illustrates its educational approach and the interrelationship between and among the following four components: (1) *The Inquirers* is a triad made up of the child, teacher and parent, who engage in the inquiry process that forms the core of the curriculum. (2) *The Cyclical Process* is the recursive model used by Blue School teachers to facilitate learning. These include planning, differentiated instruction, inquiry, observation, assessment, and reflection. (3) *The Blue School Lenses* are distinct mindsets that are assumed by the inquirers within the learning environment. These lenses are used to explore academic content areas and materials from a variety of perspectives. (4) And, finally, the *Academic Content Areas* (or *Integrated Curriculum Strands*) are the seven areas explored to help children achieve grade and developmental benchmarks: language arts, mathematical investigation, scientific inquiry, expressive arts, social/emotional learning, physical awareness, health and play, and human values/global citizenship.

Assessment at the Blue School

Assessment at the Blue School is a core component of the school. The curriculum is developed within a cycle of reflection using multiple ways of assessing what children want to know and understand in conjunction with what they need to know as identified by appropriate benchmarks. This process of "inquiry through assessment" allows teachers to pose questions about the children's learning, and to collect and organize information. This information is then used to support the identification of new threads of inquiry and clarify the next steps involved in the development of curriculum.

Typically in the field of education, assessment is culturally driven with the view that adults have something to transmit to children. The co-constructivist approach taken by the Blue School examines the mechanics of this perspective and develops processes so that the adult may be a facilitator, with both the adult and child also adopting the role of learner. The student assessments provide an illustration of a child's learning process as well as a perspective on the holistic learning of the child. Over time, these documents become a narrative of a child's learning history. Teachers collect information tracing the experiences and cycles of learning that occur over the course of the day, week, and year. The information gathered is the main form of assessment that the teachers use to inform curriculum development. The children are also brought into this process and learn skills, research tools, and different ways to collect data and information on what they know and on how they learn. For example, they are encouraged to design and use simple rubrics to assess their own work and the productivity of the groups with which they work. They become aware of learning as a constant process, understand different ways to learn, and facilitate learning from others.

Blue School teachers use observation, reflection, and assessment to identify each child's developmental profile. These developmental profiles then drive curricular content, teaching strategies, and instruction. This is referred to as a recursive model of planning and assessment. The teachers use these developmental profiles in conjunction with each grade's benchmarks, scope and sequence, and developmental expectations to engage in the authentic assessment that occurs within the moment. Teachers use observations, field notes, photographs, portfolios, and other appropriate forms of documentation to reflect upon student learning independently, with their colleagues, and with the children. This information is then linked with the curriculum model to individualize, design, and implement the curriculum that will support learning for all the children and meet both individual and grade level goals. This assessment is an ongoing, everyday process. It begins with asking a question or exploring a thread of inquiry. Its purpose is to make visible and, therefore, evaluate the holistic learning process that takes place every day in every classroom. Here assessment illustrates how a child and teacher co-construct learning and knowledge. The evidence collected informs pedagogy and curricular content. The teachers engage in a recursive method of assessment and curriculum development as illustrated in Figure 1 below:

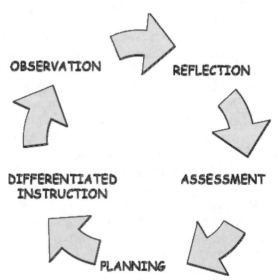

Figure 1. Recursive Model: Assessment and Curriculum Development (Blue School)

In comparison, standardized assessments focus upon a single domain (Feldman, 2010, p. 2) and do not allow for the wide range of variability in the acquisition of those early learning skills observed in the classroom, thus making them, to a great extent, inaccurate and inauthentic.

At the Blue School the benchmarks are not used as curriculum in and of itself but, rather, as a framework for curricular planning. The benchmarks are intentionally designed to guide and support the curriculum. The scope and sequence that grow out of the benchmarks are used to identify appropriate resources, and foster the reflective practices of teachers, administrators, and children. They also inform other areas of practice such as the learning environment, the schedule, and the level of family involvement. The objective is to make the identification of benchmarks more accurate and authentic while potentially teaching educators about child development. Here the purpose of assessment is not to identify deficiencies but to provide the tools to address and improve the quality of education by identifying the support needed.

The rights (and voices) of children

The United States is not the only country where play and authentic assessment are disappearing from early childhood classrooms. Article 31 of the United Nations Convention's "Rights of the Child" highlights the right of every child to engage in play and recreational activities appropriate to the age of the child. This was officially approved by the U.N. in 1989 and has since been ratified by almost every country in the world.

There are other important and relevant articles highlighted by the Convention. Article 29 states that education should be directed toward a broad range of developmental areas. Article 3 states that all action concerning the child's best interests shall be a primary consideration; Article 12 gives the child the right to express his/her views. *The United States has yet to ratify the Convention.* We are failing to listen to the voices of children, early childhood educators, and researchers. Young children have valuable contributions to make to the conversation regarding play and academic learning. Unfortunately their voices do not find their way into a large body of research (Birbeck & Drummond, 2005).

Birbeck and Drummond (2005) acknowledged the significant contribution that children's perceptions and reflections could make to research studies. King (1979) asserted that most educational research is written from an adult perspective and young children are not being asked to define play in a school setting.

Children identify frustration with having to leave a play episode to sit at the project table and complete an assignment (Russo, 2009). They have strong opinions about many classroom and curricular issues. They express clear definitions of play and work, how play is included in the curriculum, and how it is connected to learning. Children and teachers are being disempowered. Their voices are not being heard by administrators and policy makers who are pushing early childhood curriculum and assessment toward a "one-size-fits-all" system that is failing to identify the link between theory and practice. By denying children their right to play, and giving them access to authentic assessment linked to play, we are also denying them the tools to reach their potentials.

Parents' perspectives and expectations

Parents and families need to be aware of the effects of increased standardization and accountability in order to make the best choices for their children. The parents of the children at the Blue School have made conscious choices based upon the mission and values of the school. However, as expectations for learning are identified through explicit standards, many parents have adopted increased expectations. Unfortunately, this places more emphasis upon product rather than process. The increased marketing of early childhood education has added to the complexity of choice. Schwartz (2004) has noted that more choice does not necessarily make consumers (in this case, families) more comfortable with their choices.

The inquiry and experiential learning that help meet the academic objectives identified in the mission of the Blue School mean that parents and their children must be open to exploration within a lab school setting. Consequently, they have to work cooperatively with others who exhibit different points of view and perspectives. As the lead (or pilot) grade moves through the school, it is becoming apparent that, for a number of the parents, expectations are shifting. Because the school's model focuses upon development over chronological age, a great deal of trust and patience are required of parents. Therefore, a "wait and see" approach may be taken by the school as children move toward the expected goals identified by the relevant benchmarks. This somewhat more patient approach is sometimes at odds with parental expectations which devolve to a focus on content and memorization rather than higher order skills such as application.

Historically, in the upper grades, the focus on product rather than process is even more pronounced. The school's belief that children will learn the necessary content when it is presented in a meaningful way becomes challenged by the push for quantity over quality. Play in the upper grades takes on a different identity. Its role in learning is not diminished but simply changed. Play becomes group oriented and supportive of complex social skills such as sportsmanship, empathy, and compassion. Academic learning still takes place within a "playful" environment where children role play and engage in creative and imaginative activities scaffolded by the teacher to support these developmentally appropriate skill sets.

The teachers at the Blue School are there because they value the freedom to design curriculum in response to their students' needs and interests and have no desire to "teach to the test." There are many early childhood teachers at both private and public institutions who do not implement the prescribed curricula. Their curricula are also designed and developed based upon qualitative observations, authentic assessment techniques, and the individualized needs of the children. This makes it difficult for them to translate their work into very specific early learning standards.

Moving to higher grades: Different perspectives and expectations

A number of issues have arisen at the Blue School as the curriculum alignment process moves into the higher grades. The questions are complex:

- How does the Blue School move forward to meet the challenges of higher grades and the increased pressure for accountability and standardization that accompanies this transition?

- How does it address the expectations of parents within that culture?

- How does it address the increased emphasis on content while maintaining the focus on understanding, individualization, and creativity that are central components of the Blue School's philosophy?

- How will these children cope when they leave the Blue School after grade 5 and are introduced to standards-based-assessments?

These are enormously challenging questions which the Blue School community is meeting head on. The grades 3 through 5 benchmarks are in the final stages of development. They are designed to meet the needs of children's increasingly complex intellectual and social development. The educational approach for these grades will remain focused on identifying core curriculum content that is initiated by the children's inquiries. The teachers will continue to implement strategies that take into account different learning styles and developmental profiles in order to build curriculum using the information that emerges from the recursive model of assessment. This approach will provide the children with greater opportunities for further social/emotional learning, creativity, and learning through play and project work. These tenets are intended to build upon the foundation established in earlier years, deepening students' love of learning and encouraging them to branch out into new areas. As the children take on additional responsibility for integrating their personal interests and learning styles into the curriculum, their foundation of skills will allow them to benefit from more structured and rigorous assignments.

The challenge for teachers is to find the appropriate balance between academic engagement and academic challenge, while providing a learning environment that encourages and supports exploration and discovery without the stress of competition, standardization, and testing. This balance, where assessment is authentic and aligned with the objectives of the program and student needs, helps equip both teacher and child with the tools to foster individual interests and skills.

Implications for the future

It is problematic when early childhood educators are unable to articulate the tenets of early childhood education. Teachers' perspectives are extremely relevant to their chosen pedagogy. This was highlighted earlier in relation to play and its inclusion in the curriculum. Through the use of formal and informal interviews, it was clear that teachers have definitive views on the use of standardized testing and standardization. Early childhood teachers from a range of settings have many of the same concerns, as evidenced by the anecdotes below:

> With the standards as they are, the fourth grade standards people go, "Okay, third grade, second grade, first grade need to know this, okay so this is what kindergarteners need to know, okay this is what 4's need to know" completely ignoring what we know about the learning styles of young children. As a result of this, there are some very inappropriate expectations and practices going on. (ECLSSC Member # 4, Brown, 2007)

> The most inappropriate use that anybody could ever use for early learning standards is to turn it into a checklist for who is ready to go to first grade and who is not. That would be the worst use of it, ever. (ECLSSC Member #3, Brown, 2007)

> I want the benchmarks to guide me and support me, not direct me and dictate to me. (Blue School kindergarten teacher, April 2011)

> We are supposed to be the specialists. We know how children learn and we need to have the courage and support to say "Enough! Their bodies and their brains are tired. They need to rest and regroup, chat and internalize what they have learned by revisiting it through play and their interactions with each other." Then I can assess what they have learned today—using my knowledge and understanding of them as individual learners, not a work sheet or a test sheet. (Blue School second grade teacher)

Standardized tests tend to measure the acquisition and retention of facts and skills (including the skill of test taking itself) rather than genuine understanding—the very foundation of learning that we want to build for young children. Kohn (2000) states that standardized tests are more likely to be used and emphasized in schools with a higher percentage of minority students.

Predictably, this accelerates a reliance on direct instruction techniques and, according to Stipek (2006), tends to foster low-level uniformity and subvert academic potential.

It follows that the more children from low socio-economic backgrounds are presented with worksheets to complete, the more likely they are to fall behind the children from more affluent backgrounds where understanding is the primary educational objective.

Further, it is unacceptable when standardized testing is the primary source for decisions regarding placement of children in special education and gifted programs. The conditions that lead children to be labeled as "special needs" can be caused by inappropriate expectations of children who are being pushed to succeed at tasks for which they are not developmentally ready. Therefore, early learning standards need to ensure the promotion of developmentally appropriate practice. "One-size-fits-all" standards must be replaced with guidelines based upon a deep understanding of children's cognitive, social, emotional, and physical development. We need to use authentic assessment methods that are not characterized by the risks and limitations of standardized testing practices. We cannot make life-changing decisions based exclusively upon standardized tests. We must use a triangulation of methods while observing and reflecting upon the process rather than the product.

This is the model being explored by the Blue School's recursive model of assessment and it results in the development and implementation of curriculum and practice that fit the needs of each and every child.

References

Allen. K. E. & Marotz, L. R. (2010). *Developmental profiles: Pre-birth through twelve.* Wadsworth, Cengage Learning

Almy, M., & Genishi, C. (1979). *Ways of studying children.* (Revised ed.). New York: Teachers College Press.

Bergen, D. (2002). The role of pretend play in children's cognitive development. *Early Childhood Research and Practice,.* 4, 1. Retrieved October 15, 2007 from http:// ecrp, uiuc.edu/v4n2/bergenhtml.

Birbeck, D., & Drummond, M. (2005). Interviewing, and listening to the voices of very young children on body image and perceptions of self. *Early Child Development and Care,* 176, 6, 579–596.

Bodrova, E., & Leong, D. (2005). Why children need play. *Scholastic Early Childhood Today* 20, 1–6.

Bredekamp, S. (2004). Play and school readiness. In E.F. Zigler, D.G. Singer, & S.J. Bishop-Josef (Eds.), *Children's play: The roots of reading* (pp. 159–174). Washington, D.C Zero to Three Press.

Brown, C. P. (2007). Unpacking standards in early childhood education. *Teachers College Record,* 109, 3, 635–668.

DeVries, R. (2001). Transforming the "play orientated curriculum" and work in constructivist early childhood. In A. Goncu & E. L. Klein (Eds.), *Children in play, story, and school* (pp. 72–106). New York: The Guilford Press.

Edwards, C., Gandini, L., & Forman Eds.(1998). *The hundred languages of children: The Reggio Emilia approach—advanced reflections.* Ablex Publishing Co.

Elkind, D. (2001). Early childhood education: What should we expect? *Principal,* 75, 11–13.

Feldman, E. N. (2010). Benchmarks, curriculum, planning and assessment framework: Utilizing standards without introducing standardization. *Early Childhood Education Journal* May 15, Springer Science and Business Media.

Froebel, F. (1898). *The education of man.* Washington D.C.: D. Appleton and Co.

Gmitrova, V., & Gmoitrov, J. (2002). The impact of teacher-directed and child-directed play on cognitive competencies in kindergarten children. *Early Childhood Education Journal,* 30, 3, 241–246.

Good Start, Grow Smart (2001, April). U.S. Department of Education.

Helm. J. H., & Gronlund, G. (2000). Linking standards and engaged learning in the early years. *Early Childhood Research and Practice,* 2, 1, 1–20.

King, N. R. (1979). Play: The kindergartener's perspective. *The Elementary School Journal,* 80, 2, 80–87.

Kohn, A., (2000). Standardized testing and its victims. *Education Week,* September 27, 1–6.

Ladd, G. W., Herald, S. L., & Kochel, K. P. (2006). School readiness: Are there social prerequisites? *Early Education and Development,* 17, 1, 115–150.

La Paro, K. M., & Pianta, R. C. (2000). Predicting children's competence in the early school years: A meta-analytic review. *Review of Educational Research* 70, 4, 443–484.

Mashburn, A. J., & Henry, G.T. (2004). Assessing school readiness: Validity and bias in preschool and kindergarten teacher's ratings. *Educational Measurement: Issues and Practice,* Winter 2004, 16–30.

Miller, E., & Almon, J. (2009). *Crisis in Kindergarten: Why children need to play in School.* College Park MD: Alliance for Children.

National Research Council, (2001). *Eager to Learn: Educating our preschoolers.* Washington, D. C.: National Academy Press.

No Child Left Behind Act of 2001. Pub. L. No. 107–110, 115 Stat 1535, 20 USC 6361, Part B, Subpart 1, sec. 1201.

Paley, V. G. (2004). *A child's work: The importance of fantasy play.* Chicago: University of Chicago Press.

Peshkin, A. (1993). The goodness of qualitative research. *Educational Researcher,* 22, 2, 23–29.

Ranz-Smith. D. J. (2007). Teacher perceptions of play: In leaving no child left behind are teachers leaving childhood behind? *Early Education and Development,* 18, 2, 271–303.

Raver, C. C., & Zigler, E. F. (2004). Public policy viewpoint: Another step back? Assessing readiness in Head Start. *Young Children,* 59, 58–63.

Russo, H.L. (2009). Play, peer relationships, and academic learning: Exploring the views of teachers and children. Doctoral Dissertation, Teachers College Columbia University.

Schwartz, B. (2004). Paradox of choice: Why more is less. Harper Perennial.

Steinhauer, S. (2005, May 22). Maybe preschool is the problem. *New York Times.*

Stipek, D. (2006). No child left behind comes to preschool *The Elementary School Journal,* 106, 5, 455–465.

Vygotsky, L. S. (1978). *Mind in society: The development of higher psychological processes.*

Cambridge: Harvard University Press.

Walsh, G., & Gardner, J. (2005). Assessing the quality of early years learning environment. *Early Childhood Research & Practice, 7,* 1.

Zigler, E. (1987). Formal schooling for four-year-olds? No. *American Psychologist, 42,* 3, 254–260.

Zigler, E. F., & Bishop-Josef, S. J. (2006). The cognitive child versus the whole child: Lessons from Early Head Start. In D. G. Golinkoff, R. M. Singer, & K. Hirsh-Pasek (Eds.), *Play=learning: How play motivates and enhances children's cognitive and socio-emotional growth* (pp. 15–35). New York: Oxford University Press.

SECTION 3.

Leveraging Standards in Secondary Classrooms

10. Occupying the Space for Change: The Effects of Neoliberalism in a Public School in Metro Buffalo

SHAWGI TELL

Introduction

A fundamental question confronting teachers today is whether they should stay in the teaching profession in light of the nature and consequences of contemporary education reform. Given the obsession with high-stakes standardized testing, the fixation on teaching to the test, the growing use of test scores to determine teachers' effectiveness, the threat of school closures, and the increasingly multifaceted corporatization, privatization, and militarization of education (Saltman & Gabbard, 2011), educators can be rightfully concerned about their chosen career. *Is this what I want? Can I survive such conditions?* These are some of the questions teachers are asking themselves. Many feel that everything they have learned in teacher education is antithetical to what is happening in schools today.

In my role as a foundations scholar in a teacher education program in a liberal arts college in western New York, I hear these concerns every semester from both in-service and pre-service teachers enrolled in the graduate course I teach: Social Foundations of Education (SPF 501). There is a strong desire among my students to make sense of what is unfolding in the field of education and to contribute to changing education for the better. Through structured interactions with in-service and pre-service teachers, foundations scholars play an important role in situating educational institutions in the larger social, economic, historical, and political context. Equally important, they advocate and promote critical thinking and social justice in education and society.

The urgency of the concerns raised above is increasing at a rate that seems to parallel the pace of the many reforms we are witnessing in education today. Teachers are confronted by contradictions (equity vs. excellence; content quantity vs. deep understanding; a liberal education vs. test preparation) and increasingly find themselves facing tougher choices. The stressful and anti-educational conditions in K–12 public schools have, in fact, caused many to leave the profession, often with emotional and mental scars that linger long after being pushed out (Crocco & Costigan, 2006; Fair Test, 2007; Hedges, 2011; Kaczor, 2011). The teaching profession may have been rewarding (or at least tolerable) when they first entered the field, but for many it has become unbearable. The proliferation of high-stakes testing, and the belief that "data" and "metrics" can adequately measure the complexities of teaching and learning have resulted in frustration, stress, disillusionment and fatigue among teachers (as well as students, parents, and school administrators). The new "common core standards" developed recently by private entities and being implemented by President Barack Obama and U.S. Secretary of Education Arne Duncan will be linked to more high stakes standardized testing in K–12 public schools and will create more of what Karp (2010) calls the "test-punish-privatize" scheme. This process almost seems designed to assure that things will go from bad to worse. From the vantage point of many teachers, it is simply not worth staying in the profession, despite a failing economy and mounting insecurity.

Teachers today are increasingly torn between a sense of duty to their students, peers, and the profession, and their desire for self-preservation—a conflict that, in the long run, harms society. The clash between the values, interests, and motivations of current and future teachers, and the aims, nature, and consequences of corporate and market "reforms" in education has reached a new level. The chasm will only widen as the Obama-Duncan education agenda is implemented. The push for more charter schools, the expansion of performance-pay policies, the elimination of collective bargaining agreements, and the increase in standardized testing related to the "common core" standards are all part of the neoliberal agenda eroding public education and the public interest. In Giroux's (2009a) words:

> The discourse of standards and assessment dominate the Obama-Duncan language of reform, and in doing so erase more crucial issues such as the iniquitous school-financing schemes, the economic disinvestment in poor urban schools, the ongoing reduction of teachers to testing technicians, the increasing racism and segregation of American schools, turning schools over to corporate interests, and the ongoing modeling of schools after prisons and the criminalization of young people. And these are only some of the problems. (para. 2)

The title of a Diane Ravitch (2009) article, "Obama Gives Bush a 3rd Term in Education," says it all. The effects of neoliberal reform initiatives are evident and they will become even more dramatic in the next three to five years.

The 2011 documentary film *Race to Nowhere*, shown across the United States, examined the pressures faced by students, teachers, and parents in today's high-stakes education culture. In it, several teachers are shown agonizing about how unrewarding, stressful, and counterproductive teaching has become as a result of the corporate, market-oriented "reforms" being imposed on schools. Many talk about the elimination of creativity and critical thinking in teaching and learning, and how difficult it is to invent ways to cope with a worsening situation. A high level of frustration is exhibited explicitly and implicitly by the teachers in the film.

My graduate education students (most of whom have some K–12 teaching experience) frequently express similar frustration over what is transpiring in education today. They describe experiences linked to fear (higher test scores or else). The destructive effects of corporatization have many wondering if there is a way to pursue their passion in the midst of such circumstances. Does space exist to teach in such a context? And, if so, is it worth fighting corporate entities for that space? Is the alternative — leaving the profession—perhaps a better option? Any spaces that exist may, in fact, be too restricted or too superficial to make one's overall experience meaningful and rewarding.

Testing and new governance arrangements

The deleterious effects of high-stakes standardized testing cannot be emphasized enough. Standardized tests are the means by which "data" and "metrics" are generated to justify new arrangements in education (e.g., charter schools, performance-pay systems, and school "turnarounds"). "School improvement" is not the goal here; it never was (Gabbard, 2008; Garrison, 2009). Rather, the aim is to change the nature, purpose, and function of schooling by changing governance arrangements, i.e., who decides what is taught and tested, as well as when, how, and where these acts occur. Standardized testing is thus essentially about power and authority, not the three Rs (Garrison, 2009). Specifically, the tests and companion "metrics" serve to justify and facilitate the upward distribution of operational and financial control of schools, leaving students, teachers, administrators, parents, and community residents with less decision-making power (Saltman, 2010). Eliminating teacher unions, abolishing tenure, and increasing school-business alliances are some of the key features of this anti-social, anti-worker offensive. The question that emerges for educators is how to promote critical forms of education in a hierarchical, corporately controlled educational context. Which tactics and strategies could prove effective in this setting?

Gina and her students

This chapter details the ways in which a teacher of English as a Second Language (ESL) students in a school near Buffalo, New York, balances the demands of high-stakes testing and accountability with a more genuine, holistic, critical, relevant, and meaningful approach to educating her students. Teaching to the test, narrowing the curriculum, complying with test-related administrative mandates, and contending with the teacher evaluation system (increasingly defined by scores on standardized tests) are just a few of the realities that collide daily with the needs of Gina and her ESL students. How the contradictions, challenges, and frustrations unfolding in this context are perceived and confronted by both the students and their teacher reveals a complex situation—one that is degrading and offensive, but one also sprinkled with possibility and opportunity. To be sure, current conditions are not satisfactory by most measures; however, the descriptions reveal ways to make advances and to acquire a sense of purpose connected with student success.

Gina teaches in a school comprised of a relatively equal number of white students and students from several different minority groups. The diverse school setting represents a well-connected school community. According to the *New York State Report Card: Accountability and Overview Report, 2009–2010*,[1] the majority of students there receive free or reduced-price lunches (New York Stated Education Department, 2010). Eligibility guidelines for free and reduced-price school meals are set by the federal government and are determined by household size and income. School meals are a useful indicator of a school's poverty concentration. It is also worth noting that the school's "academic performance" is consistently rated as "poor" or "failing" by a local business publication and the state.[2]

The school is located in a community that has seen steady decline (disinvestment and deindustrialization) for more than 25 years. And like many other traditional public schools, Gina's school competes with area charter schools.[3] For this chapter, Gina was interviewed for two hours and asked to produce a five-page description of her classroom experiences. Interview questions were open-ended, semi-structured, and focused mainly on her experiences negotiating the contradictions and tensions outlined above (see Appendix for questions).

Education is a right

The human rights perspective used to interpret and discuss this layered reality begins with the principle that education is a basic human right that government must guarantee. I argue that corporations and the government are violating students' rights to an adequate education by imposing corporate and market ideology and practice on schools in the guise of raising standards. High-stakes testing, choice, competition, performance-pay, and other features of the neoliberal agenda all serve to lower the quality of education and they reflect the elimination of government responsibility for guaranteeing the rights of students. The right to an education, I maintain, should not be based on wealth, geography, skin color, gender, nationality, ability, or whether or not one passes a test. What kind of system allows for so many youth to be left behind in the name of leaving "no child behind"? The law of the jungle and/or corporate values cannot serve as the basis for a modern education system. Social Darwinism has no place in contemporary society. In short, I argue that market notions of education, relationships, and culture—the commodification of all aspects of life—negate human rights, including the right to education.

Impact of high-stakes testing on teaching and learning

To set the context for Gina's experience, it is helpful to begin with a brief presentation of some of the research on testing and teaching. One of the most negative effects of high-stakes testing is the narrowing of the curriculum. Price (2008) sums up the situation this way:

> In Chicago, where we work with teachers sharpening their knowledge and craft in graduate school and preparing for National Board Certification, teachers are overburdened and discouraged by the relentless before, during and after school preparation for standardized testing. They are told to not worry about social studies, and in many cases, to not even teach science as mathematics and reading consume the bulk of their curriculum. More and more teachers we work with have been handed scripted curriculum written by outside private contractors. (Charter Schools to the Rescue, para. 1)

In this way, teachers are deprofessionalized, learning is degraded, and privatization is fostered. For-profit companies, not teachers, determine the scope, pace, and content of curriculum and instruction. And instead of comprehensive and balanced instruction in different subjects, math and reading are given disproportionate attention. What teacher could feel enthusiastic about such arrangements? Abrams (2004) provides this summary of the relevant research:

> A common finding is that teachers report giving greater attention to content areas on which students will be tested. For example, of the 722 Virginia teachers surveyed, when the state test was first implemented, more than 80 percent indicated that the Standards of Learning (SOL) test had affected their instruction, especially the content focus of daily lessons. It only makes sense that increased attention to tested content would result in decreased time spent on other areas of the curriculum. In Kentucky, 87 percent of teachers agreed that their state test, the Kentucky Instructional Results Information System (KIRIS), had "caused some teachers to de-emphasize or neglect untested subject areas." Results from a

national survey of 4,200 teachers confirm these state-level findings—76 percent of the responding teachers indicated that they have increased the amount of time they spend on tested content areas, while more than half (52 percent) indicated they had decreased the amount of class time devoted to content areas not covered by the state test. (pp. 5–6)

Narrowing the curriculum has a particularly negative impact on students from nondominant cultures who are often marginalized. In short, they leave high school without access to the experiences, knowledge, and skills they will need to be successful in the 21st century. Even recess has been restricted or eliminated altogether in many schools across the country in the name of more "time on task" for testing purposes. The focus on test prep is demoralizing for many teachers—consequences Giroux (2010) discusses at length in *When Generosity Hurts: Bill Gates, Public School Teachers and the Politics of Humiliation*. Taken together, current conditions in education lower teacher engagement, reduce student motivation, degrade education, and harm the public interest (Au, 2009; Kohn, 2000, 2011). The answer here is not, as some have suggested, to use high-stakes standardized tests to "assess" neglected content areas; this will only make matters worse by multiplying the detrimental effects we have seen from their use in testing ELA and mathematics skills. The solution is to eliminate such tests altogether and replace them with assessments consistent with a humanist, nonpunitive, and democratic philosophy.

It is also dispiriting to know that test scores can be increased without improving learning (Allington, 2000; Berliner, 2008; Kohn, 2000). Drilling students on high-stakes standardized tests may cause students to learn to gain higher scores but that performance is not necessarily linked to meaningful achievement and learning. The incidents of cheating engendered by high-stakes testing also undermine deeper learning. What millions of students have learned to do under the current corporate testing and accountability regime is to memorize and regurgitate information, pencil-in bubble sheets, and then forget much of the decontextualized content shortly after the test. Many have not acquired the ability to be creative, to think critically, to research and discuss skillfully, or to find their bearings in different situations.

Using a variety of data sources, Nichols and Berliner (2005) give numerous examples of test-related cheating in schools across the country. The following are two representative instances of this growing phenomenon:

In Texas, an administrator gave students who performed poorly on past standardized tests incorrect ID numbers to ensure their scores would not count toward the district average. Nearly half of 2,000 students in an online Gallop poll admitted they have cheated at least once on an exam or test. Some students said they were surprised that the percentage was not higher. (p. ii)

Cheating is common in many public and charter schools.[4] An August 10, 2011, *Huffington Post* headline read: *Schools Caught Cheating in Atlanta, Around the Country* (Resmovits, 2011). Cheating is rampant within the culture of fear caused by the corporate-government program of testing. While cheating has always been part of education, it has grown with the increase in high-stakes standardized testing (Nichols & Berliner, 2005).

Wrecking and resistance at a public school in Metro Buffalo

The concept of "teaching to the test" has always existed in education. Such preparation generally took up a few days or, perhaps, a week out of the school year; but many teachers confirm Gina's observation that "test prep" now extends for months, and is more intense:

> During the months of November through January, all kinds of measures are directed at teachers to teach to the standardized tests. Administrators are under pressure by their supervisors to make success happen and are doing juggling acts to try to comply. Teachers are last in line for these ever changing regulations in order to comply with the ccss [common core state standards] hysteria. Even a conscious, enlightened teacher is swept into the destructive and anti-learning measures from NCLB to Race to the Top. I know as a teacher, who day in and day out lives and feels the effects of these measures in a direct way, I can conclude that it is not sound practice for learning. It is not good for my students. It is not how students learn and develop cognitively in the classroom.

Many of the practicing teachers in my graduate education classes echo these sentiments. A sense of arbitrariness surrounds the implementation of testing and accountability policies in schools across the country.[5] Consistent with past accounts shared in class, one teacher recently reported that the principal in her school had met with all the teachers in her department to reprimand them about the poor test performance of the special education students. Teachers were told that they need to "get those scores up" or there was going to be "trouble." Naturally, this left the teachers disturbed, even shaken. They wondered whether the principal understood that these students were being set up to fail through the state's testing system. Did he really believe that the state's approach to "academic success" was the best way forward? Many special education students perform below grade level and need extensive one-on-one instruction to advance. The state tests simply ignore how, to use Gina's words, "students learn and develop cognitively in the classroom." In Gina's case, the state expects ESL students to take the same tests as their English-language peers well before literacy, language, and cognitive development indicate they should be ready to take such a test; in effect, setting them up to fail (Crawford & Krashen, 2007). Gina and her peers have fought for years to get the state to understand the simple truth that you cannot test English Language Learners in English when they do not know the language. At minimum, these students need a few years to master the level of English being tested. How is it possible for students and teachers to succeed under such circumstances?

Gina goes on to explain how she works to ensure an educational environment conducive to the needs of her students within the context of high pressure, high-stakes standardized tests, and corporate-developed standards:

> For years now I taught ELLs and one of the best ways that I found to help students learn and develop under these constraints (school, district, state, federal) is to first and foremost establish a safe environment for enlightenment. As best as possible, try to make the classroom a nurturing and affirming space for students so they can discuss what's on their mind.

And this is no easy condition to establish, as Gina stresses:

> That's a big task since you are going against the grain. I had to come up with lessons that not only met the demands and rubrics of district, state, federal mandates, but also that students could identify with and use.

Clearly, testing mandates are seen as an obstacle to learning and disconnected from the identities and lives of Gina's students. There is a sense that doing what is needed means "going against the grain." Adding complexity to the situation, Gina explains that she has to "modify these lessons on a yearly basis depending on my class make up." Her student population changes relatively frequently. For example, during the U.S. war in what was then Yugoslavia (1992–1995), she had an influx of refugee students from the region. "I learned so much from them about what was really going on in a part of the world I wasn't too familiar with," she remarks, and then she describes what actions she took to affirm her students' identities and to expand their knowledge base:

> It was difficult to get my hands on literature for these students, let alone dictionaries. Students love to read about their background, culture, history because it affirms who they are and grounds them in the here and now. Since I couldn't find educational materials for them I decided to approach the teaching of English by having them discuss and write about their experiences and present to the class. They had to, of course, do tons of research and had to practice speaking, listening, reading, and writing. Students learned much faster after I applied this method to even slow learners.

This is significant because, as Vogler and Virtue (2007) conclude, "Teachers under the pressure of high stakes tend to use teacher-centered instructional practices, such as lecture, instead of student-centered approaches, such as discussion, role play, research papers, and cooperative learning" (p. 56). Gina is clearly student centered. She gives priority to the needs of her students by developing ways to merge knowledge of their identity with improvements in reading, writing, listening, and speaking. This process of making learning and teaching relevant and student centered unfolds as Gina keeps the standardized tests—their use, role, and significance—in the back of her mind, restricting what she is able to do in class but not fully determining what is taught and learned in the classroom. Further elaborating on her pedagogy with diverse students, Gina explains:

> Discussion and student/student interaction as well as teacher/student interaction propel the whole class forward so that by the end of the school year, the whole class has moved forward through group effort. Older students assist the younger or slower students especially in overcrowded classrooms where it is impossible to do one-on-one instruction. Every September, it is drilled into their heads thru modeling and practicing that they all have responsibilities and duties to themselves and classmates. Establishing a regular routine where the student is respected and also has duties is another thing the teacher must instill in the students through discussion and practice.

In this way, cooperation and mutuality (as opposed to the stress and competition fostered by high-stakes standardized tests and high-pressure accountability) become the norm. Learning and growing together becomes a means to counter the anti-educational pressures affecting today's classroom. Gina adds:

> So in addition to the standard curriculum that must be taught, there are these more fundamental aspects to teaching and learning that must take place. A teacher will have to be very creative and driven in order to continue enlightening students in a humane way while also trying to fulfill the new common core curriculum standards now being implemented in a frenzied and many times haphazard manner. Teachers are constantly being reminded that student progress is the goal which is tied to teacher accountability. The threat of layoffs and union busting has awakened many teachers to these developments in public education. Teachers are supposed to teach to the standards set forth.

Here again the state's testing system is seen as undermining a humane and meaningful approach to student learning. Gina feels she has to be "very creative and driven" to provide students with what they need as opposed to what the state requires her to do. But this "creativity" and "drive" is precisely what may put teachers in a precarious position vis-à-vis those who demand that all teachers "stick to the script" (see McNeil, 2000). What makes this situation even more untenable is that while the state is increasingly holding schools, principals, and teachers "accountable," it is becoming even less accountable to students and teachers in this era of neoliberalism and globalization. The state is essentially demanding that teachers and schools perform miracles with fewer resources, fewer protections, greater insecurity, and less autonomy. No longer are students and teachers humans and citizens with rights that government must guarantee. Rather, they are first and foremost customers or consumers who must also "perform." Within this view, "failure" brings punishment while "success" brings rewards.[6]

Gina goes on to highlight other complexities arising from the conflict between relevant and critical learning versus corporate-government testing and accountability dictates:

I try to encourage the students to be themselves so their true essence can be expressed to the world when they speak or write. Of course you need to have a safe space to learn and to assert and affirm. It is becoming much more difficult to provide that space under so much pressure to test student progress in all areas at every turn. Students do not internalize their learning when they are just memorizing information from a workbook or a computer program at such a frenetic pace. Don't get me wrong, a workbook or computer program is an essential tool in the teacher's toolbox but it is not a replacement for the complex lessons that I take long hours to prepare with my students in mind. The trend now in the mandates being forced down our throats is to force as much disparate bits of information into students' heads as fast as possible in order to measure students' proficiencies. The end result of all this is to see growth in student test results. This somehow is supposed to make our students more enlightened and able to "work in today's global economy." This kind of teaching misses the essence of the student, the human being. The organic process of learning is then stifled by the student who believes that most of this stuff they are learning has no significance in their day-to-day life—so they tune you out.

The emphasis on memorizing and regurgitating information and facts may improve students' ability to perform well on tests, but good test performance is not the same as genuine learning and meaningful growth. As noted earlier, it is possible to raise test scores without deep learning and, because students tend to forget much of what is tested (if they ever knew it well to begin with), many arrive at college needing remedial work. For example, according to the U.S. Department of Education:

In 2007–08, about 36 percent of undergraduate students considered to be in their first year [of college] reported having ever taken a remedial course, while 20 percent had actually taken one in that same year. At public 2-year institutions, about 42 percent of students had ever taken a remedial course. (Aud et al., 2011, p. 70)

To the extent that the current corporate-government testing and accountability policies thwart deep learning, creativity, and genuine subject mastery, it may be argued that it fails to prepare many youth for the future. This conclusion was also brought out in powerful ways in the film *Race to Nowhere*. Being able to fill in bubbles on a scantron sheet cannot be called preparation for the complexities and challenges of life. Using high-stakes testing in Texas as an example, McNeil (2000) explains that:

Advocates of TAAS sometimes argue that being able to pass the reading skills section of TAAS is better than not being able to read at all. However, teachers are reporting that the kind of test prep frequently done to raise test scores may actually hamper students' ability to learn to read for meaning. In fact, high school students report that in the test-prep drills and on the TAAS reading section, they frequently mark answers without reading the sample of text: they merely match key words in the answer choice with key words in the text. And elementary teachers note that so many months of "reading" the practice samples and answering multiple-choice questions on them undermines their students' ability to read sustained passages of several pages. The reading samples are material the students are meant to forget the minute they mark their answers; at all grade levels this read-and-forget activity is using up the school year with a noncurriculum. (p. 731)

Who has not experienced this phenomenon in middle school and high school?

Gina supplies another example of how she negotiates the need for being student centered with the dictates of corporate-government testing and accountability:

> I try to use the state rules and regulations to the advantage of the student. For example, students know first hand what it is like to come to this country in the 9th grade as a beginner student of English proficiencies and is still expected to pass the regents exams that even native speakers of English have difficulties with. Students feel frustrated, humiliated, dehumanized, and sometimes hopeless in the face of such daunting tasks. We discuss these issues as part of our class discussion that eventually will lead to an article or story to be read in class based on that discussion and then each student will do some research to write an opinion piece on the discussion issue which students can change or modify. Along the way, we correct our grammar, punctuation, syntax, spelling...A lesson like this can take anywhere from 2–4 weeks depending on all kinds of factors such as student proficiency levels, upcoming exams, absences, unscheduled school events...The students' initiatives are unleashed when they have a stake in the learning.

Gina attempts to negotiate two countervailing tendencies in a way that preserves the integrity of her students, herself, and the learning process. It is easy to imagine how much more all three would flourish in the absence of the current testing and accountability schemes. While more than a few of Gina's students "fail" the high-stakes tests once or twice, most end up going on to graduate from a community, state, or private college in the area. Gina's tenacity and creativity are instructive for others; it is possible to prevail under difficult conditions.

Public education, standardized testing, and the neoliberal state

How did education end up here? What accounts for the increased corporatization and degradation of education? The period between 1945 and 1975 is generally recognized as the era of the social welfare state. While conflicts and contradictions existed during this 30-year period, an understanding of sorts prevailed between labor and capital—essentially "labor peace."[7] In this context, labor promised the ruling elite that it would not strive to overthrow capitalism if the ruling elite ensured fair wages, salaries, benefits, and pensions—a piece of the American pie. In return, capitalism would be "allowed" to exist so long as the economic needs of workers were met. As a result, government funding for a variety of social programs, projects, and initiatives expanded significantly during the New Deal and War on Poverty eras, providing millions with employment and a safety net, while also serving to funnel money to the ruling elite to "maintain order" (Fox Piven & Cloward, 1971, 1982). Within this framework of "prosperity for all," workers' *political* rights were generally left out of the equation while the political power of the capitalist class remained intact.

But beginning in the mid-70s, another crisis of capital accumulation (over-production and under-consumption) had surfaced and this necessitated the beginning of the dismantling of the social welfare state, the erosion of worker rights, the elimination or scaling down of numerous social programs and institutions, and the intensification of the dictate of capital at home and abroad. Instead of upholding the "basic bargain" that prevailed during the 1945–1975 period, government (Reich, 2011) became focused on "slashing public goods and investments—cutting school budgets, increasing the cost of public higher education, reducing job training, cutting public transportation and allowing bridges, ports and highways to corrode" (section The Middle-Class Squeeze, 1977–2007, para. 5).

This trend, which continues unabated today, was launched to reverse the declining profitability of capital and it marks the beginning of the neoliberal period and the end of Keynesian policy. Free market dogma tailored to the new conditions has been brought back with a vengeance. Privatization, deregulation, and the abdication of government responsibility for the well-being of the people have all escalated since the late seventies and early eighties resulting in maximum profits for the political and economic elite. Neoliberalism essentially represents the political-economic structure created over the last 30 to 40 years to benefit the rich at the expense of everyone else. However, all the measures taken by the ruling elite and their governments have failed to diminish inequality and poverty which have only grown since the early eighties (Economic Policy Institute, 2011) and the polity remains marginalized. None of the neoliberal claims about greater accountability, efficiency, and prosperity have materialized.

Harvey (2007) states that, "There has everywhere been an emphatic turn towards neoliberalism in political-economic practices and thinking since the 1970s" (p.2). Gabbard (2008) adds that neoliberalism does not operate alone, it is closely linked to neoconservatism, which embodies Christian, right-wing, and "traditional" values. Saltman (2010) explains that:

> At its most basic, neoliberal economic doctrine calls for privatization of public goods and services and the deregulation of state controls over capital, as well as trade liberalization and the allowance of foreign direct investment. As an ideol-

ogy, neoliberalism aims to eradicate the distinction between the public and private spheres, treating all public goods and services as private ones. It individualizes responsibility for the well-being of the individual and the society, treating persons as economic entities—consumers or entrepreneurs, and it has little place for the role of individuals as public citizens or the collective public responsibilities of democracy. (pp. 36–37)

Under neoliberalism, the power of the state is not undermined, weakened, or restricted; rather, its roles and functions change to expand and enforce the dictate of capital which, in turn, escalates the destruction of the social and natural environments. According to neoliberal doctrine, anything that does not serve the interests of the ruling class is considered irrational. Schemes to pay the rich (e.g., bailouts for banks and Wall Street, cuts to social programs, free trade agreements, fewer regulations, tax cuts for corporations, greater household debt, and ongoing wars) are thus considered rational and progressive. The state's role is to implement these arrangements swiftly—and violently, if necessary (Gabbard, 2008; Nader, 2011; Perlo, 1972; Porfilio & Malott, 2008).

In the sphere of education, neoliberal ideology holds that parents and students are not citizens—they are customers or consumers; school leaders are not public servants—they are entrepreneurs, managers, or CEOs; teachers are not credentialed and qualified autonomous professionals—they are implementers of corporate-government standards, curricula, and assessments; education is not a social human responsibility—it is a commodity to be bought and sold. Government, in this view, does not affirm human rights; instead, it puts all the social and natural assets of society at the disposal of corporations in the name of being competitive in the global market, thereby depriving social programs (including education) of much-needed resources. One of the most distinctive expressions of neoliberalism in U.S. education is the rapid rise of for-profit education management organizations (EMOs). Molnar et. al. (2010) reveal that, "Since the first *Profiles* report was produced for the 1997–1998 school year, the number of schools managed by for-profit EMOs has increased to 729 from 131" (p. v). This, I believe, is the tip of the iceberg.

High-stakes standardized testing is another expression of neoliberal ideology and practice in public education (Hursh, 2000, 2008). It is a key feature of the market-oriented 2001 No Child Left Behind Act and the more recent federal Race to the Top initiative, in particular. Webb et. al. (2009) explain that, "The dominant policy discourse over the last two decades in education has been performance accountability via high-stakes testing. NCLB is the most recent articulation of performance-accountability in the USA" (p. 5). The "data" and "metrics" associated with these tests are used to, among other things, lower labor costs (e.g., through performance-pay plans for teachers and principals) and to justify the privatization of education (e.g., converting poor-performing schools to charter schools run by for-profit EMOs).

Also, high-stakes standardized testing, along with neoliberalism's individualization of responsibility and social problems, contributes to the disempowerment and deprofessionalization of teachers, while simultaneously lowering the quality of teaching and learning by narrowing the curriculum (Ohanian, 1999; Au, 2007; Valli & Buese, 2007). In today's neoliberal context, little authority and power rest with teachers, who know their students and content best. Big business and the government now determine, to a great extent, the nature, functions, and purposes of teaching and learning. Top-down "reform" is intensified under neoliberalism (Kroll, 2009). Viewed from this angle, it is easy to make sense of the corporate-government teacher bashing and union busting taking place today.

Conclusion: Education as a right and glimmers of hope in a neoliberal world

A modern education system requires modern definitions and a modern outlook. A promising approach to the problems generated by corporate-government testing and accountability is through the reclaiming of education reform discourse using a human rights perspective. By viewing problems and issues from a human rights perspective, it becomes easy to understand and sort through all the ideas, misinformation and confusion surrounding change, progress, and reform and to point the way forward to a bright future. Almost all problems can be viewed through the prism of human rights. Homelessness exists because the right to shelter is not recognized by government, the representative of society. Similarly, hunger exists because the government fails to recognize the right to food. As a result, access to both shelter and food has become a "privilege" in our society, just like work, health care, and education. In this way, one's most basic needs are treated as privileges and access is equated to the ability to pay. This represents wealth discrimination. The existence of problems thus signifies the absence of the affirmation of rights, meaning that solving problems entails guaranteeing rights.

Corporate-government policies such as high-stakes standardized testing and a punitive accountability culture violate the right to an education. Once it is established that education is a right, that this right cannot be taken away, that it is inalienable, irrevocable, and inviolable, and not based on age, skin color, sex, wealth, ability, merit, or the ability to pass a test, it becomes clear that the right to an education requires the replacement of the existing neoliberal policies with student-centered and democratic policies and practices. The competitive character, behaviorist foundations, and corporate aims of standardized testing have nothing in common with a humanist education.

In society, a human right can be either affirmed or suppressed. High-stakes standardized testing systems and their accompanying accountability schemes and punitive measures harm all students, particularly minority, special education, homeless, English as a Second Language, and low-income students. Many of these students are marginalized and pushed out of school through these policies, thereby directly contravening their right to education, as well as their right to mental, emotional, and physical well-being. Further, when it is understood that the policies in question perpetuate the social status and values of the power elite, then the magnitude of the injury being inflicted becomes clearer.

While U.S. law does not recognize education as a basic human right (*Plyler v. Doe*, 1982; *San Antonio School District v. Rodriguez*, 1973; Verges, 2009), education is nevertheless an irrevocable right that emerges from the conditions of existence and must be affirmed in a manner commensurate with the level of development of society. There is no reason why the right to education cannot be guaranteed by government. In practical terms, this includes ensuring that teachers have a greater say over curriculum, instruction, and assessment, as well as the financial and operational matters in their schools. It means teachers must have a meaningful say over their work conditions. It also means using assessments to assist, nurture, and cultivate youth rather than humiliate, stress, and punish them. One slogan that captures well these points is: *Teachers' Working Conditions Are Students' Learning Conditions.* This slogan was inscribed on the banners of thousands of striking teachers in Ontario, Canada, in 1997. This was the largest teachers' strike ever in North America; more than 125,000 teachers participated. It is hard to see how a student's right to education can be affirmed if teachers have no control over their working conditions.

The voices of students, parents, and community members must be affirmed as well, particularly through spaces that empower them to express their views and be heard. Regularly—and particularly in high-poverty districts—parents and community members are excluded from deciding the affairs of their schools. Parental "input" is generally reduced to signing up to speak for a minute or two at poorly advertised "public" meetings. These meetings are typically brief, dominated by the meeting organizers (boards of education or corporate sponsors), and designed to give the illusion of community involvement. Meeting organizers value control over open debate and the sharing of ideas. Last, but not least, affirming the right to education means restricting corporate influence in the schools, increasing funding for schools, and addressing long-standing social and economic conditions undermining public schools.

Not surprisingly, there is broad resistance to neoliberalism nationally and internationally. Students, youth, women, and workers are joining hands to say: "Another world is possible, and we will create it." Some examples of this resistance include the 2011 "Arab spring," the Wisconsin battle for labor rights, the growing demand to bring the wars in Afghanistan and Iraq to an immediate end, and opposition to austerity measures in Europe, among others. This resistance is bound to grow until the needs and rights of the peoples of the world have been affirmed in practice.

For specific examples of resistance to corporate-government testing and accountability schemes in the U.S., visit the following websites: http://www.fairtest.org and http://www.substancenews.net.[8]

In the final analysis, it is the struggle for rights, including the right to an education, that will open the path of progress to the society. As former slave and abolitionist Frederick Douglass (1818–1895) once said, "If there is no struggle, there is no progress." The forces of neoliberalism are not invincible and, in the long run, cannot overcome the forces of history, justice, and progress. A world fit for all (instead of a world where only "the fittest survive") is the demand of the times.

Appendix

Interview Questions

Gina was asked the following questions:

1. How would you characterize the main teaching and learning issues, problems, and contradictions confronted by you and your students in the course of contending with the state's standards and testing program?

2. Within this context, how do you and your students confront these realities?

3. Specifically, which practices do you deploy to promote teaching and learning?

4. Please try to contextualize your own and your students' experiences when possible.

Notes

1. The URL for this report has been deliberately omitted so as to protect the identity of the teacher and her school.
2. The newspaper is called *Business First* and it is the voice of business in the western New York region. It is published weekly. One issue per year provides area school rankings based on standardized test scores. Schools with large minority, low-income populations consistently rank at the bottom of the scale.
3. For a summary of some of the negative effects of such competition, see Lubienski & Weitzel (2010).
4. See http://charterschoolscandals.blogspot.com for regular reports on scandals and unethical practices in charter schools.

5. For more on the wrecking associated with high-stakes standardized testing, see Susan Ohanian's website at http://www.susanohanian.org. See also Substance Magazine's website at http://www.substancenews.net.
6. See Alfie Kohn's (1999) *Punished by Rewards* for a useful discussion of the behaviorist origins of this outlook.
7. Former U.S. Secretary of Labor Robert Reich, a liberal, uses the expression "basic bargain" to characterize arrangements between capital and labor during this period. See Reich (2011, June 1).
8. Both provide rich resources, including links to other sites dedicated to affirming the rights of students and teachers.

References

Abrams, L.M. (2004). *Teachers' views on high-stakes testing: Implications for the classroom.* Tempe: Education Policy Research Unit (EPRU). Retrieved from http://coe.unm.edu/uploads/docs/coe-main/research/epsl-0401-104-epru.pdf

Allington, R. (2000). How to improve high-stakes test scores without really improving. *Issues in Education,* 6, 115–24.

Au, W. (2007). High-stakes testing and curricular control: A qualitative metasynthesis. *EducationalResearcher,* 36(5), 258–267.

Au, W. (2009). *Unequal by design: High-stakes testing and the standardization of inequality.* New York: Routledge.

Aud, S., Hussar, W., Kena, G., Bianco, K., Frohlich, L., Kemp, J., & Tahan, K. (2011). *The Condition of Education 2011* (NCES 2011–033). U.S. Department of Education, National Center for Education Statistics. Washington, DC: U.S. Government Printing Office. Retrieved from http://nces.ed.gov/pubsearch/pubsinfo.asp?pubid=2011033

Berliner, D. (2008, November 3). Why rising test scores may not equal increased student learning. *Dissent Magazine.* Retrieved from http://dissentmagazine.org/online.php?id=156

Crawford, J., & Krashen, S. (2007). *English language learners in American classrooms: 101 questions, 101 answers.* Scholastic Teaching Resources.

Crocco, M. S., & Costigan, A. T. (2006). High-stakes teaching: What's at stake for teachers (and students) in the age of accountability. *The New Educator,* 2, 1–13.

Economic Policy Institute. *The state of working America.* (2011, May 6). Retrieved from http://www.stateofworkingamerica.org

Fair Test. (2007). *The dangerous consequences of high-stakes standardized testing.* Retrieved from http://fairtest.org/dangerous-consequences-highstakes-standardized-tes

Fox Piven, F., & Cloward, R. (1971). *Regulating the poor: The functions of public welfare.* New York: Pantheon Books.

Fox Piven, F., & Cloward, R. (1982). *The new class war: Reagan's attack on the welfare state and its consequences.* New York: Pantheon Books.

Gabbard, D. (Ed.). (2008). *Knowledge and power in the global economy: The effects of school reform in a neoliberal/neoconservative age.* Second edition. New York: Lawrence Erlbaum Associates.

Garrison, M. (2009). *A measure of failure: The political origins of standardized testing.* Albany, NY: SUNY Press.

Giroux, H. A. (2009a, July 24). Obama's view of education is stuck in reverse. *Truthout.*

Retrieved from http://www.truthout.org/072409A

Giroux, H.A. (2009b, September 21). The politics of lying and the culture of deceit in Obama's America: The rule of damaged politics. *Truthout*. Retrieved from http://archive.truthout.org/092109r

Giroux, H.A. (2010, October 5). When generosity hurts: Bill Gates, public school teachers and the politics of humiliation. *Truthout*. Retrieved from http://www.truthout.org/when-generosity-hurts-bill-gates-public-school-teachers-and-politics-humiliation63868

Harvey, D. (2007). *Brief history of neoliberalism*. Oxford, GBR: Oxford University Press.

Hedges, C. (2011, April 10). Why the United States is destroying its education system. *Truthdig*. Retrieved from http://www.truthdig.com/report/item/why_the_united_states_is_destroying_her_education_system_20110410

Hursh, D. (2000). Neoliberalism and the control of teachers, students, and learning: The rise of standards, standardization, and accountability. *Cultural Logic*, 4(1).

Hursh, D. (2008). *High-stakes testing and the decline of teaching and learning: The real crisis in education*. Lanham, Md.: Rowman & Littlefield Publishers.

Kaczor, B. (2011. July 31). Researchers warn of school "accountability shock." *Associated Press*. Retrieved from http://www.ctpost.com/news/article/Researchers-warn-of-school-accountability-shock-1674316.php#ixzz1V6LjFAtM

Karp, S. (2010). School reform we can't believe in. *Rethinking Schools*. Retrieved from http://www.zcommunications.org/school-refore-we-cant-believe-in-by-stan-karp

Kohn, A. (1999). Punished by rewards. Boston: Houghton Mifflin.

Kohn, A. (2000). *The case against standardized testing: Raising the scores, ruining the schools*. Portsmouth, NH: Heinemann.

Kohn, A. (2011). *Feel-bad education: And other contrarian essays on children & schooling*. Boston: Beacon Press.

Kroll, A. (2009, January 19). The Duncan doctrine. The military-corporate legacy of the new secretary of education. *TomDispatch.com*. Retrieved from http://www.commondreams.org/view/2009/01/19–8

Lubienski, C., & Weitzel, P. (Eds.). (2010). *The charter school experiment: Expectations, evidence, and implications*. Massachusetts: Harvard Education Press.

McNeil, L. (2000). Creating new inequalities: Contradictions of reform. *Phi Delta Kappan*, 81 (10), 729–734.

Molnar, A., Miron, G., & Urschel, J. (2010, December). *Profiles of for-profit educational management organizations. Twelfth annual report*. Retrieved from http://nepc.colorado.edu/publication/EMO-FP-09–10

Nader, R. (2011). *Cutting corporate welfare*. New York, NY: Seven Stories Press.

New York State Education Department. (2010). *New York State Report Card: Accountability and Overview Report, 2009–2010*.

Nichols, S., & Berliner, D. (2005, March). The inevitable corruption of indicators and educators through high-stakes testing. East Lansing: The Great Lakes Center for Education Research & Practice. Retrieved from http://greatlakescenter.org/docs/early_research/g_l_new_doc/EPSL-0503–101-EPRU.pdf

Ohanian, S. (1999). *One Size Fits Few: The Folly of Educational Standards*. Portsmouth, NH: Heinemann.

Perlo, V. (1972). *Robbing the poor to fatten the rich: Inflation, wages, prices and profits*. New York: New Outlook Publishers.

Plyler v. Doe, 457 U.S. 202 (1982). Retrieved from http://www.law.cornell. edu/supct/html/historics/USSC_CR_0457_0202_ZO.html

Porfilio, B., & Malott, C. (Eds.). (2008). *The destructive path of neoliberalism: An international examination of education.* Rotterdam, New York: Sense Publishers.

Price, T.A. (2008, September 27/28). Bailing out the foes of public education. *Counterpunch.* Retrieved from http://www.counterpunch.org/price09272008.html

Ravitch, D. (2009, June 13). Obama gives Bush a 3rd term in education. *Huffington Post.* Retrieved from http://www.huffingtonpost.com/diane-ravitch/obama-gives-bush-a-3rd-te_b_215277.html

Reich, R. (2011, June 1). The truth about the American economy. *Truthout.* Retrieved from http://www.truth-out.org/truth-about-american-economy/1306953884

Resmovits, J. (2011, August 10). Schools caught cheating in Atlanta, around the country. *Huffington Post.* Retrieved from http://www.huffingtonpost.com/2011/08/08/atlanta-schools-cheating-scandal-ripples-across-country_n_919509.html

Saltman, K. (2010). The *gift of education: Public education and venture philanthropy.* New York: Palgrave Macmillan.

Saltman, K., & Gabbard, D. (Eds.). (2011). *Education as enforcement: The militarization and corporatization of schools* (2nd ed.). New York, NY: Routledge.

San Antonio School District v. Rodriguez, 411 U.S. 1 (1973). Retrieved from http://caselaw.lp.findlaw.com/scripts/getcase.pl?court=us&vol=411&invol=1

U.S. Department of Education, National Center for Education Statistics, *2003/04 Beginning Postsecondary Students Longitudinal Study, First Follow–up* (BPS:04/06).

Valli, L., & Buese, D. (2007). The changing roles of teachers in an era of high-stakes accountability. *American Educational Research Journal*, 44(3), 519–558.

Verges, J. (2009, April 9). Judge: Education not a right. *Argus Leader* (Sioux Falls, S.D.). Retrieved from http://www.argusleader.com/article/20090409/NEWS/904090333/1001

Vogler, K.E., & Virtue, D. (2007, March/April). "Just the facts, Ma'am": Teaching social studies in the era of standards and high-stakes testing. *The Social Studies, 98*(2), 54–58.

Webb. P. T., Briscoe, F. M., & Mussman, M. P. (2009). Preparing teachers for the neoliberal panopticon. *Educational Foundations*, Summer–Fall, 3–18.

11. *The Race to Somewhere: Experiential Education as an Argument for Not Teaching to the Test*

Rosemary A. Millham

Background

In reading this chapter about how I could practice critical pedagogy and create transformative experiences for my students, and still have students succeed on high-stakes tests, it is important to note that critical pedagogy and transformative education both play critical roles in the "how" and "why" of my classroom success (Dewey, 1925, 1938; Gamson, 1984; Giroux, 1998; McLaren, 2000; Mezirow, 2000; Freire, 1998; Shor, 1996). Therefore, it is best to begin by sharing something about these progressive constructs as a way to explain my thinking as I planned setting up my students for success in a high-stakes testing environment. Short descriptions are provided below followed by my thoughts on their impact on teaching and learning. I encourage you to read the works on critical pedagogy and transformative education listed at the end of this chapter as a guide to classroom transformation.

Critical pedagogy

Henry Giroux (1998) describes critical pedagogy as an educational movement, guided by passion and principle, to help students develop consciousness of freedom, recognize authoritarian tendencies, and connect knowledge to power and the ability to take constructive action. Giroux's description is linked with Maxine Greene's (1986) perception as those who "see freedom as the power to act and choose and to overcome obstacles which keep us from defining ourselves and being the best we know how to be" (p. 430). This illustrates that critical pedagogy allows for student freedom in conscious thought, and it empowers them to participate in all aspects of their education.

For me, this meant that my students had to be actively engaged in the process of teaching and learning. They needed to know that my classroom provided a space for safety and equity and that all voices would be heard (hooks, 2003). They needed to feel that they had a say in how things were accomplished and be given the power to design and implement instructional activities that would provide them with the ability to think critically. They needed to learn that they could make mistakes and learn from them. They needed to know they would not be criticized for making mistakes; and, most important, they needed to believe that not all educational activities had a single correct answer.

Transformative education (learning)

Transformative education can be defined in numerous ways, but it is closely linked with critical pedagogy. There are several guiding principles which provide the underpinnings for transformative education. They include perspective, a sense of freedom, and the ability (desire) to know oneself, to identify one's convictions, and, if necessary, change one's thinking.

The following are brief descriptions of what transformative learning means to three leading transformative educators. Mezirow (1996) describes transformative learning as "learning that is understood as the process of using a prior interpretation to construe a new or revised interpretation of the meaning of one's experience in order to guide future action" (p. 162).

Boyd and Myers (1988), whose view of transformative learning is rooted in analytical psychology, see it as a "fundamental change in one's personality involving [together] the resolution of a personal dilemma and the expansion of consciousness resulting in greater personality integration" (p. 277). Boyd suggests that transformation calls upon thought beyond the rational (i.e., imagination, emotions, abstractions, etc.) in applying symbols, images, and archetypes to assist in creating a personal vision of what it means to be human (Boyd & Myers, 1988; Taylor, 1998; Cranton, 1994).

Finally, bell hooks (2003) ties the concept of transformation to the role of the teacher, noting that, "Teachers must be aware of themselves as practitioners and as human beings if they wish to teach students in a non-threatening, anti-discriminatory way. Self-actualization should be the goal of the teacher as well as the students" (p. 33).

The intrinsically connected critical pedagogy and transformative education paradigm creates a classroom environment wherein students identify what they know, they gather new information and form new constructs while operating in a democratic, diverse, and tolerant setting. Such an atmosphere is necessary for learning, and is an essential ingredient in assuring equity in teaching and learning. In short, the approach provides a voice for all students.

Critical pedagogy and transformative educational practices are particularly effective when misconceptions occur and content and concepts need to be re-evaluated, reorganized, and possibly discarded. For my classroom, it also means involving students in the learning process. The result is an increase in intrinsic motivation through the development of processing and critical thinking skills. Consequently, students feel valued as members of our classroom's learning community. Within this transformed classroom, students experience success in all forms of assessment and evaluation—as well as on the high-stakes standardized tests.

Introduction

This chapter will describes a journey through the implementation of critical pedagogy that created transformative experiences for my students. This approach assured that my students were *experiencing* their education (Dewey, 1925, 1938) and discovering the meaning behind the activities that provided them with the ability to think critically, and to apply and communicate what they learned. All standards-driven (NYS Core Curriculum, 1997) and curricular mandates that dictated *what* (content, concepts, skills) I needed to teach my students were morphed into activities that empowered my students with choice, voice, and the opportunities to make decisions about their education. The *what* was standardized—the *how* was not.

Many researchers agree that inquiry instruction incorporating student investigation is highly effective in developing critical thinking and processing skills (Shor, 1996; Thousand, Villa, & Nevin, 2002; Singleton, & Newman, 2009). These skills are necessary for students to understand and apply what they learn in the classroom. Even basic content and concepts can be learned by default in the inquiry process as students work to find solutions to essential questions or solve problems. During the process, I posed questions to guide students into thinking through what they knew, what they are learning, and how it all fit into their current understandings. This process allowed students to build on prior knowledge, adjust their schema, and move forward successfully. In fact, empowering students with the ability to think through the process of inquiry based investigations resulted in impressive levels of achievement on classroom assessments that were mirrored by a 96% passing rate (consistent over several years) on the related on standardized tests. This success was due, in large part, to the fact that my students *experienced* their education and were active participants in learning as a transformative process (see the methods section).

I chose student-directed inquiry on the premise that it creates (1) personal meaning for the learner through experience, (2) interest and empowerment, (3) positive relationships with fellow students and the teacher, and (4) conceptualization competencies (Dewey, 1916, 1925, 1934). The use of inquiry is not new. Transformative philosophies of education have been around for decades (Dewey, 1902, 1916, 1925, 1934; Rich, 1979; Mezirow & Taylor, 2009; Gamson, 1984; Giroux, 1983).

Educator and philosopher John Dewey was a proponent of experiential teaching and learning in the late 1890s. In his book *Democracy and Education* (1916), he states:

> The educator's part in the enterprise of education is to furnish the environment which stimulates responses and directs the learner's course. (p. 188)

In *Experience and Education* (1938), he elaborates:

> It is [the educator's] business to arrange for the kind of experiences which, while they do not repel the student, but rather engage his activities are, nevertheless, more than immediately enjoyable since they promote having desirable future experiences. The central problem of an education based upon experience is to select the kind of present experiences that live fruitfully and creatively in subsequent experiences. (p. 27)

Hence, we acknowledge that if students are provided with opportunities to think, share, communicate, and make the cognitive connections necessary for understanding, we are able to transform them from passive to active participants in their education and, ultimately, create a population eager and interested in learning every day of their lives.

More recently, the work Mezirow (1997) reflects Dewey's perspectives by suggesting that common themes are central to a student's success. Edward Taylor (1998) lists three common themes related to Mezirow's theory: the centrality of experience, critical reflection, and rational discourse in the process of meaning structure transformation. Mezirow strongly supports critical pedagogy and transformative experience as an essential strategy for best practice in teaching and learning.

Unfortunately, many students never experience inquiry or student-centered investigative studies in the K–12 setting. Traditional teaching (teacher centered, lecture based, presentational in nature) continues to be the most common method used by educators. It is by far the most controlling method (regarding what is taught, how it is taught, and how learning is assessed) for delivering content through what has been referred to as "talk and chalk" where students are passive participants. And, even though teachers acknowledge that inquiry-based, student-centered experiences are more meaningful and have a greater impact on student engagement and understanding than traditional teaching methods, they are reluctant to discard traditional methods when standardized test results become a measure of teacher effectiveness, retention, and tenure.

In fact, when federal dictates drive states to accept a top-down model in order to secure federal funds for education, experts in education do not always blame teachers for practicing traditional pedagogy. As Diane Ravitch observed in her speech at the 2010 Representative Assembly of the National Education Association criticizing NCLB testing, "No Child Left Behind...it's a disaster. It has turned our schools into testing factories." Like Ravitch, many education experts continue to witness frustrated teachers teaching to the test as a means of just getting through what Ravitch (2010) calls the business of educating.

I agree that state and federal mandates put a tremendous amount of pressure on teachers to get their students to pass high-stakes tests (no matter how the material is taught). However, I know from experience that teachers can practice critical pedagogy and apply standards-based transformative methods and still enable their students to be successful on high-stakes tests.

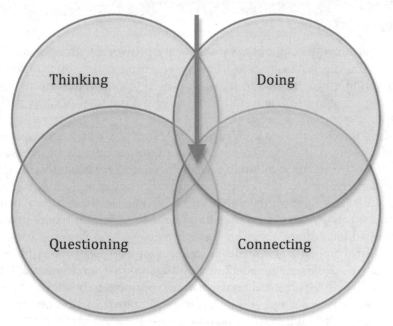

Application – Understanding - Learning

Thinking

Doing

Questioning

Connecting

Figure 1.0. An interpretation of the integrated process for learning combines thinking, questioning, and connecting concepts whereby the ability to successfully and cognitively apply what is "learned" results in understanding, which translates into true learning. Credit: Author.

Therefore, I began my search for the ideal teaching and learning strategies for my classroom by identifying the best qualities of existing theories and designing original methods that would have the greatest impact on student success. As you will see in this chapter, developing a transformative critical pedagogy takes time and thought, but the benefits are irrefutable.

The setting

My former high school is located in the Mid-Hudson Valley in New York and encompasses several townships in two counties. The student population is comprised of urban, rural, and suburban neighborhoods. School starts the first Wednesday after Labor Day, and ends at the end of June when the New York State Regents Examinations are completed. With a block schedule of alternate A/B days, the "A" days consisting of 90-minute periods followed by "B" days with 45-minute periods, students had a significant amount of time to conduct investigations, discuss results, clarify information, and present their findings to the class.

Of the 144 students who attended my earth science classes each year, about 25 percent were ninth graders, 15 percent were tenth graders, and the remainder were eleventh and twelfth graders trying to get a second Regents science course to meet graduation requirements (and not because they were fond of the earth science). Of the total number of students in my classes each year, generally about 10 percent comprised students with Individual Education Plans (IEPs). These are students with special needs (e.g., requiring assistance or additional time for a range of academic activities. Some were hearing impaired and needed supplementary written instructions and others were sight impaired and needed larger print size. On average, over 97 percent of my students were required to take the NYS Regents in Earth Science—the state's standardized, high-stakes test for that subject.

Planning for critical pedagogy and transformative experiences

I begin with the belief that the practice of experiential transformative education based on critical pedagogy and subsequent student success on standardized tests are not exclusive. When I first agreed to work at our high school after years in the middle school, I needed to determine how I could teach my students what they needed to know and understand to succeed in our classroom while, at the same time, prepare them for the high-stakes examination at the end of the school year.

Although I did not want to give up engaging my students in active investigations (in the middle school for ten years, my instruction had been predominantly investigation oriented), I thought that I would have to resort to "talk and chalk" at the high school just to cover all the material. It was almost overwhelming to review what needed to be taught in one school year. I spent the summer thinking about what I could do to make sure my high school students *experienced* their education just as my middle school students had. As Henry Giroux (1998) so eloquently stated, "It is important to stress that teachers must take active responsibility for raising serious questions about what they teach, how they are to teach, and what the larger goals are for which they are striving" (p. 97). I decided that my high school classroom would run pretty much like my classroom had at the middle school—only the students would be older and would know what I was asking of them, i.e., they would be active participants and investigators in my student-centered inquiry classroom. I wanted them to be transformed in their thinking, empowered by what they did and learned, and be able to think critically while learning how to process what they learned. And, most important, I wanted them to reflect on all aspects of the learning process. As Mezirow (2000) stated, students need to be "more critically reflective of their assumptions and aware of their context" p. 19).

By the time school started in the fall, I was ready.

The methods

Employing engaging critical pedagogy, I led my classes into the world of scientific processes to find answers to essential questions and responses to problems posed. I incorporated the 5E's (engage, explore, explain, expand, evaluate) constructivist approach with groups consisting of four students applying a process I developed to connect all of the parts in investigations. I called it the "BIDDI process" (brainstorm, investigate, debrief, debate, and identify). The BIDDI process provided students with opportunities to reflect in a structured way and to communicate expectations that I believed necessary for ownership of their learning (i.e., transformative in nature).

The 5E's constructivist approach required me to engage the students in the lesson topic. I demonstrated a discrepant event (something that caused unexpected results) or showed a short video clip that left them asking questions and/or wanting to know more.

The 5E's model, as described by Gabler and Schroeder (2002), is a learning strategy that draws on students' existing knowledge, beliefs, and skills. In the process, students synthesize new understandings with knowledge and make connections with the new information.

The constructivist teacher poses essential questions and/or problems and monitors student exploration, guides student inquiry with additional questions, and helps promote the development of process skills. Working mostly with raw data, primary sources, and interactive material, the constructivist teacher asks students to work with their own data and learn to direct their own explorations and thinking. Ultimately, students begin to think of learning as accumulated and evolving knowledge. Communication of group thoughts and findings is an essential part of the constructivist process.

The 5E model

This is an elaboration of the steps in the 5E model: **Engage:** an "engage" activity should do the following: Allow students to make connections between past and present learning experiences; and excite and focus student thinking on outcomes for current activities. Students should become cognitively and socially engaged in the concept(s), processes, or skills to be learned. **Explore:** students identify and develop concepts, processes, and skills as they actively explore their environment, design and conduct investigations, and/or manipulate materials. **Explain:** students explain what they have learned. They have opportunities to discuss conceptual understanding and to demonstrate new skills or behaviors. This provides opportunities for teachers to introduce formal terms, definitions, and explanations for concepts, processes, skills, and behaviors. It is also a useful place to address misconceptions. **Expand:** this provides an opportunity for students to share their conceptual understanding and to practice skills and behaviors. The learners develop deeper and broader understandings of major concepts, obtain more information, and refine their processing and thinking skills. **Evaluate:** this encourages learners to assess what they did as well as assess their understandings and skills.

The BIDDI process

As noted earlier, BIDDI is an acronym for brainstorm, investigate, debrief, debate, and identify. The BIDDI process provides a venue for those conditions I felt needed a more student-centered focus with multiple opportunities for reflection and communication.

This is an elaboration of the steps in the BIDDI process: **Brainstorm:** whether introducing a topic, a problem, or posing an essential question, students are to brainstorm some aspect of the learning process. Brainstorming begins as the whole class discusses a problem or responds to an essential question so students clearly understand what is being asked of them. Discussion includes background information and the identification of prior knowledge. This activity often reveals students' misconceptions. Students are also asked to brainstorm how they will design and implement an investigation and how they will identify the evidence they would need to support their findings. **Investigate:** once designed, students begin the investigation or experiment and conduct research. They observe, measure, record, collect, compile, organize, and identify the data while documenting the evidence to support findings and draw conclusions. **Debrief**: in this portion of the process, student teams share their investigative design, methods, data, and presentation format (graph, chart, essay form, poster, etc.) and present their findings and evidence to the class. After each group shares in the debrief, they decide, as a class, which of the teams succeeded in answering the problem or essential questions posed at the beginning of the investigative process. This is determined in the debate step. **Debate:** by citing evidence, students argue for their methodology and findings. Each team is provided with a rubric designed to assist in evaluating the investigative process, the methodology and collection of data, the findings, and the evidence to support the findings. Occasionally, two or more teams merge as their findings and evidence are similar. The individual or combined groups then debate the issue of methodology, findings, and evidence as a class. The goal is to identify the team(s) whose process is the soundest. **Identify:** As a class, the students identify the team results they believe to be the most scientifically accurate. A rationale is expected. This does not mean that only one group has the correct finding(s). It means that with the information presented, specific results and/or methods best answered the essential question(s) posed and are supported by the best evidence.

Once students have been involved in a whole process from the start, comparing and contrasting their group work with others, they have a clearer sense of what worked, what didn't, and how data were collected, results obtained and evidence identified. They have been engaged to think critically about the whole process.

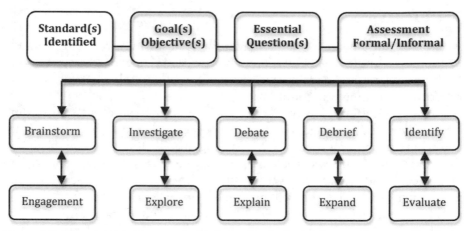

Figure 1.1. This schematic illustrates the Understanding by Design framework connected with the BIDDI and 5E's instructional process. Credit: Author.

Combined, the 5E Model and the BIDDI Process worked to ensure that the students were actively engaged, could think through what needed to be accomplished, could successfully conduct investigations, and could communicate findings/results. For example, if I were *engaging* students with a "hook" to get them interested in sediment deposition, I might show them a video clip of a mudslide in California that included homes and roads taken out in the slide. Then the students would *brainstorm* how and why the mudslide happened, *explore* existing research, develop a hypothesis, and design and conduct an *investigation* that required them to continue exploring and test their hypothesis. Following the investigations, the students would *debrief (explain)* and share their findings/results, then *debate (expand)* the results/findings, and decide which investigation succeeded in more accurately addressing the hypothesis, essential question or problem *(Identify/Evaluate)*. During the process, students needed to think about what they were doing, reflect on their work and communicate with their peers.

BIDDI in action

For this portion of the chapter, I will describe how the BIDDI Process and the 5 E's were used as an integral part of actively engaging students in the process of learning.

I started by looking at the prescribed New York State standards and core curriculum. Then I asked myself questions to focus on what I needed to accomplish in a high-stakes testing classroom. These included: "What mandates could I translate into short-term or long-term educational experiences? What curricular mandates did I need to address in the short-term or long-term to ensure that my students understood concepts? Could any given concept be better developed through engaging students in the process of understanding using student-centered or teacher-directed activities? Could I identify the embedded concepts within the content that students would need to discover before they could truly understand the content itself?

It was through the deliberate posing of these questions that I identified what needed to be taught and I made decisions about how it would be discovered by my students. My goal was to increase their ability to actively participate in their learning, to build a community of learners, to foster independent thought, *and* to assure student success on the standardized test.

First, I am a constructivist, and I wanted my students to work in groups and be engaged in their learning. I preferred the Understanding by Design (UbD; Wiggins & McTighe, 2005) lesson approach, which required me to look carefully at (1) the standards I wanted to address (2) the assessments I would implement and (3) the questions I would need to ask students before I planned for any activities.

With these frameworks in mind, I planned for success. I identified what I thought were the long-term and short-term concepts that needed to be developed by asking myself if the students would benefit more from a long-term study of some critical concept, or a short-term investigation. Knowing the state standards and aligning them with our curriculum, I came up with three concepts that could be developed more comprehensively if conducted over a long period of time. All other concepts would be developed during regular class time.

BIDDI for short-term projects

The BIDDI Process (embedded with the 5 E's) was used on a daily basis for all lessons throughout the year. Each lesson (including research, readings, investigations, and experiments) was standards driven and curriculum based. No 45-minute lesson was dominated by "chalk and talk." Rather, lectures were limited to 10–15-minute segments. I practiced a "little chunks of information" philosophy as a means to assure that the students knew and could apply a concept before moving on to a new one. Students became proficient at conducting the steps for the BIDDI-embedded 5 E's by November and were leading investigations by the end of March. In addition, implementing this method every week allowed for students to become comfortable enough with the structure that their long-term projects were done exceptionally well.

SAMPLE SHORT-TERM PROJECT

Daily Motion of the Sun: Recording shadows for a full day provides information necessary to understand the daily motion of the Sun.

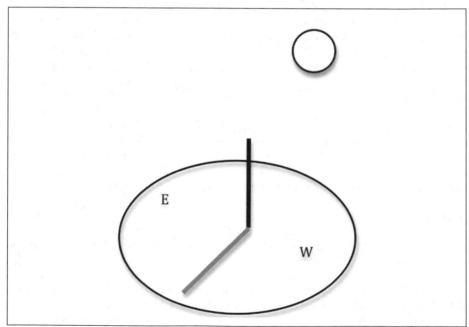

Figure 1.2. Sun-Stick Diagram: The diagram illustrates the sun stick and the shadow created by the stick when the Sun strikes the stick from the opposite direction. Credit: Author.

Students record the shadow cast by a stick to determine the apparent path of the Sun during the course of the day. Each student places an 8-inch stick in the ground in the schoolyard in an open place where shadows from trees or buildings would not interfere with the project. Using a large sheet of butcher paper, the students draw the shadow created by the stick at 45-minute intervals and record the time. The paper is positioned in the same spot all day with N, S, E, and W labeled on the paper's edges. This activity requires cooperation of other teachers because the students will need 5 minutes every 45 minutes to record the shifting shadow. A sundial will produce the same results. However, recording the sundial shadow is a more passive activity than constructing one's own shadow stick.

BIDDI for long-term projects

Long-term projects are a little more difficult to implement. Beginning, again, with a close look at the standards and core curriculum mandates, I asked myself what mandates could be translated into long-term educational experiences. I also needed to design a method to check on student progress throughout the length of the projects to be sure students were actually keeping up with the work.

From the first day of class, we discussed the long-term projects and how the data were to be compiled into some kind of data table that provided the information necessary to determine the connections that existed. Please note that I did not teach any of the concepts developed in the long-term projects until late in the school year and found that the projects were so effective that little teaching was needed; only guiding questions and investigations to expand the data they had already collected, compiled, and interpreted. Such activities exceeded many expectations of the NSES and the AAAS benchmarks, especially in the areas of inquiry (although guided in many cases) and a scientist's approach to research. The NSES see inquiry as:

> a multifaceted activity that involves making observations; posing questions; examining books and other sources of information to see what is already known; planning investigations; reviewing what is already known in light of experimental evidence; using tools to gather, analyze, and interpret data; proposing answers, explanations, and predictions; and communicating the results. Inquiry requires identification of assumptions, use of critical and logical thinking, and consideration of alternative explanations. (p. 23)

SAMPLE LONG-TERM PROJECT

The Apparent Path of the Sun: Tracking the apparent path of the Sun over an extended period of time connects concepts related to daily motion using shadows cast by the Sun, identifying the position of the Sun relative to seasonal change, providing data to determine the angle of incoming solar radiation (which is directly related to seasonal change), and allowing students opportunities to apply their knowledge of our global grid system (longitude and latitude). Below are the New York Standards and Performance Indicators related to this project.

STANDARD 1 Analysis, Inquiry, and Design

SCIENTIFIC INQUIRY: The central purpose of scientific inquiry is to develop explanations of natural phenomena in a continuing, creative process.

STANDARD 6 Interconnectedness: Common Themes

PATTERNS OF CHANGE: Identifying patterns of change is necessary for making predictions about future behavior and conditions.

PERFORMANCE INDICATORS 1.1: Explain complex phenomena, such as tides, variations in day length, solar insolation, apparent motion of the planets, and annual traverse of the constellations. 1.1g Seasonal changes in the apparent positions of constellations provide evidence of Earth's revolution. 1.1h The Sun's apparent path through the sky varies with latitude and season.

Sun data were collected at the start of each class every Wednesday beginning in the fall. Students plotted the shadow cast by the Sun at the same time (relatively) and location every week. We used rectangular blocks positioned permanently on the school grounds that were oriented and marked N, S, E, and W. The papers used to plot the shadows were labeled and positioned to the north for control purposes. Once a shadow was completed, the students measured the length of the shadow and the arc distance change from one week to the next. Each week the data were entered on a graph. At the end of two months the students' graphs illustrated the change in the length of the shadow and the shadow's slight shift to the northwest.

By spring, the shadow length and direction had changed and it was heading back to its position from the previous fall. Students could predict how the shadow length and direction would change over the next three months and they knew what the completed yearly graph (analemma) would look like. I never really had to "teach" anything about the apparent motion of the Sun or how it changed during the course of the year. Students had already figured it out (for a more detailed explanation, please feel free to contact the author). Today there are websites with angle and shadow length calculators available for free. However, they only provide information—like looking at a digital clock to see what time it is. They do not teach the concepts surrounding the motion of the Sun's shadow. Therefore, the chances of a true understanding of the apparent path of the Sun are minimized. It is the gathering, compiling, and interpreting data that make this project a conceptual success for students.

Assessing student understandings

In the course of each ten-week quarter, I used a number of formative and summative assessments to determine my students' conceptual understandings.

The formative (generally informal) assessments include what I call a "walk-about." Armed with a clipboard, a list of the students in the class, and a particular question, I walk around the room and individually quiz each student. If students responded correctly, they received a check plus. If their understanding seemed weak, they received a check. Answers reflecting a complete lack of understanding earned a check minus.

Exit tickets (a question posed and then answered on a slip of paper handed in at the end of class), questions of the day, and random questioning were also used in the formative assessment process. These assessments did not go into any grade book. They were used as tools for reflection on the teaching and learning process, and they helped me identify where I needed to work on my instruction. If my goal was for students to be successful on the Regents examination, I needed to know if the methods I employed were actually setting the students up for success. The ways the students thought and communicated understandings were critical elements for self-reflection to determine the effectiveness of my instructional practices.

The investigations themselves were both formative and summative, especially the BIDDI process, where students were evaluated primarily on the outcomes of the investigative process and on how well they defended their findings. Any misconceptions or false findings were eliminated during the debrief and debate steps. The process was also graded (summative evaluation) using a rubric to assess the information in the students' journals and investigation reports.

Additionally, every topic was followed by a test or quiz with questions mirroring the Regents format. This was intended to maintain student familiarity with the state test and provide the repetition necessary to focus students on the type of testing in which they would be evaluated in a high-stakes arena.

A word about homework

Homework is a complicating factor because I cannot control what happens once a student leaves my room. As teachers, we do not know if students will have any control over the out of school time needed to complete assignments, or what level of assistance they might need—or be getting from classmates or family members. To attempt to address these variables, I assigned three to four homework assignments on the first morning of the week; all assignments were due on Friday. I did not assign weekend or holiday homework. Additionally, I do not count homework assignments in the overall class average. I used homework completion to decide whether or not a student is consistent in completing the work in a reasonable amount of time and I factored it, minimally, into the quarterly grade. Overall, the process seemed effective. I also noted that students who completed homework assignments passed the Regents examination.

Conclusion

Instead of becoming overwhelmed with anxiety over test questions and content-specific issues, I aligned the state standards, the prescribed core curriculum, and the expectations of the standardized Regents Examination in Earth Science to identify what my students needed to know, understand, and be able to do.

Then, I designed investigations to develop those competencies. I tied in the BIDDI process with constructivism and provided opportunities for reflection and practiced standard summative evaluation questions based on the content covered.

Overall, the process proved to be extremely successful in teaching students to think, to reason, and to participate in discourse as part of a comfortable classroom community. By default, the process taught concepts and embedded themes in a manner that allowed students to own their understandings and provided them with the ability to apply what they learned. Our passing rate on the Earth Science Regents averaged 96 to 97 percent over the years. Is this a measure of success? I believe it is. The process fundamentally engaged students in their learning and created "habits of mind" for lifelong learning. By applying a pedagogy that encourages and supports empowerment, critical thinking, and process skills, the students excelled in the classroom.

References

Journals

Boyd, R. D., & Myers, J. G. (1988). Transformative Education. *International Journal of Lifelong Education*, 7 (4), pp. 261–284.

Giroux, H. A. (1983). Ideology and agency in the process of schooling. *Journal of Education*, 165, 1, pp. 12–34.

Greene, M. (1986). In search of a critical pedagogy. *Harvard Educational Review*, 56, 4, pp. 427–441.

Mezirow, J. (1996). Contemporary paradigms of learning. *Adult Education Quarterly*, 46, 3, pp. 158–173. (Retrieved March 2011 from the Sage Social Science Collections.)

Mezirow, J. (1997). Transformative learning: Theory to practice. *New Directions for Adult and Continuing Education*, 74, pp. 5–12. San Francisco: Jossey–Bass.

Singleton, A., & Newman, K. (2009). Empowering students to think deeply, discuss engagingly, and write definitively in the university classroom. *International Journal of Teaching and Learning in Higher Education*, 20, 2, pp. 247–250.

Books

The American Association for the Advancement of Science. (1993). *Benchmarks for science literacy*. (1993). New York: Oxford University Press.

Cranton, P. (1994). *Understanding and promoting transformative learning: A guide for educators of adults*. San Francisco: Jossey-Bass.

Dewey, J. (1902). *The child and the curriculum*. Chicago: University of Chicago Press.

Dewey, J. (1916). *Democracy and education*. New York: The Free Press.

Dewey, J. (1925/2000). *Experience and philosophic method*. In J. J. Stuhr (Ed.), *Pragmatism and classical American philosophy* (2nd ed.). (pp. 460–471). New York: Oxford University Press.

Dewey, J. (1934). *Art as experience*. Carbondale, IL: Southern Illinois University Press.

Freire, P. (1998). *Pedagogy of freedom: Ethics, democracy, and civic courage*. Lanham, MD: Rowman & Littlefield.

Gabler, C., & Schroeder, M. (2002). *Seven constructivist methods for the secondary classroom: A planning guide for invisible teaching*. Upper Saddle River, NJ: Allyn & Bacon (Pearson).

Gamson, Z.F. (1984). *Liberating Education*. San Francisco: Jossey-Bass.

Giroux, H. A. (1998). *Teachers as Intellectuals: Toward a critical pedagogy of learning*. Westport, CT. Bergin and Garvey Publishers, Inc.

hooks, b. (2003). *Teaching community: A pedagogy of hope*. New York: Routledge.

McLaren, P. (2000). *Che Guevara, Paulo Freire and the pedagogy of revolution*. Lanham, MD: Rowman & Littlefield.

Mezirow, J. (2000). *Learning as transformation: Critical perspectives on a theory in progress*. San Francisco: Jossey-Bass.

Mezirow, J., & Taylor, E. W. (2009). *Transformative learning in practice: Insights from community, workplace, and higher education*. San Francisco: Jossey-Bass.

Rich, A. (1979). *Claiming an education*. In A. Rich (Ed.), *On lies, secrets, and silence* (pp. 231–236). New York: Norton.

Shor, I. (1996). *When students have power: Negotiating authority in a critical pedagogy*. Chicago: University of Chicago Press.

Taylor, Edward W. (1998). *The theory and practice of transformative learning: A critical review*. Information Series no. 374. Columbus, Ohio: ERIC Clearinghouse, Ohio State University.

Wiggins, G. & McTighe, J. (2005). *Understanding by design*. Alexandria, VA. ASCD.

Edited Works

Thousand, J. S., Villa, R. A., & Nevin, A. I. (Eds.). (2002). *The Practical Guide to Empowering Students, Teachers, and Families* (2nd ed.). Baltimore, MD: Paul H. Brookes Publishing Co., Inc.

Web Resources

New York State Core Curriculum (1977). http://www.p12.nysed.gov.ciai/mst/scirg.html.

NSES Content Standard D: Earth and Space Science: Origin and evolution of the earth system (1996). Grades 9–12, page 23. http://www.p12.nysed.gov/ciai/mst/scirg.html

Ravitch, D. (2010). Speech to the Representative Assembly of the National Education Association. http://www.nea.org/grants/40246.htm

Teacher Web Resources

Constructivism and 5 E's

http://www.thirteen.org/edonline/concept2class/constructivism/index.html
http://www.learning-theories.com/constructivism.html
http://userwww.sfsu.edu/~foreman/itec800/finalprojects/eitankaplan/pages/home.htm
http://enhancinged.wgbh.org/research/eeeee.html

Transformative Learning:

http://transformativelearningtheory.com/corePrinciples.html
http://www.hent.org/transformative.htm

12. Making Writing Matter: Creating Spaces for Students in the Research Process

Katie Greene & Peggy Albers

April showers bring May flowers, but spring research papers bring moans and groans. Every year, as warm weather teases us with the promise of Spring Break, students and teachers (often) begrudgingly begin the research paper process. As quickly as students create note cards, teachers are expected to grade them. As swiftly as students draft introductory paragraphs, teachers check them off their to-do lists. Although, as teachers, we—along with our students—work through those spring days as efficiently as possible, we have begun to realize that the research paper process has, to some point, alienated students from authentic inquiry. In addition, large class sizes and mandated testing detract from valuable class time, making it difficult for teachers to schedule individual conferences to mentor each student throughout the research process. Sadly, we have begun to realize that the research paper process, often presented as a multiple-step process, has turned into a research paper checklist: a series of events that do not recognize the research processes that students themselves bring to the classroom.

As a high school English teacher and a university professor, we are aware that we must meet state and national standards which require our students to learn and demonstrate that they can conduct research; but we also wish to invite them to use multimedia resources as part of the research process. In short, we want to offer students ways to integrate their own experiences with digital technologies, including the Internet; print-based sources; and visual and audio information (e.g., YouTube, podcasts). Further, as we have come to know through our own teaching, students' research must be situated in their own content interests, as well as their interest in new technologies (Albers, Vasquez, & Harste, 2008; Doering, Beach, & O'Brien, 2007; Hagood,

Stevens, & Reinking, 2003; Knobel & Lankshear, 2008; Lankshear & Knobel, 2007; Short & Burke, 1991).

In this chapter, we wish to present effective practices involving the research process; practices grounded in critical pedagogy where choice is central, where students study significant social issues that affect them, where dialogue about learning is essential, where dominant forms of communication prevail (written language), and where representation and demonstration can cut across communication systems.

Critical pedagogy and critical writing

Within the past 40 years, a great deal of literature has focused on the writing processes of students. In 1971, Janet Emig wrote a groundbreaking study entitled *The Composing Processes of Twelfth Graders*. This study ignited interest in theorizing the writing process. In the 1970s, writing was seen as a linear process, with three primary stages: prewriting, writing, and postwriting (Hume, 1983) with attention paid to the product. However, as additional scholarship emerged, writing was seen as a dynamic, recursive set of processes interacting between the text and the writer (Flower & Hayes, 1981).

Despite the preponderance of research in the writing process, traditional models of instruction prevail, such as teachers asking students to follow specific stages in writing research: brainstorming, prewriting, note cards, outlines, draft, read-revision, and final draft. Topics are often controlled by the teacher and remain disconnected from student interest. Assessment and evaluation in this teacher-centered model focus on whether students have correctly followed the stages—not whether students have engaged in the research itself. That is, using the research process to write and the writing of research to learn. In this model, often constricted by time, students are research automatons: they select a topic to explore (one in which they may or may not be invested), and move automatically (and, passively) through other stages of the process (Christenbury, 1994). Within this model, they engage little in the research process (Flower, 2003). Further, the paper itself is primarily an individual effort; students had to prove that they could do independent research, even if others in the class had similar topics. Rather than offer authentic experiences to collaborate on research, students could discuss ideas and changes only in the peer-review stage, often an artificial step in which students were asked to comment on others' drafts. One of the major flaws in this approach is its emphasis on individuality and the artificiality of the collaborative nature of writing research. We suggest that this is not what real researchers/writers do. We believe that they engage in the sharing of ideas, see others as potential resources in helping them develop their work and thinking, and, in essence, participate in learning as a social activity (Harste, Short, & Burke, 1987).

As teachers and researchers interested in supporting students' voices, experiences, and backgrounds, we pose this question: "How do we engage students in culturally situated and significant issues as they demonstrate how they conduct, write, and present research?"

The positioning of situated knowledge (the knowledge and experiences that students bring into the classroom) necessitates a critical stance that provides democratic spaces for student research. We align our pedagogical work within critical literacy (Albers, Vasquez, & Harste, 2008; Harste, 2003; Janks, 2000, 2010; Shannon, 1993; Vasquez, 2004). That is, literacy is taught within the context of important societal issues. We argue that teachers must prepare students not only to read and write but to develop literacy practices that engage them in examining and writing about their world and its assumptions about learning. Those assumptions include the high school requirement—how to write, including the research paper.

In short, critical literacy moves issues of literacy from decoding and encoding of words in order to reproduce the meaning of a text to one in which a person begins to, as Shannon (1995) states, "understand one's own history and culture, to recognize connections between one's life and the social structure (p. 83). That is, students should understand the research paper not just as part of a school's requirement, but one that arises from their own experiences and backgrounds. In such a critical practice, teachers provide spaces for students to use a range of media (art, photographs, written text, podcasts, etc.) to question commonplace assumptions about social issues they wish to investigate (Lewison, Leland, & Harste, 2008), and to delve into topics that matter to them.

Unlike the traditional model that privileges the reading of only published texts (often found in their school libraries), this model of inquiry offers students opportunities to design and write research using a range of media. However, as critical literacy scholars argue (Albers, 2004; Albers, Vasquez, & Harste, 2011; Vasquez, 2004), merely writing in multiple media is not enough. Students must be aware of how their media choices position those being researched and/or the topic under investigation. We believe that students must be aware of how they represent people, events, and situations in their research, as well as the medium/media they select to report this research. We argue that when students are asked to examine their topics and the media choices they make, they are positioned to make decisions on what knowledge they wish to include in their research, and why and how this knowledge allows them to present this research in ways that might be limited by print.

Redesigning the research paper: A teacher's perspective

In order to address the academic and motivational needs of her students, Katie, the first author, designed a research project to help her students learn to write for a purpose and to use rhetorical devices. In previous years, research papers that Katie's students had written had centered on student-selected topics that related, either thematically or through a literary device, to a piece of literature that they had studied earlier in the year. For example, some students (inspired by the setting in Edgar Allan Poe's "The Cask of Amontillado") chose to research catacombs. Others studied arranged marriages (a connection to their study of one of the conflicts in Shakespeare's *Romeo and Juliet*). While this allowed students to create and choose from a variety of topics, they were not vested completely in their chosen topic, and it was difficult for Katie to monitor students' individual progress throughout the unit. With 150 students completing research materials simultaneously and working concurrently with a checklist full of dates, Katie found it challenging to schedule multiple conferences with each student.

As a result of Katie's observations and the annual frustration associated with teaching *the* research paper, she designed an action research project that allowed for social learning to take place. This project provided opportunities for small groups of students to collaborate in collective inquiry to create a single, standards-based research paper. In so doing, Katie hoped that her students would share valuable resources and generate a more substantive and thorough product. Further, Katie invited students to draw from their own interests in digital and visual media to design and represent their inquiry through an action research project. These action research projects would position students not as automatons, but as researchers inquiring actively into social issues of personal significance. Just as she invited her students to open themselves up to an unfamiliar approach to writing research, Katie herself, as their teacher, opened herself up to the various ways in which students could represent their projects. The newly designed project required each group to create a coherent technical writing piece that incorporated digital technologies to help students demonstrate an understanding of the writing process as it is situated in an increasingly digitalized world. Thus, students were positioned as 21st century inquirers, a stance that allowed them to situate the action research project within their interests and backgrounds, to select the media they would need to communicate their learning, and to experience multiple opportunities to share their learning.

Working within standards-based writing

Writing with a purpose and writing as a member of a social group are two important principles addressed in NCTE's position statement "Beliefs about the Teaching of Writing" (2004). Members of NCTE's Writing Study Group and authors of this statement describe conditions they believe will elicit competent writing. They state that "it is important that teachers create opportunities for students to be in different kinds of writing situations, where the relationships and agendas are varied" (p. 3). It was the intent of Katie's action research project to help students write for different purposes and she hoped that her students would engage more meaningfully with the research process. She wanted to avoid the pervasive sense of compliance identified by the Writing Study Group; namely, that "students write only to prove that they did something they were asked to do" (p. 3).

The Writing Study Group encourages the idea of writing as a social process. Writers must be aware of their audiences, and writers ought to reflect continuously on who their audiences will be once their works are complete. During the action research project, Katie encouraged her students to reflect on their purposes and their audiences so that her students could convey their research findings in the ways that they believed were most appropriate.

Wiggins (2009), Wiggins and McTighe (2005), and Atwell (1998) each stressed the importance of writing for particular audiences and engaging students in the writing process. In designing this new approach to inquiry, Katie anticipated that her students would address social issues of importance to them and, through reading and exploring their topics via a variety of viewpoints, collaborate with one another. She also speculated that her students would increase their understanding of rhetorical devices such as ethos, pathos, and logos, and apply those devices to their own writing.

In addition to its social and collaborative nature, the action research project was positioned within critical literacy. From past experiences in teaching the research paper and from students' written and oral responses to writing assignments, Katie understood that students engaged more completely in the research process when they deliberately and actively interacted with information versus neutral researchers who simply relayed static information to the reader (Greene, 2011). Consequently, she encouraged her students to work collaboratively to analyze authors' purposes, rhetorical strategies, and technical writing throughout the action research process.

Design of the research project

As a teacher with a socially conscious perspective and a desire to support students of all abilities, backgrounds, languages, and experiences, Katie wanted this inquiry project to become more than just written text on paper. With an eye toward critical literacy, Katie knew that these projects had the potential to demonstrate that students met the English language arts standards while, at the same time, they were learning about and addressing social changes in the community. It was out of this critical perspective that this action research project arose.

Prewriting activities

To connect the students' experiences to this project, Katie asked them to complete a Standards-Based Pre-Writing Survey which addressed the NCTE/IRA Standards. Students responded to eleven items and indicated the degree to which they understood the writing process: "Strongly Agree," "Agree," "Disagree," and "Strongly Disagree." From this survey, Katie learned that 79% of her students strongly or mostly agreed that they understood what it meant to write for a purpose, while only 52% responded that they felt comfortable using traditional rhetorical strategies. Seventy-eight percent agreed that different types of writing required different manuscript forms, but only 51% felt confident that they could produce a technical document. Based on information gathered in this survey, Katie designed an action research project that synthesized the eleven areas in the prewriting survey. The project had three major foci: (1) writing for a purpose (2) using the various rhetorical strategies of narration, exposition, persuasion, and description in writing research, and (3) producing a technical document.

Katie started the unit by describing an overview of the research process: that this research would be collaborative and conducted in small groups, and that the research would focus on social issues in their community. Katie explained that at the end of the unit, each small group would disseminate their individual and collective findings through a multimedia project such as a small journal, magazine, or newspaper, or media presented by the group.

Each class generated lists of "researchable" topics they wished to investigate. Students also discussed to what extent they would be able to locate information in a range of print-based and electronic-based resources. Interestingly, each of the classes eventually settled on the same six topics: music, sports, celebrities, business, fashion, and technology.

In order to create groups of four, Katie assigned each student a number. After all of the students in the class received a number, she drew numbers at random. When she called a student's number, the student selected one of the six topics. When four students had signed up for the topic, the topic was no longer available as an area for research.

The research process

Once the groups were formed, each designed a guiding research question based on the general topic. For example, in one of Katie's classes, the music group decided to research the question, "Who Wrote Only One-Hit Wonders?" Students generated researchable areas within this question. For example, in this group, each student researched a music artist or group who had only one famous song. As each of the students researched individual

TABLE 1. Standards-Based Pre- and Post-Writing Survey and NCTE/IRA Standards

Standard(s)	Next to each statement please write 1 for "Strongly Agree", 2 for "Agree", 3 "Disagree", or 4 for "Strongly Disagree"
NCTE/IRA4	I know what it means "to write for a purpose".
NCTE/IRA 11	I participate in class discussions.
NCTE/IRA 6	I produce writing that establishes an appropriate organizational structure, sets a context and engages the reader.
NCTE/IRA 4,6	My writing maintains a coherent focus throughout, and has a clear conclusion.
NCTE/IRA 5	I understand the manuscript form, and that different forms of writing require different formats.
NCTE/IRA 7,8	I use technology to support my writing.
NCTE/IRA 5	I can compose a technical document
NCTE/IRA 5	I use the writing process to develop, revise, and evaluate my writing.
NCTE/IRA 4	I realize that the proper use of the English language involves the appropriate application of conventions and grammar.
NCTE/IRA 8,11	I deliver focused, coherent, and polished presentations that convey a clear and distinct perspective, and demonstrate solid reasoning.
NCTE/IRA 5	I combine traditional rhetorical strategies of narration, exposition, persuasion, and description in my presentations.

artists, the group's members shared information with one another and helped each other locate print-based and electronic-based information.

As the students continued their research, the groups generated several documents: a proposal explaining the group's interest in the topic and the general research question, the preliminary research findings, and how the research would benefit the class and the community. For example, members in the "One-Hit Wonders" inquiry group indicated that each member played an instrument and that the members did not want to suffer the fate of producing only one great song. Their preliminary research findings helped them focus their proposal on the biographies of "one-hit wonder" artists and their songs. Group members also agreed that they could include a range of media in their presentation in the way of music, lyrics, and song lists. The proposal enabled each group to set a purpose for individual and collective research while staying focused on the research process.

Katie noted that in the research process, students were more articulate in their ability to describe their purpose and focus. For example, one student from a group that researched influential musicians focused her inquiry on Michael Jackson. She explains her reasoning in her section of her small group's proposal:

> Our group's topic is "The Most Definitive Music Group/Artist in the Past Century," which immediately led me to think about Michael Jackson. I chose Michael Jackson for three main reasons, and because of those three reasons, I believe my research will benefit the class. Jackson was, hands-down, the "King of Pop," and ever since the genre's creation, pop music has influenced our culture greatly. Secondly, Jackson's an interesting enigma, not only was he thrown into the music business at a very young age, but he branched out and became a hit. And lastly, his music is simply amazing. He has affected so many people, that I just *have* to research him.

This student's ability to define her research aims offered her a way to expedite her inquiry throughout the research process. This initial proposal continued to inform her research as she revisited her proposal each week.

Throughout the unit, students continued to conduct research and, at times, interviewed subjects if it suited the students' purposes. In order to help students employ the various rhetorical strategies of narrative, exposition, and persuasion, each group disseminated the group's collective and individual findings through the creation of a publication (e.g., a small journal, magazine, or newspaper). In order to assess students individually, each student also summarized his/her findings in a separate written abstract that accompanied the group's final project.

In addition to interacting with the research process, students also explored their roles as members of various school and local communities. As part of the proposal, students were asked to identify a charity or foundation that could be linked to their research topic. For example, the members of the music group identified particular charity concerts at which their artists had performed. Another group, who chose to research sports injuries, decided to include information about a local, not-for-profit spinal cord rehabilitation center that assisted people with serious injuries. Students were asked to include information about the charities or foundations in their final presentation in order to increase awareness among their peers and to situate their learning as meaningful. As a result, students were encouraged to research for a critical purpose—a purpose which supports organizations that rely on community involvement. They researched from a critical perspective with a conscious awareness of the organization to which this inquiry would matter. Katie discovered that many students enjoyed this particular part of the research process. "I am glad you asked us to research a charity," shared the student who researched sports injuries. "I decided after the project to volunteer at the center to help people who have sports injuries. I wouldn't have known about the center unless I did my research."

Other groups, however, had a difficult time locating charities or foundations that linked to their topics. One group, researching a large automotive corporation, resigned themselves to the fact that the company did not, as they stated, actively participate in charitable opportunities. "They give away money, but that's it," one student claimed in a group conversation, "but they do not *do* anything." Although disappointed, students learned from these experiences as well. Katie's students realized that they held personal assumptions about their topics and that they, themselves, place relative importance on social participation and civic responsibility.

The final steps

In order to help the students maintain their purposes throughout the unit, each group regularly reflected on the purpose, audience, and format for their journal, magazine, or newsletter. While many groups (such as the "One-Hit Wonders" music group) did not need to significantly revise their topics, a few groups did as they delved deeper into their research. For example, one of the technology groups proposed researching the "Best Inventions of the Century," but soon discovered that the topic was too broad. The group settled on researching "Best Inventions of the 2000s." As the unit drew to a close, each group presented its journal, magazine, or newsletter to the class, identified the best audience for their projects, and explained why they chose the format that they did for disseminating the group's findings.

The results

After the research unit ended, Katie asked each student to respond again to the same Standards-Based Writing Survey they had taken at the start of the action research project. However, in addition to the Likert items used in the initial survey, the postwriting survey included open-ended questions which invited students to write comments in response to the action research process. As Katie analyzed the data, she paid particular attention to the statements related to writing for a purpose; identifying an audience; using rhetorical devices for narrative, expository, and descriptive writing; and writing a technical report.

An analysis of this survey indicated that the action research project increased students' understandings of writing for a purpose, writing for an audience, and using rhetorical strategies. After completing the research paper project, 92% of Katie's students agreed that they understood what it meant to write for a purpose and, most notably, 82% agreed that they felt comfortable using traditional rhetorical strategies. In addition, the analysis indicated that that 91% percent of Katie's students agreed that different types of writing required different manuscript forms; and 85% now felt confident that they could produce a technical document.

Open-ended comments supported the numerical findings. "The process taught me a lot about technical writing," wrote one student, "and how to cite using MLA format." Another student commented on the small group structure and the opportunities for students to choose from different topics. "I liked working in small groups because it helped with our discussions," he wrote, "and I felt that the [research] process was helpful because we didn't just get a grade for the final essay. I enjoyed this project because we could choose topics that we found interesting."

The redesigned research paper as an action project also had a quantitative impact. The small group scores, on average, were nine points higher than the individual research papers submitted the previous year, rising from a 79 to an 88 (based on 100%), and working in groups increased the rate of on-time project submissions. In years past, handfuls of students asked for extra time or turned in their papers late. This year, only one group (out of thirty-one) asked for additional time.

In this era of neoliberalism—when everything is measured and commodified—schools are pressured to produce data that show that students have demonstrated "competence" or "mastery" on a standardized test. But what is most important to us is that students became aware of how to do their own research and, of equal importance, how it could have an impact on their community. When students volunteer to assist community organizations as a result of their action research, it serves as testament to the power of the writing process, the power of collaboration, and the power of choice within the classroom. We also want to reconsider how this research mandate can impact the community in more substantive ways. Although this project did not start out with an aim for social action, the implementation of the research guidelines enabled the students to direct their interests and energies toward social awareness and social justice.

As we reflected on ways to improve this unit of instruction—reconceptualizing a research project that invites social action—we suggest the following: invite students to walk around and study their neighborhoods, to take pictures and video shorts of areas that they believe are issues of concern to their community; and have them share these snapshots and observations with the rest of the class. By identifying issues of concern in their communities and creating multimedia projects that demonstrate the need for social action, students can engage in research that does so much more than "meet a standard." It is research that is relevant, life changing, and life affirming.

Conclusion

While the research paper may always elicit some moans and groans from students, the process does not have to be disengaging. While Katie's students worked in groups and wrote for particular audiences, her students learned to view writing as a social process. And, while April may continue to tease us with promises of Spring Break and warmer weather, the month also provides the perfect environment in which to plant the seeds of engagement, collaboration, and social change.

References

Albers, P. (2004). Literacy in art: A question of responsibility. *Democracy and Education, 15*(3–4), 32–41.

Albers, P., Vasquez, V., & Harste, J.C. (2011). Making visual analysis critical. In D. Lapp & D. Fisher (Eds.). *Handbook of research on teaching the English language arts* (3rd ed.). (pp. 195–201). New York, NY: Routledge.

Atwell, N. (1989). *In the middle: New understandings about writing, reading, and learning*. Portsmouth, NH: Boynton/Cook.

Britton, J., Burgess, T., Martin, N., McLeod, A., & Rosen, H. (1975). *Development of writing abilities (11–18)*. London, England: Macmillan.

Burke, C., & Short, K. (1991). *Creating curriculum: Teachers and students as a community of learners*. Portsmouth, NH: Heinemann.

Christenbury, L. (1994). *Making the journey. Being and becoming a teacher of English language arts*. Portsmouth, NH: Heinemann.

Doering, A., Beach, R., O'Brien. (2007). Infusing multi-modal tools and literacies into an English education program. *English Education, 40*(1), 41–60.

Emig, J. (1971). *The composing processes of twelfth graders*. Urbana, IL: The National Council of Teachers of English.

Flower, L. (2003). Talking across difference: Intercultural rhetoric and the search for situated knowledge. *College Composition and Communication, 55*(1), 38–68.

Flower, L., & Hayes, J. R. (1981). A cognitive process theory of writing. *College Composition and Communication. 32*(4), 365–387.

Greene, K. (2010). From reluctance to results: A veteran teacher embraces Research. *English Journal, (99)*3, 91–94.

Greene, K. (2011). The power of reflective writing. *English Journal, (100)*4, 91–94.

Hagood, M.C., Stevens, L.P., & Reinking, D. (2003). What do THEY have to teach US? Talkin' 'cross generations! In D. Alvermann (Ed.), *Adolescents and literacies in a digital world* (pp. 68–83). New York: Peter Lang.

Harste, J. C. (2003). What do we mean by literacy now? *Voices in the Middle, 10*(3), 8–12.

Harste, J. Short, K., & Burke, C. (1987). Creating classrooms for authors and inquirers. Portsmouth, NH: Heinemann.

Hume, A. (1983). Research on the composing process. *Review of Educational Research, 53*, 201–216.

Janks, H. (2000). Domination, access, diversity, and design: A synthesis for critical literacy education. *Education Review, 52*(2), 175–186.

Knobel, M., & Lankshear, C. (2008). Remix: The art and craft of endless hybridization. *Journal of Adolescent and Adult Literacy, 52*(1), 22–33.

Lankshear, C., & Knobel, M. (2007). Sampling "the new" in new literacies. In M. Knobel, & C. Lankshear, (Eds.) *A new literacies sampler* (pp. 1–24). New York, NY: Peter Lang.

Lewison, M., Leland, C., & Harste, J.C. (2008). *Creating critical classrooms: K–8 reading and writing with an edge*. Mahwah, NJ: Lawrence Erlbaum.

Shannon, P. (1993). Developing democratic voices. *The Reading Teacher, 47*(2), 86–95.

Shannon, P. (1995). *Text, lies, & videotape*. Portsmouth, NH: Heinemann.

Vasquez, V. (2004). *Negotiating critical literacies with young children*. Mahwah, NJ: Lawrence Erlbaum.

Wiggins, G. (2009). Real-world writing: Making purpose and audience matter. *English Journal, 98* (5), 29–37.

Wiggins, G., & McTigh, J. (2005). *Understanding by Design*. (2nd ed.). Upper Saddle River: Prentice Hall, 2005.

Writing Study Group of the NCTE Executive Committee. 2004. NCTE Beliefs about the Teaching of Writing. October 2010. http://www.ncte.org/positions/statements/writingbeliefs?source=gs

13. Traditional Language Arts Viewed through a Media Lens: Helping Secondary Students Develop Critical Literacy with Media Literacy Education

KATHY GARLAND & MARION MAYER

Classroom lessons: Introduction

Culturally relevant pedagogy can bridge the gap between students' socially and culturally acquired knowledge and the academic concepts they are expected to learn in school settings (Banks, 1994; Delpit, 1995; Gay, 2000; Ladson-Billings, 1994). Oftentimes, social and cultural backgrounds refer to students' ethnicity, race, gender, or socio-economic status. However, scholars have suggested that media, such as popular culture, is such a ubiquitous presence in students' social and cultural lives that it should also be considered culturally relevant (Banks, 1994; Gay, 2000). Consequently, because of the influence of popular culture, theorists have advocated for the use of media literacy education as culturally relevant pedagogy (Buckingham, 2003; Hobbs, 2007; Morrell, 2004).

Media literacy education is the formal study of media where students "access, analyze, evaluate, and communicate information in a variety of forms, including print and non-print messages" (National Association for Media Literacy Educators, 2011). Though the term "non-print messages" encompasses a variety of multimedia, for this chapter, non-print messages and media refer to popular culture texts, such as films. Accessing, analyzing, and evaluating popular films require students to develop a process for engaging actively with media. Instead of passively viewing films for entertainment purposes, actively engaging with media helps students develop critical literacy—the ability to view everyday texts through multiple points of view (Lewison,

Flint, & Van Sluys, 2002). Although critical literacy is traditionally associated with reading and writing, researchers have documented ways that deconstructing popular culture texts (such as music and films) in classroom settings can help develop critical "readings" (Alvermann, Moon, & Hagood, 1999; Callahan, 2002; Kist, 2005; Morrell, 2004; Morrell & Duncan-Andrade, 2004). Subsequently, deconstructing popular culture texts promotes "critical consciousness," as students develop a new perspective for viewing popular culture (Freire, 1998).

In this chapter, we will (1) provide two standards-based examples for using media literacy education to teach about popular film; (2) illustrate how these culturally relevant methods for teaching about popular film were designed to develop students' critical literacy; (3) describe the results of research that examined students as they participated in formal lessons centered on examining popular film; and (4) reveal students' perceptions about literacy and texts as a result of studying popular culture in academic context.

Background

Pineview High School (a pseudonym) is situated in a rural, north Florida district. The average high-school student population is just below 2,000 and is 92% White, 4% African American, 3% Hispanic, and 1% Asian. Twenty-four percent of the students qualify for free or reduced lunch (Florida Department of Education, 2009).

I (Marty) have taught a range of traditional English language arts classes at Pineview for more than 30 years. However, I have also had the opportunity to teach a course I created called Literature in the Media. The course is an honors English language arts elective that provides an interdisciplinary media literacy education to secondary students by combining state standards in English language arts, theater, visual arts, and music. Pedagogy for this class is supported by a theory of media literacy education and critical literacy. For example, lessons require students to develop a process for recognizing the parallels that exist between print and multimodal texts. What follows are descriptions of two lessons in which students critically analyze film images.

Lesson 1: Deciphering trailer

Getting 21st century children to recognize societal differences is vital to the study of literature. Without an elemental awareness of how social customs which initially appear "stupid" are not, few modern teenagers will give works like *The Great Gatsby* (1925), *The Importance of Being Earnest* (1895), or *Jane Eyre* (1847) the chance they deserve. Students may judge them as irrelevant to their world.

Teaching students to reflect on societal differences and similarities is not difficult if you begin with a visual example. I use movie trailers to demonstrate how easy it is to become aware of instances of societal traits that have changed and those that have remained the same.

I begin by screening the trailers for *The Maltese Falcon* (1941) and *Mission Impossible* (1996), explaining that each starred the heartthrob of its day. When the screenings end, students list differences other than (the obvious) black and white versus color. Their lists usually include the fact that *Falcon* has a lot more printed words and much fewer images while *MI* is a fast-paced collage of images. Questions such as, "What does *Falcon*'s use of printed words suggest about the education level of its audience?" and "Why would the audience for *MI* be initially unimpressed by *Falcon*'s trailer?" led students to note that *Falcon*'s audience was more educated and "could read faster than we can" and that *MI*'s audience had shorter attention spans but could multitask. Class discussion suggested possible rationales for those differences and whether or not one era's audience was "better" than another.

As an extension of this lesson, one could show three versions of *King Kong*: 1933, 1976, and 2005. After airing the trailers, ask the students what differences and similarities they saw and how they would validate those differences and similarities. These could include how the heroines demonstrated differences in female strengths and weaknesses appropriate to the movie's original audience as well as how the portrayals of the natives and King Kong reflected what audiences considered "realism in film." For another lesson extension, air trailers for *The Road to Zanzibar* (1941), *A Shot in the Dark* (1964), and *Ratatouille* (2007), asking students to consider how comedy has and has not changed over time and what those changes suggest about the respective social milieu.

NCTE/IRA STANDARD	FLORIDA DOE STANDARDS
• Students read a wide range of print and non-print texts to build an understanding of texts, of themselves, and of the cultures of the United States and the world; to acquire new information; to respond to the needs and demands of society and the workplace; and for personal fulfillment. Among these texts are fiction and nonfiction, classic and contemporary works	Florida LA.910.2.1.8 and LA.1112.2.1.8 (FCAT 2.0): The student will explain how ideas, values, and themes of a literary work often reflect the historical period in which it was written. Florida LA. 910.2.1.9 (FCAT 2.0): The student will identify, analyze and compare the differences in English language patterns and vocabulary choices of contemporary and historical texts

Figure 1.

Lesson 2: Genre murals as symbols

The concept of genre seems simple but it is not. Superficially, it is a methodology for categorizing literature and other art forms using *conventional* standards. This is problematic because what constitutes "conventional" in one era does not constitute it in another. Just think of the changes in broadcast television fare and commercials in the last 30 years! Encouraging students to consider genre offers an exercise enabling them to perceive examples of shades of meanings as well as develop rationales for assigning symbols to those meanings.

Begin by screening this statement, "Several thousand years ago the Chinese philosopher Confucius is reputed to

NCTE/IRA STANDARD	FLORIDA DOE STANDARDS
Students apply a wide range of strategies to comprehend, interpret, evaluate and appreciate texts. They draw on their prior experience, their interactions with other readers and writers, their knowledge of word meaning and of other texts, their word identification strategies and their understanding of textual features.	• LA. 910.2.1.4 (FCAT 2.0): The student will identify and analyze universal themes and symbols across genres and historical periods, and explain their significance. • LA.910.2.1.7 (FCAT 2.0): The student will analyze, interpret, and evaluate an author's use of descriptive language, figurative language (e.g., symbolism, metaphor, personification, hyperbole).

Figure 2.

have noted that 'A picture is worth 10,000 words.'" Next screen an image of a woman or child screaming and have a short discussion about the "why" and the "what" of that open mouth: Screaming? Yelling? Fearful? Excited? Exuberant? You will discover myriad possibilities offered by your students, probably not the 10,000 suggested by Confucius but enough to make the point that a single image can generate multiple meanings. (Note: I found wonderful images at Creative Commons and Flikr.)

Now, bring the discussion to task by defining "genre" for your students and having them compile a class list of their favorite ones. (Though film genres were necessary for my class, you could ask for a genre list more compatible with your classroom situation: books, video games, television shows, toys, etc.) My students generally end up with about 10–15 categories resembling those listed on CreateYourScreenplay.com's Movie Genres Chart. Next, break the class into small groups that will each generate a list of 3–5 examples for every genre. Post the shared lists around the room and invite each group to defend its examples. The subsequent discussion emphatically demonstrates the concept of shades of meaning as varied groups categorize *Bad Boys* (1995) as a comedy, crime film, buddy film, or action film.

Have the student groups choose one genre they wish to explore. Do this during a class discussion so each group knows the others' genres and there is no duplication. Give the groups time to come to consensus about the Top 10 films, books, games (whatever your topic is) that identify their genre over a span of time. My students had to use films spanning a minimum of 20 years.

After a discussion of symbols and imagery in film, each group creates a list of 5–10 images that metaphorically captures the essence of each of their Top 10 films. When the lists are completed, I screen the famous *Greetings from Austin* mural that has inspired so many signs and postcards and tell the students they are to apply that mural concept to their chosen genre by spelling their genre in outline letters on a 4' x 6' sheets of paper and filling in each letter with at least one image from a film from their Top 10 list. I request one film per letter. No text is allowed. If they chose wisely and illustrate effectively, then students around the school would be able to recognize the films when the murals were hung outside the cafeteria. The project takes a long time to complete but the results are amazing. On Mural Hanging Day, each group hangs its mural and delivers an oral report defining their genre, delineates its rationale(s) for the films it selected, and explains the metaphors inherent in the symbols and images used to "capture the genre essence" of each film. Also, each student submits an individually written reflection responding to two prompts: "Rationalize three images you would have used instead of the ones chosen by your group" and "Explain whether or not your personal definition of this genre was altered by this project." The two examples below illustrate how students interpreted the "ACTION" genre project.

Conducting research: The ACTION mural

In 2009, I (Kathy) was able to capture how the students who created the 2009 ACTION mural (Figure 4) participated during the Genre Mural project that Marty noted in the first section. My study was designed with students' voices in mind. While other examinations of media literacy education in language arts classes have focused on either the teacher or the pedagogy (Alvermann, Moon, & Hagood, 1999; Callahan, 2002; Kist, 2005; Morrell, 2004), my research presents an understanding of how secondary students participate when formally studying popular culture text. This study also highlights students' views of learning about media texts as a literacy activity. To understand how students participated during the Genre Mural project, I collected data from several sources (videotaped and audiotaped observations, a weekly media diary and curricular artifacts). A description of each data source follows:

Observations. Classroom observations formed the base of my examination of the students. Observing students as they participated in classroom activities allowed me to view the classroom context in ways that the participants may

Figure 3. 2008 ACTION mural

Figure 4. 2009 ACTION mural

not have been able to describe fully (Patton, 2002). Each classroom observation was videotaped and audiotaped in order to capture student discussions and actions. My goal was to be noninvasive, so I would speak with students before and after class, and I did not contribute to lessons.

Media Diaries. Media diaries were composition notebooks that I provided for each student to reflect on lessons centered on popular culture. The first question: "How do you define literacy?" required that students create their own operational definition. However, subsequent media diary questions prompted them to relate the previous week's lessons with their initial (and sometimes shifting) conceptions of literacy.

Curricular Artifacts. Curricular artifacts were materials generated as a result of curricular activities (Pace, 2006, 2009). Because texts were integral to Marty's lessons, curricular artifacts included focus and generative texts. Focus texts such as teacher handouts, Power Points, or film were those used in class to focus instruction. Generative texts, such as Genre Mural posters, were those created by students as a result of instruction.

Literacy practices

Observing the students as they formally examined film genres revealed an understanding that they were either using familiar literacy practices they had developed elsewhere or that they were developing new ways to practice literacy with familiar texts, such as popular film. I noted that students were engaging formally with film images in ways that we, as language arts teachers, expect with traditional texts. Therefore, a combination of media literacy education theory (Hobbs, 1996) and research (Pace, 2009), the National Council of Teachers' definition for 21st Century Literacies (2008), and critical theory (Freire, 1998; Kellner & Share, 2005) informed the categories for literacy practices that I used to describe students' engagement with film.

Media literacy education theory and research have suggested that media literacy education can support students' use of analytical, interpretive, evaluative, and communicative literacy practices (Aufderheide, 1993; Hobbs, 1996; Pace, 2009). Consequently, literacy organizations such as NCTE have begun to recognize the importance of including lessons about media in the traditional language arts classroom. This organization believes that language arts instruction should include teaching methods that require students to "create, critique, analyze, and evaluate multi-media texts" (NCTE 21st Century Literacies Framework, retrieved in 2011; published in 2008), resulting in a 21st century literate student. Critical theorists have suggested that students who develop new perspectives on how to use texts in social and cultural settings can develop critical literacy (Freire, 1998; Kellner & Share, 2005). Critical literacy is a process that includes developing critical consciousness, an awareness for how new perspectives for using texts shape existing understandings. Data analyses suggested that the ACTION genre group used and developed the literacy practices described in Table 1. The following section provides isolated descriptions of how each group member used and developed the five practices. It should be noted that oftentimes students used and developed multiple literacy practices simultaneously.

The ACTION group

Four students chose to represent the ACTION genre visually. Three 12th graders, Devina, Shean, and Brandon, were each in the Drama Club. Between the extracurricular activities of the Drama Club and their outside engagement with popular culture, these students had a wealth of popular film knowledge. An 11th grader, Adam, also possessed an impressive range of popular film knowledge. He had an older brother who introduced him to classic movies and a younger sister who asked him to watch movies with her. While Devina and Brandon had completed previous group assignments together, the Genre Mural project was the first opportunity for the four to collaborate. For this project, students followed two general rules to convey their visual message on a 4' x 6' poster:

- The only printed letters allowed on the poster were the title of the genre.

- Popular culture texts had to be recognizable films.

These two rules implied an expectation of intertextuality. Students would have to think of a popular film that would embody a specific genre, and they were also required to represent identifiable letters of the genre. For these students, communicating the ACTION genre with recognizable visual images for their high school peers became more prevalent than other literacy practices. For this chapter, the group's literacy practices are described as separate categories. However, analytical, interpretive, and evaluative practices became imbedded within the communicative practices students used to

TABLE 1. Defining the ACTION Genre: One Group's Literacy Practices

Literacy Practices

Analytical Practices
- Students apply formal concepts to texts.
- Students use formal concepts to examine texts.

Communicative Practices
- Students create multimodal texts for a specific audience.
- Students sequence and organize ideas to convey messages.

Interpretive Practices
- Students develop a process for responding to texts.
- Students construct meaning from texts.

Evaluative Practices
- Students value and judge the meaning of texts within existing understandings.
- Students value and judge the meaning of texts as they participate in formal study of such texts.

Critical Literacy Practices
- Students develop an awareness of the constructed nature of texts.
- Students develop the ability to question the power of texts in shaping social and cultural views.
- Students' new perspectives of texts empower them to actively engage with such texts.

design their genre mural. Subsequently, as students became more aware of ways to manipulate visual texts, they developed a critical consciousness. However, because a student's critical consciousness is not tangible, critical literacy practices are revealed by how Adam, Shean, and Devina discussed the project in their media diaries. Brandon chose not to participate in this research component.

Analytical practices

Analytical practices illustrate how students used the concept of genre to categorize visual media. The Genre Mural project required the group to develop their own concept of what constitutes an *action* movie. On the first day, each group member brought printouts of film they believed represented the ACTION genre. Students drew on existing understandings of popular culture and suggested films such as *Watchmen* (2009), *Spiderman* (2002), *Quantum of Solace* (2008), and *xXx* (2002). There was little questioning *if* each movie was representative of the ACTION genre; the group's problem was rooted in how to communicate accurately their ACTION genre message to their high-school peers. Students were familiar with using analytical practices. They had been introduced to concepts of genre and were able to apply the concept to specific categories of film. The next section differs because students had to develop communicative practices in order to express their message to the high school audience.

Communicative practices

Communicative practices require students to convey organized multimodal messages to a specific audience, in this case, the general high school population. Adam and Shean had never used film images to communicate meaning. Therefore, the following exemplifies how they developed communicative practices for this project. On the first day of production Adam brainstormed ways to organize popular film images to convey letters. He suggested that the group think of single popular film images that could symbolize each letter of the word *action*. For example, a Spiderman image would represent "N." This led to the use of a "007" image to represent the dot for the letter "i" in the word *action*. The next day, Adam was skeptical about using the image because students could misinterpret the letter as a capital "E." Adam had a valid concern. Misinterpreting the letter could lead to a misinterpretation of the word *ACTION* because it would be read as *ACTEON*, resulting in a misconception of the overall message. Adam expressed his concern for how the audience would interpret the image and the letter "i." The following conversation ensued:

Adam: What's a movie we can use the dot for?

Shean: Ah. *The Mortal Kombat* sign for the "i." We can use the *Mortal Kombat* sign.

Adam: We're gonna do the *Mortal Kombat* sign for the I. (referring to the dot over the "i")

Shean's proposal of the popular action film *Mortal Kombat* (1995) was appropriate for two reasons; it was one circle or "dot" that Adam was searching for to present a lowercase "i," and it was an action movie that accurately represented the way they defined the ACTION genre. The group used the *Mortal Kombat* image as a representation of both a dot for a lowercase "i" and a popular culture film that supported this group's concept of *action*. The criteria for the Genre Mural project helped students develop communicative practices because they were expected to create an unfamiliar text (the word *action* without words) using only multimodal texts (images of film) in order to communicate a message ("these are action films") to their high school peers. The following section describes how students used interpretive practices as a method for creating a recognizable message.

Interpretive practices

Interpretive practices require students to make meaning from texts. The group also had to consider how the audience would interpret the representation of genre. Interpretive practices became problematic for the group when Brandon suggested they re-create the symbols from the popular film *The Matrix* (1999). Using *The Matrix* was challenging because the group had various interpretations of the symbols in that film. Brandon interpreted the symbols as letters and numbers while Shean interpreted them as Japanese characters. Several days into the project, Brandon brought in a copy of *The Matrix* symbols and the group discussed how to use visual details to interpret the signs. Brandon reiterated that the symbols were letters and numbers; Shean was adamant that "They are not even letters." The group recognized they had conflicting understandings, and that these differences would affect creating an accurate portrayal. How could they create an organized, visual representation for others to read and interpret if they could not accurately read and interpret the visual text?

Devina: So, how are we doing this?

Brandon: I have absolutely no clue.

Shean: Draw random letters slash numbers?

Adam: Take this and do lines. Like lines down here and paint it black and make it look like letters.

Devina's initial question moved the conversation back to communicative practices; she was really asking how the group will organize the symbols for others to interpret. Adam's answer provided a solution for both the problem of interpretation and of organization. His suggestion indicated the group could organize the multimodal texts to resemble *The Matrix* symbols. This organization served as a guide for the audience to match the group's interpretation. Adam implied that it was more important for the group to organize *The Matrix* characters in a way that appeared like symbols rather than for the group to actually decipher the signs. This example illustrates how important it was to begin with interpretive practices. Students used interpretive practices as a method for constructing meaning from the symbols. Although the use of interpretive practices yielded different results, the group was able to determine an effective method for helping the intended audience match each group member's interpretation. The following section describes how the group developed ways for comparing texts.

Evaluative practices

The ability to juxtapose existing understandings of texts with new interpretations underscores the importance of evaluative practices. Juxtaposing texts in this way is also referred to as intertextuality. The group's secondary goal of symbolizing each letter with one film created an element of intertextuality because each member had to compare film images as action movies (existing understandings) and as representative of letters (new interpretations). Consequently, conversations similar to the following occurred:

Shean:	I'm trying to see if I can do a Greek column that's an "I."
Adam:	That's fine. Isn't there a Greek movie that's an action movie?
Shean:	*300*.
Brandon:	Yeah.

This brief conversation illustrates the intertextual connections that supported Adam's and Shean's use of evaluative practices. Initially, Shean drew on his existing understandings of Greek architecture to describe how he would represent the letter "I" in the word *action* as part of the poster. Adam acknowledged that Shean's connection was a good idea, but that it wasn't a movie. Shean acknowledged Adam's question and then drew on his existing concepts of popular culture to propose the popular film *300* (2007). In this exchange, the students used their existing understandings of movies to judge an appropriate movie that would fit the criteria of genre that the group had conceptualized and one that would fit in with the use of a Greek column for the letter "I" in the visual. The film *300* was appropriate in that it was an *action* movie and could accurately represent an "I." Students had no experience with judging how well a film's image could represent a letter. As a result, evaluative practices were developed in similar ways throughout the Genre Mural project. In the final section, three group members describe how they had developed critical literacy practices as a result of this project.

Critical literacy practices

Critical literacy practices refer to the new perspectives students develop as a result of studying how texts are constructed to shape societal and cultural views. These practices also describe the ways that students are empowered as they develop new perspectives for using texts in their lives. As described earlier, students created their own operational definitions for literacy, and the media diary entries required students to re-examine their definitions. The media diary responses provided a way for me to "see" students' emerging perceptions about literacy, and thus understand how they were developing critical literacy practices. Excerpts from Devina's, Shean's and Adam's media diary responses before and during the Genre Mural project provided commentary about their ACTION poster and its role in helping them to develop literacy practices or concepts about literacy.

> *Media Diary Question #6: How is the current project you're working on helping you understand media? How is it helping you become more literate?*

Adam: By forcing me to analyze movies, it is helping me see movies in a different light. Helping me be [*sic*] more literate.

Devina: It opens our view of the vast variety of things there are in one genre.

Shean: On the genre project I am working on right now, I am seeing how visual representation can take the place of words.

These three group members describe developing a new perspective for interpreting and constructing visual media. Adam's answer suggests that he has used analytical practices that have helped ("forced") him to view film differently. Devina began to recognize genre as fluid concept, as opposed to a static category (Dean, 2008). Shean's new perception is one of semiotics; he now perceives similarities between visual and printed texts. These responses suggest that as students developed new understandings about media, they began to equate shifting understandings with a form of literacy.

> *Media Diary Question #7: Aside from the title of your genre, you cannot use any words to represent the genre. If there are no words, how is what you've created an example of literacy?*

Adam: Literacy is being able to comprehend what is in front of you whether it's words or images. This assignment assesses are [*sic*] comprehension of not only the genre but our definition as well. In our group we have Action and all the images represent those words that would describe the genre to us.

Devina: Literacy is defined as the understanding of knowledge. The project we did shows that we understand what we are doing. We understood what movies were classified under our genre. It is an example because we are creating examples of what we have learned and displaying it as a type of media.

Shean: It is an example of literacy because it still requires analytical skill to read what the images express.

Each student uses terminology typically associated with reading alphabetic symbols, even though their work was primarily centered on organizing visual texts. Adam suggests that the group has proven its "comprehension" of the ACTION genre by providing accurate images for others to interpret. In his view, the project is an example of literacy. Devina chooses the terms "knowledge" and "understand" to describe how completing the genre mural exemplifies literacy. From her perspective, gaining knowledge and understanding of how to communicate their media genre visually equals literacy. Shean's terms "analytical skill" and "reading" explain how their project demonstrates literacy. His word choice demonstrates that one can analyze and read visual texts, and that these skills demonstrate one's literacy. Students understand that being literate requires one to read different types of texts that may include visual images. Each student recognized the power of using visual images to convey messages. Subsequently, their responses indicate that they began to see how literacy is socially and culturally constructed.

Conclusion

The lessons described in this chapter address both the NCTE/IRA and Florida Department of Education Standards. With increasing nationwide adoption of the Common Core State Standards and Race to the Top initiatives, it seems that standards-based education and high-stakes testing are permanent fixtures in education. However, unlike prior state standards, each state's Common Core Standards illustrate components that value the importance of media literacy education. For example, a close look at the *Reading Standards for Literature* indicates that students are required to evaluate similarities and differences between print and film versions of stories. The *Media and Technology* strand suggests that it is integral for students to analyze aspects of media (Common Core State Standards, 2011). We are not advocating for the standardization of language arts instruction because of the unintended consequences of such a policy. However, we hope that the standards-based lessons and the descriptions of literacy practices that we have provided strengthen language arts teachers' rationale as a way to use standards *for* their secondary students.

References

Alvermann, D. E., Moon, J. S., & Hagood, M. C. (1999). *Popular culture in the classroom: Teaching and researching critical media literacy.* Newark, DE: International Reading Association.

Aufderhide, P. (1993). Media literacy: A report of the National Leadership Council on media literacy. The Aspen Institute Wye Center, Queenstown, MD, December 7–9, 1992. Washington, DC: Aspen Institute.

Banks, J. (1994). *An introduction to multicultural education.* Needham, MA: Allyn and Bacon, Inc.

Buckingham, D. (2003). *Media education: Literacy, learning, and contemporary culture.* Malden, MA: Polity Press.

Callahan, M. (2002). Intertextual composition: The power of the digital pen. *English Education, 35*(1), 46–65.

Common Core State Standards for English Language Arts. Retrieved April 5, 2011, from http://www.corestandards.org/assets/CCSSI_ELA%20Standards.pdf

Dean, D. (2008). *Genre theory: Teaching, writing, an being.* Urbana, IL: National Council of Teachers of English.

Delpit, L. (1995). *Other people's children: Cultural conflict in the classroom.* New York, NY: The New Press.

Florida Department of Education (2009). FCAT scores and report. Retrieved August 24, 2009 from http://feat.fla.e.org/results/default.asp.

Freire, P. (1998). *Pedagogy of freedom.* Lanham, MD: Rowman & Littlefield.

Gay, G. (2000). *Culturally responsive teaching: Theory, research, and practice.* New York, NY: Teachers College Press.

Hobbs, R. (1996). Expanding the concept of literacy. In R. Kubey (Ed.), *Media literacy in the information age: Current perspectives* (pp. 163–183). New Brunswick, NJ: Transaction Publishers.

Hobbs, R. (2007). *Reading the media: Media literacy in high school English.* New York, NY: Teachers College Press.

Kellner, D., & Share, J. (2005). Toward critical media literacy: Core concepts, debates, organizations, and policy. *Discourse: Studies in the Cultural Politics of Education, 26*(3), 369–386.

Kist, W. (2005). *New literacies in action: Teaching and learning in multiple media.* New York, NY: Teachers College Columbia University.

Ladson-Billings, G. (1994). *The dreamkeepers: Successful teachers of African American children.* San Francisco: Jossey-Bass.

Lewison, M., Flint, A.S., & Van Sluys, K. (2002). Taking on critical literacy: The journey of newcomers and novices. *Language Arts, 79* (5), 382–392.

Morrell, E. (2004). *Linking literacy and popular culture: Finding connections for lifelong learning.* Norwood, MA: Christopher Gordon-Publishers, Inc.

Morrell, E,. & Duncan-Andrade, J. (2004). What they don't learn in school: Hip-hop as a bridge to canonical poetry. In J. Mahiri (Ed.), *What they don't learn in school: Literacy in the lives of urban youth* (pp. 247–268). New York, NY: Peter Lang Publishing.

The National Association for Media Literacy Educators. Retrieved July 27, 2011, from http://namle.net/publications/media-literacy-definitions/

The National Council of Teachers of English Framework for 21st Century Literacies. (2008). Retrieved March 25, 2011, from http://www.ncte.org/positions/statements/21stcentdefinition

Pace, B.G. (2006). Between response and interpretation: Ideological becoming and literacy events in critical readings of literature. *Journal of Adolescent and Adult Literature, 49*(7), 584–594.

Pace, B.G. (2009). Critical connections: Media literacy and transformed practice as learning. Paper presentation at the 2009 National Association of Media Literacy Educators.

Patton, M.Q. (2002). *Qualitative research and evaluation methods.* Thousand Oaks, CA: Sage Publications.

Popular Culture References

Apelian, L., & Kasanoff, L. (Producers), & Anderson, P.W.S. (Director). (1995). *Mortal kombat* [Motion picture]. Argentina: New Line Cinema.

Gordon, L., Levin, L., & Snyder, D. (Producers), & Snyder, Z. (Director). (2009). *Watchmen* [Motion picture]. United States: Warner Bros. Pictures.

Hitchcock, P., Cruise, T., Badra, E., Wagner, P. (Producers), & DePalma, B. (Director). (1996). *Mission: impossible* [Motion picture]. United States: Paramount Pictures.

Jones, P. (Producer) & Schertzinger, V. (Director). (1941) The *road to Zanzibar* [Motion picture]. United States; Paramount Pictures.

Lewis, B., Lasseter, J., Stanton, A., & Susman, G. (Producers), & Pinkava, J., & Bird, B. (Directors). (2007). *Ratatouille.* [Motion picture]. United States; Walt Disney Pictures.

Miller, F., Nunnari, G., Silver, J., Canton, M., & Goldmann, B. (Producers), & Snyder, Z. (Director). (2006). *300* [Motion picture]. United States: Warner Brothers.

Moritz, N.H. (Producer), & Cohen, R. (Director). (2002). *xXx* [Motion picture]. United States: Columbia Pictures.

Silver, J. (Producer), & Wachowski Brothers. (Director). (1999). *The matrix* [Motion picture]. United States: Warner Brothers and Village Roadshow Pictures.

Simpson, D., & Bruckheimer, J. (Producers), & Bay, M. (Director). (1995). *Bad boys* [Motion picture]. United States: Columbia Pictures.

Wallis, H.B. (Producer), & Huston, J. (Director). (1941). *The maltese falcon* [Motion picture]. United States: Warner Bros.

Wilson, M.G., & Broccoli, B. (Producers), & Forster, M. (Director). (2008). *Quantum of solace [Motion picture]. United Kingdom: Metro-Goldwyn-Mayer Columbia Pictures.*

Ziskin, L., Bryce, I., Fugeman, H., Saeta, S.P., Curtis, G., Arad, A., & Lee, S. (Producers), & Raimi, S. (Director). (2002). *Spiderman* [Motion picture]. United States: Columbia Pictures.

Additional Resources for Classroom Lessons

A Shot in the Dark. Trailer. http://www.youtube.com/watch?v=FNNOh4wG7–4 Create Your Own Screenplay Genre Chart. http://www.createyourscreenplay.com/genrechart.htm

Greetings from Austin original mural photograph. http://austintexasdailyphoto.blogspot.com/2009/07/greetings-from-austin.html

King Kong 1933. Trailer. http://www.youtube.com/watch?v=H0WpKl2A_2k

King Kong. 1976. Trailer. http://www.youtube.com/watch?v=aanYNjjoCQo

King Kong. 2005. Trailer. *http://www.youtube.com/watch?v=B5j_2sRUTbU*

The Maltese Falcon. Trailer. http://www.youtube.com/watch?v=yRSCV2qc2IY

Mission Impossible. Trailer. http://www.youtube.com/watch?v=Uks_lHTua30

Ratatouille. Trailer. http://www.youtube.com/watch?v=c3sBBRxDAqk

The Road to Zanzibar. Trailer. http://www.youtube.com/watch?v=0BhR8X-B5Jo

SECTION 4.

Teacher Education:
Modeling Critical Approaches

14. Teaching from the Test: Using High-Stakes Assessments to Enhance Student Learning

Julie A. Gorlewski

Introduction

Prepositions matter. One of my favorite academic cartoons depicts a pig standing on a corner, holding a sign that reads, "Will work as food." The caption offers an ironic epilogue: the pig's grammar mistake led to a position, but not one that he wanted. I generally share this image with my English education students early in the semester, intending to remind them of the importance of accuracy in language—even with seemingly innocuous words like prepositions. A more subtle but equally relevant example of preposition power is reflected in the title of this chapter. Educators—with good reason—bemoan the causes and effects of teaching *to* standardized tests. In this chapter, I explore the considerable possibilities that arise from a shift in the preposition; instead of teaching *to* the test, we can encourage educators to plan instruction with standards and assessments in mind. That is, we can show future educators how to avoid the deleterious consequences of standardization and retain their professional roles by teaching *from* the test.

The purpose of this chapter is to explore how the typically negative effects of standardization on curriculum and instruction can be used to develop critical pedagogies intended to advance student empowerment and promote social justice. Specifically, this chapter describes how I used high-stakes tests to expand (rather than narrow) the curriculum and enhance (rather than inhibit) student learning in a teacher education program.

Context

Despite a wealth of scholarship demonstrating the reductive effects of high-stakes examinations on curriculum and instruction (Hillocks, 2003; Ketter & Pool, 2001; Neill & Gayler, 2001; Nelson, 2001; Nichols & Berliner, 2007; Popham, 2001), in the United States today the trend in education is toward increasing accountability with more and more standardized assessments. These assessments then drive curriculum and instruction (Gorlewski, 2011; Garrison, 2010; Apple, 1996). Although standards, as broad frameworks for setting learning targets, are not necessarily problematic, when they are operationalized as high-stakes assessments, test-based pedagogies emerge and frequently dominate curriculum, leaving little room for construction of knowledge or critical pedagogies. This phenomenon is evident at all educational levels. Energies that might be devoted to social justice and critical pedagogies are drowned in the ocean of norm-referenced data that serve political ends without doing much to improve the teaching/learning process. Legislation that legitimizes testing as the central measure of learning undermines the ability of educational institutions to inspire excellence and ameliorate inequities. In addition, critics maintain that high-stakes assessments serve to perpetuate current class structures by maintaining skill gaps and controlling ideology, particularly beliefs in individualism, meritocracy, and what counts as knowledge (Dorn, 2003; Hillocks, 2002).

The experience described in this chapter began with the results of a critical ethnography I conducted in 2006 which investigated the experiences of students and teachers in a working-class high school. The study consisted of participant and non-participant observation, in-depth semi-structured interviews with 11th grade students and teachers across the four major disciplines (English language arts, social studies, science, and mathematics), and analysis of a wide range of documents created by teachers, administrators, students, and state education department officials. Data analysis, grounded in constant-comparison methodology, indicated that high-stakes standardized assessments resulted in narrowed curriculum, teacher deprofessionalization, and student alienation from schooling. In this K–12 setting, it was clear that teaching to the test, particularly in the area of writing (which connects closely to thinking), had negative effects on student performance, teacher professionalization, and writing instruction.

In an attempt to reduce the effects of standardization, I implemented instructional activities designed to integrate aspects of standardization while simultaneously reinforcing tenets of critical pedagogy, i.e., the awareness that "every dimension of schooling and every form of educational practice are politically contested spaces" (Kincheloe, 2007, p. 2). To be effective, the activities could not be strictly strategic (focused on measuring bits of knowledge easily assessed on multiple choice tests). Addressing student performance from a critical pedagogical perspective required, instead, that students understand that the assessments themselves are socially constructed and that using assessments as means of self-reflection could offer possibilities of bridging the gap between standards and culturally responsive instruction. This view of standardized assessments, grounded in the concept of "resistance literacy" (Gorlewski, 2011), provides a context in which high-stakes tests can be a lever for critical pedagogy—a context that certainly seemed transferable to a higher education classroom.

From K–12 to teacher education

Although I had taught graduate-level teacher education courses on a part-time basis over the previous five years, in 2009 I began teaching full time in a teacher certification program in western New York State. This program had two unique characteristics. First, it was an accelerated, cohort-based program; students began classes in the fall, and—in most cases—were student teaching by the following fall. Second, although the college was a U.S. institution, the cohort was primarily composed of Canadian students, many of whom drove for hours to attend classes.

This college program was particularly attractive to Canadian students who had been closed out of teacher education programs (which were quite selective) in their native country because Ontario (the province from which most of our Canadian students came) accepted New York State teacher certification as equivalent to its own certification. Therefore, if the Canadian students in our program earned New York State certification, they would also be certified to teach in Ontario (which, for most of them, was the ultimate goal).

In addition to course work, to earn state certification in New York, students are required to pass a set of assessments. Generally, the Canadian students who enrolled were solid students who had little difficulty meeting the requirements of our New York State certification program. There was, however, one significant hurdle.

The Content Specialty Test

For these students, New York State certification requisites included three examinations: the Liberal Arts and Sciences Test (LAST), the Assessment of Teaching Skills—Written (ATSW), and the Content Specialty Test (CST). Pearson Education, Inc. (2008) which publishes the assessments as part of its New York State Teacher Certification Examinations™, describes these tests as follows:

> The New York State Teacher Certification Examinations are criterion referenced and objective based. A criterion-referenced test is designed to measure a candidate's knowledge and skills in relation to an established standard rather than in relation to the performance of other candidates. The explicit purpose of these tests is to help identify for certification those candidates who have demonstrated the appropriate level of knowledge and skills that are important for performing the responsibilities of a teacher in New York State public schools. (CITE, p. 2)

The CST, as its name implies, is specific to the core area discipline that adolescent education students intend to teach. Its development and format are explained in the test booklet:

> Each test is designed to measure areas of knowledge called subareas. Within each subarea, statements of important knowledge and skills, called objectives, define the content of the test. The test objectives were developed for the New York State Teacher Certification Examinations in conjunction with committees of New York State educators.
>
> Test questions matched to the objectives were developed using, in part, textbooks; New York State learning standards and curriculum guides; teacher education curricula; and certification standards. The test questions were developed in consultation with committees of New York State teachers, teacher educators, and other content and assessment specialists.
>
> An individual's performance on a test is evaluated against an established standard. The passing score for each test is established by the New York State Commissioner of Education based on the professional judgments and recommendations of New York State teachers. Examinees who do not pass a test may retake it at any of the subsequently scheduled test administrations. (Pearson, 2008, p. 2)

In New York State, the CST is required for certification in the following subject areas:

- Agriculture
- American Sign Language
- Biology
- Blind and Visually Impaired
- Business and Marketing
- Cantonese
- Chemistry
- Dance
- Deaf and Hard of Hearing
- Earth Science
- Educational Technology Specialist
- English Language Arts
- English to Speakers of Other Languages
- Family and Consumer Sciences
- French
- German
- Gifted Education
- Greek
- Health Education
- Hebrew
- Italian
- Japanese
- Latin
- Library Media Specialist
- Literacy
- Mandarin
- Mathematics
- Multi-Subject
- Music
- Physical Education
- Physics
- Russian
- Social Studies
- Spanish
- Students with Disabilities
- Technology Education
- Theatre
- Visual Arts

The graduate students had no difficulty with the LAST and the ATSW; their undergraduate experiences had prepared them well with respect to general studies and literacy skills necessary to achieve a passing score on these examinations. In fact, many students opted to take these exams just after acceptance and had already passed them before taking the methods class I taught. The CST, however, posed a challenge. Despite the fact that these students had earned bachelor's degrees in English, the scope of the exam and its focus on American literature created anxiety that was not entirely without merit. That is, students had reason to be concerned about this exam, since they could not assume that the material it covered would have been included in their English degree programs at Canadian colleges and universities.

Even though students had the option of retaking the exam if they earned an inadequate score, the fee ($79 per administration) and the efforts associated with the test increased anxiety associated with the possibility of failing to achieve certification.

In short, the intent of the test is to serve as an assurance that New York State certified teachers possess and can demonstrate particular sets of knowledges, dispositions, and skills—characteristics that are set forth through the "established standards" claimed by the assessors in their descriptive document. This is certainly a laudable goal; no educator would support the certification of candidates unworthy of the designation. However, in a school of education, we faced a specific, significant challenge as we sought to help our candidates meet the standards meant to be measured by this assessment. Primarily, the challenge involved preparing students for the assessment without resorting to test-prep pedagogy. In fact, I believe that we, in schools of education, have an obligation to model—consistently—critical pedagogies. Therefore, in this class, the challenge for me was to foster critical pedagogies even as we explicitly prepared students for the CST.

Course goals

Since I had no intention of subordinating our program or course goals to the assessment (however positive its intent), I decided to begin instructional planning with the course goals, which had been developed through a collaborative process aligned with Teacher Education Accreditation Council (TEAC) standards. The goals for this course, which was entitled Methods of Adolescence Education: English, were:

Teacher candidates will understand

1. Student diversity and how to be effective with a variety of students.

2. National and State standards and how to build units and lessons that meet these standards.

3. Formative and summative assessment techniques that can be used to guide practice.

4. A wide variety of proven techniques from which to select to teach English effectively.

Naturally, these goals were supported and extended by a detailed set of course objectives—none of which were explicitly aligned with the certification examinations.

The course goals and objectives had been developed in accordance with a set of four claims that the department faculty had composed as part of the accreditation process. These claims were aligned with the guiding principles and the mission of the department, the college, and the accrediting agency.

> Claim 1: (Our) College graduates know the subject matter in their certification area(s).
>
> Claim 2: (Our) College graduates meet the needs of diverse learners through effective pedagogy and Best Teaching Practices.
>
> Claim 3: (Our) College graduates demonstrate scholarship supported by the use of technology.
>
> Claim 4: (Our) College graduates are caring educators.

In addition, the school of education faculty had created a set of common core assessments linked to specific courses. Within the context of the comprehensive program, these assessments were meant to target the specified claims and goals of the department. Common core assessments included a Philosophy of Education, an Annotated Bibliography, a Lesson Plan, and a Unit Plan. Materials associated with the common core assessments incorporated descriptors and rubrics; however, the content allowed for academic freedom with respect to both substance and pedagogical approach. As might be expected, the common core assessments associated with the methods class consisted of lesson plans and a unit plan.

From standards to critical pedagogy

As I began to *think* about planning the course—a component of the process that seems always to precede actual planning by many, many hours—I kept returning to the two aspects of the course and the program over which I had the least control: the certification examinations (in particular, the CST, which related directly to our content area) and the common core assessments. How could I model critical pedagogical practices while ensuring that students adhered to the guidelines necessary for them to succeed at these essential tasks? The answer (or, more accurately, an answer) came to me as I reflected on my experiences in secondary education when I sought to prepare students for mandatory examinations relative to earning a high school diploma without contributing to the alienating, commodifying, and exploitative experiences of learning that standardized assessments tend to foster. Critical approaches that had been effective in this setting included transparent explication of the tasks as the social construction that they are, intentional efforts to explore and validate the knowledges and skills that students bring to the tasks (whether or not these knowledges or skills seem to be valued on the assessments), deliberate exploration of the emotional and social pressures connected to the assessments, and finally—once the cultural considerations have been unpacked and investigated—focused development of the skills necessary to succeed on the assessments. These strategies had worked well with high school students and had allowed me to connect critical pedagogies to standardized requirements without subjugating our identities (mine or my students) to state or institutional mandates. Could these ideas transfer to a graduate-level classroom? And, if so, how?

One of my recurrent professional and personal survival strategies is to seek synergy. If I am in a situation that seems confounding and overwhelming, it feels natural to find connections in order to help organize my thoughts and maximize the effects of my efforts. In this case, a possibility emerged that combined the CST with the common core assessments and was in harmony with the principles of critical pedagogy.

Embracing assessments

In accordance with curriculum planning principles of backward design, I began the semester by presenting the expectations for the course and asking students to identify connections between department claims, course goals, and their aspirations as teacher candidates. Rather than casting the common core assessments (the unit plan and lesson plan) as obstacles or impediments that hindered our ability to engage in effective learning experiences (as such assignments are often portrayed and performed in courses that require them), I introduced the assessments as opportunities for us to demonstrate the learning that would occur over the course of the semester. Furthermore, I organized our instructional activities to support the creation of unit and lesson plans; for example, when we delved into the topic of essential questions, students used the opportunity to craft essential questions related to their unit plans and lesson plans. Each week, students made progress in their understanding of the methods and strategies relative to English language arts in secondary schools, and their progress would be apparent, in part, through the development of their unit plans (of course, other assignments were built into the course, as well, both formative and summative). In addition, we discussed the terminology of the lesson plan and unit plan descriptors and rubrics with respect to the importance of common language, as well as the power relations involved in determining whose language is used. Students applied the rubrics to one another's plans during peer review sessions and, in doing so, cultivated a sense of appreciation for the challenges inherent in the development of such tools. Deep understanding of the core assessments, themselves, assisted student in two ways. First, they demonstrated planning ability and knowledge that went beyond the surface of the assessment expectations. Second, their confidence in their capacities as teachers and learners was strengthened. This increased confidence was expressed in their individual conferences with me, in their final presentations, and in their course evaluations. By rethinking the assignment in terms of its framework, analyzing it as a socially constructed instrument, and focusing on its indefinite spaces—areas that allowed for choice and exploration—I was able to shift the experience from externally focused and restricted, to authentic and purposeful.

It is important to note one significant advantage that contributed to my ability to apply critical pedagogical principles to the unit plan and lesson plan assessments: I was the evaluator of these assignments. Although the documents, along with the completed rubrics, were submitted to the school of education assessment coordinator, I was the final arbiter in terms of the grades that students received on the projects. Therefore, if we, as a class, chose to accept a more inclusive definition of "reflection," for example, I—as the instructor/evaluator—would incorporate that definition in my appraisal of the student work. Unfortunately, such flexibility is utterly absent from a standardized assessment like the CST.

To apply a critical pedagogical approach to the CST required that I bring together my students, the course goals (as addressed through the common core assessments), and the examination, itself. Fortunately, after many stressful hours of deliberation as I planned the course, inspiration struck. And the idea was much simpler than I had ever imagined: I decided to have students incorporate content from the CST into their unit/lesson plans so that their development of these plans would address potential aspects of students' content area deficiency. But how could I make this happen?

On the first day of class, we discussed the requirements of the course and the requirements for New York State certification. Reviewing the expectations for a semester's worth of work, as well as the complex, lengthy regulatory and bureaucratic specifications for certification, is an overwhelming experience for students; however, I believe that knowledge—even knowledge that is intimidating—is always more empowering than ignorance. Furthermore, I was determined to help students develop the confidence and capacity to meet the challenges they faced. Therefore, after introducing the unit plan, I distributed the 59-page Preparation Guide for the English language arts CST.

It is a daunting document. It lists the examination's six subareas:

Subarea I. Listening and Speaking

Subarea II. Writing

Subarea III. Reading

Subarea IV. Fundamentals of Literature

Subarea V. Language and Literature

Subarea VI. Fundamentals of Literature: Constructed-Response Assignment.

These subareas incorporate 24 objectives which are explicated by a series of focus statements. The objectives embody an exceptional range and scope of knowledge, skills, and information. Some are extremely general, such as Objective 0012: Understand writing for literary response and expression; Objective 0007: Understand reading for information and understanding; Objective 0019: Understand literature written for adolescents; and Objective 0017: Understand the characteristic features of various types of nonfiction.

Others are more specific but also comprehensive, such as Objective 0011: Understand the use of reading comprehension strategies; Objective 0015: Understand the historical, social, and cultural aspects of literature, including the ways in which literary works and movements both reflect and shape culture and history; Objective 0022: Understand significant themes, characteristics, trends, writers, and works in American literature from the colonial period to the present, including the literary contributions of women, members of ethnic minorities, and figures identified with particular regions; Objective 0018: Understand the characteristic features of various forms of poetry; and Objective 0024: Understand the literatures of Asia, Africa, continental Europe, Latin America, and the Caribbean, including major themes, characteristics, trends, writers, and works.

Students were understandably frustrated and anxious by the preparation guide, which seemed to warn them that everything that they had ever learned about English—as speakers, listeners, writers, and readers—was fodder for a prospective test question. No one could be expected to demonstrate proficiency in relation to all these objectives and focus statements. How might such a broad content area be focused in order to provide students with strategies to address their deficiencies without destroying their sense of expertise with respect to the assessment? Here's what I did.

After providing a few minutes for students to peruse the guide to sample questions and study tips, I instructed them to read each of the objectives (and its related focus statements) and rank the objectives 1–24 according to the students' sense of their own level of expertise and proficiency. Then I asked them to identify, in their rankings, the lowest 5 objectives and share these objectives aloud with me and their classmates. We discussed overlapping concerns, possible interpretations of overly general objectives, and ways to make the comprehensive objectives manageable. Next, I divided them into groups and asked them to each select one objective, eliminating duplication among group members and taking into consideration our previous class discussion. At the end of this process, each student had identified an objective that addressed a content area deficiency *and*—among our 25 candidates—*all* the CST objectives were accounted for.

Then, and only then, I informed them that each student's self-assigned objective was going to be the focus for his or her unit plan. I must admit that their initial reactions were hardly joyful. Many students admitted that they had envisioned creating unit plans that were devoted to areas of English language arts that reflected their passions, not their deficits. However, once I clarified the purpose of this method of selecting unit plan topics, they appreciated its intent, as well as its promise. If all went well, I informed them, the whole class would benefit from this range of unit plan topics. The advantages of purposeful application of their weakest objective were obvious; they would be immersed in an area in which they were now the least confident. Moreover, as students presented pieces of their units to their classmates over the course of the semester, our learning community would extend its expertise with respect to all the CST objectives.

Remarkably, that is exactly what happened. The unit plans and lesson plans enabled students to develop strengths in matters that many had previously avoided. In addition, the range of topics was broad and offered possibilities for applying methods and strategies that a more restricted set of selections would not have provided. When the course ended, several student comments—in person and on course evaluations—indicated that they were gratified, and even a bit surprised, to learn that they enjoyed a topic they had once disliked. Although they were still anxious about the exam, they were more confident about their ability to pass the CST.

And all of them passed on their first attempt.

Reflection

As enjoyable as it is to report the positive results, it is not the main point of this account. While passing is required to earn certification, passing was not the primary intent of the activities described in this chapter.

To me, what really matters is that teacher candidates experience and develop a critical approach to standardized assessments—wherever they appear.

The work that we did was intended to help students meet—then move beyond—the requirements of these high-stakes standardized assessments. As a result of these approaches, students developed increased confidence and expertise—characteristics that promote performance on assessments without resorting to test-based pedagogies. While the negative effects of standardization are well known, it is sometimes difficult for educators to imagine ways in which resistance can be enacted without dire consequences for teachers and students. Reconsidering our own perceptions of standards as something we can use *with* and *for* our students (rather than *on* or *against* them) enables educators to avoid having our profession devoured by high-stakes assessments.

I hope we can escape the sad fate of the unemployed cartoon pig who offered to work *as* food.

References

Apple, M. W. (1996). *Cultural Politics and Education*. New York: Teachers College Press.

Dorn, S. (2003). High-Stakes Testing and the History of Graduation. *Education Policy Analysis Archives, 11*(1).

Garrison, M. (2009). *A Measure of Failure*. New York: SUNY Press.

Gorlewski, J. (2001). *Power, Resistance, and Literacy: Writing for Social Justice*. Charlotte, NC: Information Age Publishing, Inc.

Hillocks, G. J. (2003). Fighting Back: Assessing the Assessments. *English Journal, 92*(4), 63–70.

Ketter, J., & Pool, J. (2001). Exploring the Impact of Direct Writing Assessment in Two High School Classrooms. *Research in the Teaching of English, 5*, 344–393.

Kincheloe, J. L. (2007). *Critical Pedagogy*. New York: Peter Lang Publishing.

Neill, M., & Gayler, K. (2001). Do High-Stakes Graduation Tests Improve Learning Outcomes? Using State-level NAEP Data to Evaluate the Effects of Mandatory Graduation Tests. In G. Orfield & M. L.

Nelson, G. L. (2001). Writing beyond Testing: "The Word as an Instrument of Creation." *English Journal, 91*(1), 57–61.

Nichols, S. L., & Berliner, D. C. (2007). *Collateral Damage: How High-Stakes Testing Undermines Education*. Cambridge: Harvard Education Press.

Panofsky, C. P. (2004). The Relations of Learning and Student Social Class: Toward Re-Socializing Sociocultural Learning Theory. Retrieved February 11, 2005

Pearson, Inc. (2008). *New York State Teacher Certification Examinations Preparation Guide: English Language Arts CST*. Albany, NY: New York State Education Department.

Popham, W. J. (2001). *The Truth about Testing: An Educators Call to Action*. Alexandria: Association for Supervision and Curriculum Development.

15. *Standardizing Effective Pedagogical Practices*

DAVID A. GORLEWSKI

Teacher educators are in the unique position of being in a continuous state of modeling instruction. After all, we teach about teaching. Whether our instruction is effective or not, it is, nonetheless, being modeled and our students are learning about pedagogy by what we *do* as much as by what we *say*. As pedagogical role models, our own performances are being evaluated by students during each class. We don't get a grade—but we do get judged.

Consequently, it is critically important for us to plan lessons, select materials, organize classroom activities, develop assignments, and assess student performances with that thought in mind. The best teacher educators I know will explain to students *why* they chose an activity and *why* they organized it in a particular way. It is, as Kennedy (2005) pointed out, a way to enable students to get "inside the teacher's head and learn why he/she acted in a certain way" (p. 33), for, as she noted, students have spent years in classrooms watching teachers teach but very few have an understanding of why a teacher acted in a particular way.

These principles appear to be at odds with the current neoliberal environment of standards, standardization, and accountability. The impulse to standardize content (often a by-product of accreditation and various reform initiatives) should not lead to the standardization of methodology or the standardization of student outcomes. Teachers and teacher educators can continue to model good pedagogy even in a standards-based culture.

The willingness to model good pedagogy openly and explicitly (what a colleague calls "meta-teaching") may very well be the most important disposition a teacher educator possesses because, within that context, a continuous examination of what we teach, how we teach, and how we assess can occur.

Accreditation

Three years ago, the small private college where I serve as an assistant professor in the education department went through a rigorous accreditation process. The multiple-year process sent cultural shockwaves through the institution in general, and through the education department in particular, after our self-study was heavily critiqued by accreditation representatives.

All operational aspects of our program were open to examination and many were found deficient. The accreditation representatives noted that the education department needed more (and more current) technology, class sizes had to be reduced, the department had too many adjunct instructors and not enough full-time faculty, there was a lack of alignment between instructors' credentials and the courses they taught, and, finally (when department syllabi were examined), courses bearing the same name and course description often had wildly different sets of objectives and assessments. The critiques touched a departmental nerve primarily because they were all true.

The college and the department began to address these concerns and most were remedied relatively quickly: All classrooms were equipped with computers, CD/DVD players, and Internet access; some were equipped with Smart Boards. Graduate-level class sizes were reduced from an average of 30 to a maximum of 20. Sections taught per instructor were reduced from 4 to 3 per semester. Several new full-time faculty members were hired in areas of need and the department was directed to align faculty credentials with all course assignments.

These changes were relatively easy to make and were accepted by the faculty because they represented structural add-ons that did not disturb the standard operating procedures of the institution, and this noninterference enhanced their chances of lasting (Orlosky & Smith, 1972). In addition, and consistent with the findings of Cuban (1990), these "top down" changes were required by the accreditation personnel and were easily monitored.

The accreditation process, then, called for some needed standardization—in terms of technology, maximum class sizes, percentage of full-time faculty, and faculty credentials. But it also called for the standardization of courses. As noted earlier, an examination of syllabi found that courses with the same title and course description often had profoundly different objectives, activities, readings, and assessments. The accreditation representatives insisted upon the revision of course syllabi to reflect full alignment. That is, all courses with the same name and course description had to share the same objectives. In addition, each course had to have specifically stated benchmark performances. This meant that all students taking a certain course would complete an agreed upon set of assessments as outlined in the syllabus—no matter who was assigned to teach the course.

The process of developing and reaching consensus on common objectives and common benchmark performances is a much longer one and represents Fullan's "re-culturing" concept. For Fullan (2000) "restructuring" represents changes in the structure, roles, and related formal elements of the organization. He points out that restructuring is relatively easy because it can be legislated,e.g., forming a new advisory committee, but that, ultimately, it makes no difference in the quality of teaching and learning. He posits that "re-culturing," which *can* make a difference in the quality of teaching and learning, is the *process* of developing professional communities and involves going from a limited attention to assessment and pedagogy to a situation in which teachers and others routinely focus on these matters and make associated improvements.

In terms of curriculum development, the education department did not (to this point) have a culture of collaboration and consensus building. That fact was evidenced in the inconsistent syllabi. A premium had been placed on academic freedom. Nonetheless, within a few months (and thanks to the leadership of an assessment coordinator hired by the college), all courses in the graduate education program had revised sets of course objectives and related benchmark performances. Education department members complied with these changes under the threat of losing program accreditation.

Tackling standardization through critical theory

The remainder of this chapter will be devoted to how the accreditation mandates to standardize course objectives and assessments did *not* result in the standardization of my course but, rather, were used to help students gain a deeper understanding of the content and concepts related to the objectives.

For example, Objective #6 in a course I was teaching (EDU 652—Curriculum Planning in Education) read:

> Students will evaluate current research and legislation related to curriculum planning and decision-making, including research related to contemporary political and social issues as they affect the curriculum of our schools.

The standardized performance selected and developed to meet course objective #6 as a result of the accreditation/standardization process read:

> Performance: Analyze current research related to curriculum planning in education. Assignment: Research based curriculum position paper.

I was intent on teaching to the prescribed course objectives *and* complying with the mandated "research based curriculum position paper." A simple but ineffective response would have been to assign a "position paper" on some aspect of curriculum, draft a set of guidelines (outlining format, minimum number of pages, sources, etc.), and set a deadline for the submission of the papers. That approach would meet the *letter* of the standardized assignment, but it would not represent good teaching and it would not engage students in the tenets of critical theory as posited by Apple (2001), Aronowitz (2003), and Kincheloe (2007). I believe there is no need to assume that just because a course objective is standardized or that a prescribed student performance is "benchmarked," that the instructor is necessarily stripped of his/her pedagogical knowledge and skills. And it must be noted that this essential point should be made to our pre-service teacher candidates.

Critical theory is grounded in a social view of justice and promotes a fundamental rethinking and reconceptualization of school-related issues. These include ways that power operates to create purposes for schooling that are not necessarily in the best interests of students, how teachers and students relate to knowledge, and how it affects the relationship between teachers and learners.

Apple (2001) presents a broad view of the role of critical pedagogy:

> Critical pedagogies *require* [italics in the original] the fundamental interruption of common-sense. However, while the construction of new theories and utopian visions is important, it is equally crucial to base these theories and visions in an unromantic appraisal of the material and the discursive terrain that now exists. Common-sense is already being radically altered, but not in the direction that any of us on the left would find comforting. Without an analysis of such transformations and of the balance of forces that have created such discomforting alterations, without an analysis of the tensions, differential relations of power, and the contradictions within it, we are left with increasingly elegant new theoretical formulations, but with a less than elegant understanding of the field of social power on which they operate. (p. 64)

The assignment, and the approach I used to help students develop it, is embedded in Kincheloe's (2007) concept of "dialectical authority" which involves studies that account for the importance of opposites and contradictions within all forms of knowledge. This is consistent with Apple's "fundamental interruption of common-sense." In this context, knowledge is not complete in and of itself. It is produced in a larger process and cannot be understood outside its historical development.

The standards/standardization movement continues (to a great extent) to prescribe *content:* long lists of names, places, terms, skills, and concepts that students are supposed to "know." Standardized tests are now considered the primary vehicle for determining to what extent students "know" the countless names, places, terms, skills, and concepts prescribed by state and national standards. Popham (2001) notes that such tests have been used inappropriately to evaluate individual teachers and entire schools. He asserts that they should be used, instead, to inform teachers about their students' relative achievements.

However, despite the top-down standards-based and standardized test culture that permeates K–12 education and is beginning to permeate higher education, teachers still control the teaching/learning process within the walls of the classroom.

As I considered how to address course objective #6 and its related "position paper" benchmark performance, I began the planning process by posing these questions:

1. Despite the standardization implicit in this course objective and benchmark performance, how can I create a *structure* that embraces elements of student choice?

2. What preliminary activities can I organize so that students have opportunities to delve into this topic (the "research based curriculum position paper") before actually engaging in writing it?

3. What can I do to enable students to have a deeper understanding of the topic so that the process of evaluating and returning papers does *not* represent a terminal activity? That is, how can students understand this assignment to be more than a mere collection and reiteration of facts and how can they continue to learn more about the complexities of this topic even *after* the papers are completed? (It was my hope that this would be the manifestation of Kincheloe's "dialectical authority" in which the importance of opposites and contradictions would emerge.)

Using standards for students

Learning is greatly enhanced when the classroom activities designed by a teacher are mutually supportive and interconnected. In other words, carefully planned and sequenced activities have a cumulative effect because students are given multiple opportunities through multiple modalities to learn.

Given the three questions I listed above, I decided to build my instruction around these corresponding elements:

1. Choice—Students would be able to select a particular "curriculum movement" from a teacher-developed list. This would represent student choice within a teacher-centered framework that would ensure alignment with stated standards.

2. Preliminary Activities—I decided that this paper would not be just an assignment or "event" but, instead, an integral part

of the opening weeks of class. Preliminary activities included two elements. First, students would be engaged in reading, writing, listening, and speaking activities related directly to an array of curriculum development issues in the weeks prior to the submission of the paper. Those specific activities will be outlined in the section entitled "Teaching and Facilitating—Not Just Directing." Second, I developed a detailed "Guidelines" sheet which was distributed at the outset of this project. Students were then encouraged to submit drafts of their papers at any time prior to the deadline listed in the syllabus. This allowed me to provide written feedback for the students to assure that they were following established guidelines.

3. Follow-up Activities—The point of the post-paper follow-up activities was to assure that students had an even deeper understanding of the complexities and interrelationships of their topics. This was accomplished in two ways. First, if their papers included significant misunderstandings about their chosen topics, students were given an opportunity to revise and resubmit their papers. Second, students were grouped according to the topic they chose and were engaged in post-paper discussions and presentations.

Letting students choose

Students could complete the "benchmark performance" by submitting a 5–7-page paper on any one of the following "curriculum movements": standards-based curriculum, constructivism, interdisciplinary curriculum, multicultural education, or international/global education. This allowed me to comply with the mandate to have students complete a "research based curriculum position paper" while, at the same time, provide an element of choice for my students.

Teaching and facilitating—not just directing

As noted earlier, teachers at all levels of education often fall into the "assign and assess" model of operation. There is certainly a desire to give such short shrift to mandated and standardized portions of a program. But good teaching is much more than assigning and assessing. At the beginning of this project, I reminded my students that good teaching consists of communicating, scaffolding, demonstrating, providing time for guided practice, applying ongoing assessment, and monitoring and adjusting; that it takes time for complex concepts and understandings to occur.

The first rung of this project consisted of preliminary activities designed to immerse students in a range of reading, writing, listening, and speaking activities related to the concept of "curriculum" and to the forces (psychological, sociological, and political) which affect curriculum development.

The first topic on the first day of class was introduced in the form of a question: What is curriculum? Rather than giving a lecture on the topic or offering definitions from "experts" in the field, I wanted the students to develop their own definitions through group work. The students were placed in small groups (3 to 4) and were asked to develop a *group definition* of curriculum. After each group reached consensus, a representative wrote the agreed-upon definition on chart paper and posted it for the full class to see. Then, as part of a class discussion, each group was asked to provide a rationale for the selection of its definition.

The activity had several interesting outcomes: First, definitions varied widely from group to group. Some groups saw curriculum in very narrow and *concrete* terms, e.g., "an organized plan for learning" or "guidelines for instruction," while others included an array of characteristics ("completed over a specified period of time" or "geared toward specific age groups and levels of learning").

Some groups saw curriculum as *prescriptive* and dictated by an authority ("developed by boards of education" or "dictated by governing bodies").

And finally, several groups—but not all—added a *purpose* to their definitions ("to provide internal scrutiny of student progress" and "to meet the needs of students" and "to promote student learning").

As we reviewed the range of definitions posted on chart paper and displayed around the room, areas of disagreement and confusion were evident. The following questions emerged: What if you, as the teacher, disagree with the prescribed curriculum content? What if a parent disagrees with the prescribed content? What happens if students don't learn the prescribed content within the given time frame? What if the needs of the students are at odds with the prescribed curriculum? What do we mean by "appropriate" content? Appropriate from *whose* point of view? One student provided a transition into the next phase of our project when he asked, "These definitions are really more philosophical, aren't they?"

Arriving at group definitions of curriculum opened the door to the next question: What does the literature tell us about curriculum? During subsequent class sessions, students had access to a range of curriculum-related topics, specifically literature related to the explicit curriculum, the hidden curriculum, the null curriculum, and the received curriculum, among others.

Class discussions focused on personal definitions of, and perspectives on, curriculum but now within the framework of these curricular "types." In addition, students were provided with a "Conceptual Framework for Defining Curriculum" as posited by Beane, Toepfer, and Alessi (1991) (See Figure 1.0).

That framework views curriculum along the lines of a continuum from concrete to abstract, and from school-centered to learner-centered. In the related discussions, students could position their personal definition of curriculum and the various curriculum "types" within the Beane, Toepfer, and Alessi framework, enabling them to see a graphic representation of both their personal and group definitions of curriculum.

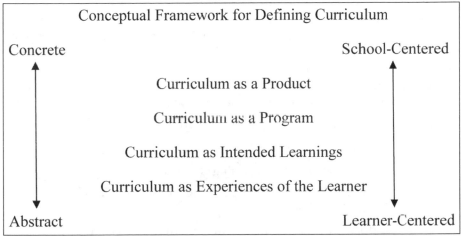

Figure 1.0. Note: Definitions of curriculum range from abstract to concrete, and from school-centered to student-centered.

In an attempt to follow the tenets of critical theory and assure greater student engagement, I wanted students to see that there was no single "correct" definition of curriculum and that one's definition of the term was based on personal beliefs about the role and purposes of schooling—from abstract to concrete, and from learner-centered to school-centered.

Readings/discussions

A great deal of literature supports the notion that the application of a range of modalities (reading, writing, listening, and speaking) enables students to develop a better understanding of complex issues. In order to immerse students in the complexities of curriculum development and curriculum delivery, assigned readings included works by Anyon on social class; Eisner on school effectiveness; Stoll and Fink on student assessment; Glasser on the concept of a quality curriculum; Gardner on teaching for understanding; Wiggins and McTighe on determining understanding; E. D. Hirsch on the core curriculum; Apple on the concept of sanctioned knowledge; and English on choice in the curriculum development process.

These readings were selected to offer students a range of perspectives on curriculum development, delivery, and assessment, as well as give them a sense of the political underpinnings of the process. Discussions of class readings were based on the use of essential questions as posited by Wiggins and McTighe (1998), who differentiate the essential question from what the authors refer to as a typical teacher question which is factual in nature and designed to seek "the" correct answer.

Essential questions have at least three different connotations: First, they involve important questions that occur throughout one's life. Second, they represent key inquiries within a discipline. Third, they help students make sense of important but often complicated knowledge, ideas, and concepts.

The questions posed as the basis for the discussions related to these readings were representative of all three connotations. They included:

1. How does social class affect teaching and learning? (Anyon)

2. What is an effective school? Teacher? Curriculum? (Eisner)

3. How should we measure learning? (Glasser)

4. What do we mean by "quality" when describing a school curriculum? (Stoll and Fink)

5. What does it mean to understand something? (Gardner)

6. Can understanding be measured? (Wiggins and McTighe)

7. What should all children know and be able to do? (Hirsch)

8. How do politics affect teaching and learning? (Apple)

9. How does power relate to curriculum? (English)

The use of essential questions in any class discussion implies that there is not necessarily "one right answer." The responses given often provoke deep thought by requiring students to provide evidence, justify answers, and consider alternatives. In a very natural way, essential questions lead to *additional questions* as students weigh various responses and begin to see the complexities inherent in trying to arrive at an answer. The application of essential questions served as a model for subsequent unit/lesson planning later in the semester. Students built their units/lesson plans around questions such as: What are the limits of power? Is change good? What does it mean to be a friend? Who has the right to decide?

The power of writing

Discussions based on essential questions were part of my standards-based instruction. However, since discussions are a poor form of assessing student knowledge and understanding (because not all students participate, not all comments are insightful, recording responses is tedious, and ranking the quality of a response can be subjective), I employed the use of in-class, on-demand writing. This represented the second rung of the project.

The course syllabus states that, on occasion, students would be asked to respond to questions during class time. I made it clear to the students that these in-class, on-demand writing activities were not designed as "check tests" or "pop quizzes." My intent was not to coerce students to do the assigned readings; rather, the writing activity was designed to allow each student extensive time to reread, think about, and write about the discussions related to the essential questions. The writing provided another mode of learning and, more important, it gave my students the opportunity to demonstrate a level of understanding and, perhaps, recast previous beliefs and assumptions.

My purpose in having students write is consistent with the concept of writing as a means of thinking. Gorlewski (2011) states that literacy, and by extension, writing, involves more than the transmission of facts or skills. Serious writing, as noted by Moffett (1988), requires investment by the writer in developing thought; while Knoeller (2004) refers to written projects as "narratives of rethinking" in which students "test perspectives and recount turning points in their understanding" (p. 149).

When asked to complete in-class writing assignments, students in my class were allowed to use any class articles, handout materials, or notes. The only restriction was that they were required to work independently. I believe that these writing activities were essential to teaching based on critical theory and critical pedagogy because the message I delivered both implicitly and explicitly was that I trusted the students (by allowing them to use reference material) and that I wanted to learn more about what they knew (by the way I would respond to their work).

Below is a sampling of the types of questions associated with several in-class writing activities:

1. Among the concepts discussed in William Glasser's *The Quality School Curriculum* were the following: a) Lead manager versus Boss Manager, b) Throwaway knowledge, and c) The coercive nature of schools. Discuss how each of these concepts appears in Jean Anyon's *Social Class and the Hidden Curriculum of Work*. Note: to adequately answer this question, you need to explain each of Glasser's concepts; then, you

need to make a direct connection between the respective concept and specific examples from Anyon's article.

2. a) Define: Curriculum. b) Provide a rationale for the selection of that definition. c) Finally, discuss how your definition fits into the "Conceptual Framework for Defining Curriculum" as posited by Beane, Toepfer, and Alessi.

3. Review pp. 1–2 of E.D. Hirsch's article *Fairness and Core Knowledge*. a) What is Hirsch's perspective on multiculturalism in the classroom? b) Do you agree or disagree with that perspective and why?

4. According to Stoll and Fink (pp. 124–125 in *Changing Concepts of Teaching and Learning*), a) list and briefly explain the three approaches a teacher can take to determine if a student has met a standard. b) Which approach do you feel is best and why?

5. Consider the concept of the Essential Question: a) Define it. b) List at least four characteristics of a good essential question. c) What role do they play in the teaching/learning process?

6. Alluding to the work of Michael Apple, a) how would you define neoliberalism? b) To what extent, if any, does neoliberalism have an impact on education today? c) Is neoliberalism at odds with Wiggins and McTighe's concept of "understanding'? Please explain your answer.

The writing activities served two purposes. First, they gave students the opportunity to explain and discuss (on an individual basis) the critical content and concepts of the course. As Bazerman (2004) noted, students in such a setting discover that

> there was more to writing good research papers than locating some sources and following correct bibliographic form. There was a journey of learning, of problem formation and reformulation, of careful and thoughtful reading, of being able to interpret and restate what sources had to say, of evaluation and comment, of synthesis, of fresh argument. (p. 60)

Second, the "open book" nature of the activity represented a subtle shift in power from the instructor to the students who had access to materials which gave them the *opportunity* to revisit and reformulate their thinking. But this shift in power had to be coupled with my *responses* to their writing. As I read their papers, I was determined to engage in a "written conversation" with my students. As a result, my written feedback was intentionally encouraging and instructive. I wanted my students to see themselves as creators of knowledge—not just recipients of it.

The research paper

After several weeks of classroom activity which included readings, discussions, group work, and writing, I believed that my students were ready to begin the mandated research paper. At the very least, my students had been exposed to a range of social, political, and cultural aspects of curriculum development and delivery. As noted earlier, the guidelines sheet for the research paper was distributed to the students at the beginning of the semester. The guidelines included the following requirements:

- Students could do a literature review on any one of these curriculum movements—standards-based curriculum, constructivism, interdisciplinary curriculum, multicultural education, or international/global education.

- The paper was to be 5 to 7 pages in length with a reference page.

- The paper was to be organized around these headings: definition(s) of the movement, historical development, perceived advantages of implementing such a movement, perceived disadvantages, and a personal reflection.

In many ways, the review, feedback, and grading of the curriculum movements research paper was the easiest part of this project.

Dialectical authority—the fundamental interruption of common sense

The third and final rung of this project was the post-paper activity. As explained earlier, the point of the post-paper activity was to assure that students had a deep understanding of the complexities and interrelationships of their topic and that the submission of the paper, itself, would not represent a terminal activity. This was accomplished in two ways. First, if a student's paper included significant misunderstandings about the chosen topic, the student was given an opportunity to revise and resubmit his/her paper. Detailed feedback, coupled with one-on-one conferences, was provided to assure that students were aware of the specific deficiencies in their papers so that adequate revisions could be made. Second, students were grouped according to the topic they chose and were engaged in post-paper discussions and presentations. It was at this point that Kincheloe's *dialectical authority* (stressing the importance of opposites and contradictions) and Apple's *fundamental interruption of common sense* became manifest.

After being placed in groups, students were asked to fill out chart paper related to their chosen curriculum movement and list, in a highly abbreviated form, a synthesis of the group's literature review findings. The findings included the "perceived advantages" and "perceived disadvantages" of each movement. As the students posted their work and presented it to the class, it became evident that there were profound contradictions within and between each curriculum movement. This result was predictable in view of the fact that Miller and Silvernail (1994) maintain that the "rub between theory and practice" occurs most productively when questions arise in the context of real students and work in progress, and where research and disciplined inquiry are also at hand.

For example, students noted that in a constructivist classroom, the benefits of active participation and the activation of prior knowledge were tempered by difficulty in assessing student-generated ideas and material.

In a standards-based curriculum, the students noted that the benefits of a commonly agreed upon set of knowledge, concepts, and skills could also give rise to a more narrowed curriculum. Perceived disadvantages included the question of whom, exactly, is the developer of these standards and to what extent could agreement be reached on what constitutes a standard.

In the interdisciplinary curriculum, the students saw that the benefits of more engagement, higher-level thinking, and "real-world" application could be offset by instructors who did not have sufficient knowledge and experience to address a wide variety of disciplines. They also saw the approach as being at odds with the current testing structure which is designed to address discrete subject areas.

In their analysis of multicultural education, the students discovered that the benefits of developing knowledge and acceptance of other cultures were also inconsistent with the standardized testing culture which did not measure these attributes. In addition, students wondered how any single teacher could become sufficiently knowledgeable about so many different cultures and subcultures within the classroom.

As my students presented their findings on international/global education, they noted that, first of all, the literature on the topic was sparse and that the literature they did find focused on business and trade—basic capitalistic topics. They also noted that the definition (the idea that schools should equip students with the knowledge, skills, and dispositions required for participation in a more globalized world) implied that there was a certainty about the positive effects of globalization—a certainty which they all did not share.

Conclusion

This chapter focused on the efforts of a graduate education instructor in a small private college who decided to address the standardization of course objectives and assessments by developing a set of activities featuring student reading, writing, listening, and speaking activities within the context of student choice and leading to an understanding of the complexities and contradictions inherent in any philosophical/theoretical approach.

Good settings for teacher learning, in both colleges of education and schools, provide opportunities for research and inquiry, for trying and testing, and for talking about *understanding* the results of teaching and learning.

The standardization of curriculum at the higher education level should not be equated to the standardization of methods, materials, assessments, and outcomes. As a result of neoliberal policies and the accreditation process, colleges and universities find their policies, practices, and programs under greater scrutiny than ever.

Nonetheless, educators have the power to apply the principles of critical theory to enable students to become more engaged in their own learning and to help them gain a deeper understanding of the knowledge, concepts, and skills that they, as future teachers, will be charged with teaching.

References

Apple, M. (2001). *Educating the "Right" Way: Market, Standards, God, and Inequality*. New York: RoutledgeFalmer, New York.

Aronowitz, S. (2003). *The Knowledge Factory: Dismantling the Corporate University and Creating True Higher Learning*. Boston: Beacon.

Bazerman, C. (2004). Intertextualities: Volosinov, Bakhtin, literary theory and literacy studies. In *Bakhtinian Perspectives on Language, Literacy and Learning*, Arnetha F. Ball and Sarah Warshauer Freedman (eds.). New York: Cambridge University Press.

Beane, J.A., Toepfer, C.F., & Alessi, S.J. (1991). *Curriculum Planning and Development*, Boston: Allyn and Bacon.

Cuban, L. (1990). Enduring resiliency: Enacting and implementing federal vocational education legislation. In *Work, Youth and School*, Kantor and Tyack (eds.), Stanford, CA: Stanford University Press, pp. 45–78.

Fullan, M. (2000). The three stories of education reform. *Phi Delta Kappan*, April, pp. 581–584.

Gorlewski, J. (2011). *Power, Resistance, and Literacy: Writing for Social Justice*. Charlotte, NC: Information Age Publishing.

Kennedy, M. (2005). *Inside Teaching: How Classroom Life Undermines Reform*. Cambridge: Harvard University Press.

Kincheloe, J.L. (2007). *Critical Pedagogy*. New York: Peter Lang Publishing.

Knoeller, C. (2004). Narratives of rethinking: The inner dialogue of classroom discourse and student writing. In *Bakhtinian Perspectives on Language, Literacy and Learning*, Arnetha F. Ball and Sarah Warshauer Freedman (eds.). New York: Cambridge University Press.

Miller, L., & Silvernail, D.L. (1994). Wells Junior High School: Evolution of a professional development school. In *Professional Development Schools: Schools for Developing a Profession*, Linda Darling-Hammond (ed.). New York: Teachers College Press.

Moffett, J. (1988). *Coming on Center* (2nd ed.). Portsmouth, England: Boynton/Cook.

Orlosky, D., & Smith, O.B. (1972). Educational change: Its origins and characteristics. *Phi

Delta Kappan, 53(3), 412–414.

Popham, W.J. (2001). Uses and misuses of standardized tests. *NASSP Bulletin* 2001; 85; 24 DOI: 10.1177/019263650108562204, pp. 27–28.

Wiggins, G., & McTighe, J. (1998). *The Six Facets of Understanding. Understanding by Design*. Alexandria, Virginia: ASCD.

16. A Counternarrative of Subversion and Resistance: Hijacking NCATE to Promote Equity and Social Justice in a College of Education

Lauren P. Hoffman & Brad J. Porfilio

There has been a seismic shift in the function of higher education over the past decade in the United States. Academic institutions across the country have been infiltrated by hegemonic ideologies and practices "of militarism, corporatism, and political fundamentalism" (Giroux, 2007, p. 1). The ruling elite's desire to commodify social life and to promote a "new world order" predicated on the ideals of free-market fundamentalism, on Eurocentric values, and on American superiority have been braided to threaten the university as an interconnected, counterinstitution "that has evolved over hundreds of years" (Brodsky, 2002; Giroux, 2007; Porfilio & Yu, 2006; Washburn, 2005). The commercial, political, and military ethos embedded within academic settings can be witnessed in the following practices: Academic institutions are frequently run by former CEOs; numerous programs and research projects serve military personnel; the CIA influences collegiate life; privatized educational institutions (e.g., Kaplan, the University of Phoenix, and Walden University) train students to become dutiful workers inside and outside educational environments; and conservative "watchdog" groups, such as the National Association of Scholars, are behind the McCarthy-like movement to remove any scholars, programs, or practices that may question the racist, sexist, classist, or status quo in schools and in society (Fassbinder, 2006; Giroux, 2007; Porfilio & Yu, 2006).

Critical scholar-practitioners who educate future and current teachers, school administrators, and other school personnel in schools or colleges of education have been particularly affected by the changing nature of higher education (Butin, 2007; Cochran-Smith, 2009; Hinchey & Cadiero-Kaplan,

2005; Porfilio & Yu, 2006; Sleeter, 2008). Political leaders in the United States, Western CEOs, educators, psychologists, and think tank organizations have been able to sell the public the false idea that it is the teacher education system (rather than unjust policies, systemic inequalities, and historical forces) that perpetuates a dysfunctional educational system nationwide. They have played upon the public's fear that strained racial relations, youth alienation, an inequitable distribution of wealth and resources, as well as heightened unemployment will only be altered if teacher educators are held "accountable" through a battery of standards and assessments, or if traditional teacher education is gutted entirely (Taubman, 2009, p. 3).

Consequently, many midcareer changers and others who hope to land a teaching or school administrator job believe traditional teacher education programs will hinder, rather than help, them in becoming effective teachers or school leaders. In fact, over one-third of such candidates now gain their state certifications or advanced degrees through alterative programs (Wetzel, 2011). Critical scholars and their beliefs, ideas, and pedagogical projects are not supported by the vast majority of these programs. Many students who enroll in alternative certification programs—like the future teachers and school leaders who enroll in online commercialized education programs—never take a single course dedicated to the multicultural foundations of education.

Moreover, critical educators whose passion and "main interest is in interpreting—and enabling others to interpret—the social, political, and economic factors that affect and influence the processes of education" (Green, 1976, as cited in Butin, 2007) have become, at best, marginal actors within traditional education programs. They are frequently viewed with consternation by fellow teacher educators or administrators who support practical, technical, or "scientific" approaches to educating school personnel. There are two reasons for the marginalization of critical scholars in traditional teacher education programs: First, more scholars during the past decade have secured doctorates focusing on *practitioner* practices rather than the sociological/philosophical foundations of education. And, second, administrators in traditional schools of education are reacting to the pressure to compete with their commercial/fast-track counterparts for student enrollment and tuition dollars (Butin, 2007; Hinchey & Cadiero-Kaplan, 2005; Porfilio & Yu, 2006). To attract students to their institutions, college and university administrators often streamline their programs by removing course work that is not deemed practical in an attempt to make students feel confident they will be able to secure school-based jobs. The streamlined programs are better able to compete with the commercial/fast-track institutions. By obtaining national teacher education accreditation through the National Council for Accreditation of Teacher Education (NCATE), a school of education has the ability to inform potential students that it is an institution committed to "high-quality" education.

For the past two decades, NCATE officials have generated a successful propaganda campaign to associate "teaching excellence" with that organization (Johnson, Johnson, Farenga, & Ness, 2005).

The shrinking group of critical scholar-practitioners who remain in teacher education has been openly critical of allowing standards and assessment organizations to be the sole arbiters of whether or not their programs are preparing effective school personnel for employment in American schools. The NCATE accreditation process is based on the belief that effective preparation of teacher candidates includes the *standardization of syllabi* (using NCATE codes and standards generated by professional organizations such as the National Council of Teachers of English) and the *analysis of student assessments* as a valid indicator of learning. Many scholars will not support these notions (Johnson, Johnson, Farenga, & Ness, 2005). Other scholars believe that using standards to evaluate the effectiveness of a teacher education program will sap teacher creativity and drive teacher educators to "only teach items that are evaluated by the standards" (Johnson, Johnson, Farenga, & Ness, 2005, p. 104). Aside from the problems associated with the way in which NCATE evaluates the effectiveness of teacher education programs, critical scholars have condemned the organization for promoting standardized assessments at all education levels, for withdrawing its support for the promotion of social justice in schools of education, and for failing to take an overt stance against the social actors and structures promoting injustice in schools and in society (Johnson, Johnson, Farenga, & Ness, 2005; Taubman, 2009). In any event, the accreditation process is another force behind the marginalization of critical multicultural education educators and their ideas, beliefs, and scholarship.

Although we fully agree with some of the concerns our colleagues have with NCATE and other accreditation organizations (which often compel teacher educators to focus on meeting the standards of the professional organizations rather than to think creatively about how to guide students in becoming agents of change), we believe educational foundation organizations and scholars must become involved in the national teacher accreditation process. Direct involvement is necessary in order to have accreditation agencies hear our concerns by articulating our opposition to how they evaluate the preparation programs of teachers and school leaders—as well as to have an impact on key policy decisions and issues affecting teachers, schools, and society (Butin, 2007). We also believe this input is necessary if critical pedagogy is to gain momentum in impacting the preparation of teachers and school leaders in the 21st century. Consequently, this chapter is designed to illustrate how the national teacher accreditation process provided fertile ground for us, two critical scholar-practitioners, to transform a conservative and commercialized college of education. The NCATE accreditation process provided the opportunity to develop and implement programs, assessments, and standards that are designed to provide a salient contribution to the amelioration of injustice and inequality through the preparation of educators who believe all can learn, and who challenge marginalizing discourses and honor diversity rather than perpetuating education policies antithetical to personal and social transformation.

However, as we illustrate through our narrative below, the road to moving from a conservative educational context to a socially transformative one is fraught with problems, so much so that clinical, commercial, and technical aspects are coming to overshadow the critical and transformative initiatives, policies, and programs we put in place over the past several years. Based on our experiences, we do not feel it is accreditation agencies such as NCATE that have blocked us from sustaining and furthering critical multicultural dimensions in our College of Education. Rather, it is our clinical colleagues and administrators who are sapping the critical lifeblood from our program. Their views relative to the purpose of schooling, the role faculty must play in eliminating social inequalities in schools and in the wider society, and the purpose of engaging in scholarship to understand and eliminate social injustices, are at the heart of our goal to make our College of Education a beacon of criticality, rather than an appendage of the commercial and corporate elite.

We conclude our chapter by highlighting how commercialized forces have become a threat to the humanizing and transformative nature of teacher education as well as a threat to critical scholar-practitioners through our College of Education's recent struggle with NCTQ (the National Council on Teacher Quality). The organization's attempt to dismantle traditional teacher education as well as to produce compliant schoolteachers appears to be undoing some of the transformative work we accomplished during the NCATE process. This example is meant to show that it is imperative for critical scholars to be aware of how commercialized forces have infiltrated teacher education, and to be active in raising their opposition to its takeover of education.

Introduction

The purpose of this section is to discuss how we used the NCATE accreditation process and the development of unit standards to build a critical theoretical foundation for our College of Education. We begin by situating this work with a brief description of the rationale for leading this phase of the NCATE accreditation process and a review of the educational and political context in which this activity was done. This is followed with a discussion of how we used the standards to support critical pedagogy across the College of Education, and it includes a description of the tensions that arose during the process.

Having just failed three out of six NCATE standards on the first NCATE visit, the dean of the College of Education was in need of leadership and support. She knew the university president expected the colleges and programs to obtain the appropriate accreditation credentials and this failure was considered a major disappointment by a college that is depended on to bring in significant credit hours and tuition dollars. The fear of having to close the College of Education and the subtle threats of losing faculty jobs were palpable after news spread about the disastrous NCATE results.

After a dialogue with the dean about the severity of the situation and the pressure she and the provost were under to pass the remaining three NCATE standards, the department's faculty members agreed to lead the charge for the next phase of the NCATE accreditation process. We made it clear to each other, and to the dean, that we did not support NCATE in any way. We were offended by their power in dictating a narrow and technical agenda for education and found their reductionist, rigid, and bureaucratic principles, procedures, and surveillance methods limiting and dangerous for the profession. However, there was a sense of inevitability that NCATE accreditation would be obtained, even if it required bringing in teams of "experts," along with spending thousands of dollars, to make it happen. At that moment, we decided to seize this as an opportunity to resist NCATE's standardized ways of conceptualizing vision, mission, unit standards, and assessments and build a critical framework for the College of Education.

However, we knew this would be difficult due to the educational and political context of our College of Education. Instructors in our college treat education as primarily a technical issue, which is perhaps not different from many other colleges across the country. They appear immersed in the positivist tradition that presents teaching as a precise and scientific understanding and sees teachers and leaders as technicians responsible for carrying out predetermined programs and strategies. The emphasis in the programs is on the right "methods" to improve academic achievement for all students while giving lip service to the issues of students who have historically been oppressed. Bartolome (1994) refers to this as a "methods fetish" that serves to cover up the more pressing concern about why subordinated students do not generally succeed academically in our schools and how schools reproduce the asymmetrical power relations among cultural groups.

Along with this technical and uncritical orientation to education is a culture of private conversations where faculty members build coalitions to either support or oppose ideas. There is fear and resistance when faculty members are asked to explore educational ideas that differ from their own, especially when they are asked to do so publicly. Dialogue is difficult and appears to be engaged only for the purpose of seeking a single, convergent method aimed toward their view of Truth, as opposed to recognizing that agreement and common understanding are complex, fluid, and quite rare (Burbules & Rice, 1991). Faculty members tend to eliminate difference of opinion and, instead, seek consensus.

What makes this context frustrating is the fact that the university has a religious affiliation that promotes the value of justice in its mission. The university embraces programs that reflect an ethical and social orientation and it seemed possible to capitalize on this fact and assume some level of leadership in promoting social justice in education.

The following section outlines how we created critical NCATE unit standards in this uncritical context. It also outlines how we used the unit standards to drive many of the College of Education policies and procedures, including program and unit assessments, professional development, program development, and faculty hiring.

Developing a critical NCATE plan and critical unit standards

We entered this work with a critical view of knowledge that promotes the concept of "paradox where there is certainty, open-endedness where there is finality, multiple perspectives where there is objectivity, and de-familiarization where there is comfort and security" (Kincheloe, 2008). We would not be passive recipients of knowledge nor pawns in the commercialized accreditation machine. We quickly learned the NCATE regime is based on a politics of knowledge that utilizes an

> evidence-based science that excludes complexity, context, multiple modes of research design, ever-changing nature of phenomena, subjugated knowledge from diverse social and geographical locales, and the multiple realities perceived and constructed by different peoples at divergent historical times and cultural places, and where dominant power brokers regulate what people view as legitimate knowledge. (p. 38)

We resisted this ideology by continually raising questions about the intent and purpose of the NCATE practice, gaining clarity about the marginalizing effects of the practice, and reinterpreting the standards and requirements within a critical frame of reference. We quickly learned there were alternative ways to meet the requirements of NCATE *without* assuming its neoliberal and technical orientation to education. We began by establishing a vision and mission for the College of Education that embraced a critical foundation.

The vision compels the College of Education to understand the central role of education to be the creation of a more equal and just society. Therefore the College of Education views its work as making a salient contribution to the amelioration of injustice and inequality, and it envisions the school as an important location for challenging and transforming social ills. The mission emphasized a culture of critique, possibility, and inquiry where students and faculty recognize the political, social, moral, and economic dimensions of education; submit their own beliefs and understandings to scrutiny; challenge dominant discourses; and understand their responsibility as a social advocate for all students, especially the marginalized. Having an explicit vision and mission are required by NCATE; however, *content* of that vision and mission is not dictated. Although there was significant controversy several years ago when NCATE decided not to include social justice in its standards for dispositions (Butin, 2007; Haybach, 2009), it should be noted that they do not criticize or penalize a College of Education for including it in its own NCATE plan. Our plan was explicitly critical whereby social justice was evident throughout—and there were no concerns from the NCATE evaluators regarding our inclusion of these ideals.

NCATE also requires the development of unit standards to guide the preparation of all candidates. This is where we reflected our commitment to critical pedagogy in an explicit manner. Following are the unit standards that were developed: All teacher and leader candidates will be prepared to be (1) knowledgeable critical transformative educators; (2) multicultural educators; and (3) social justice advocates. There was significant discussion with various groups in the College of Education, the NCATE assessment committee, and the leadership team to agree to the standards. We are fortunate to have strong social justice values in the University Mission and we continually referred to that to build understanding and support for the unit standards. Even so, faculty members asked why we should concern ourselves with marginalized groups. They even suggested that our students would not get jobs because school districts would be fearful that our students would "cause too much trouble." They also had questions about how to emphasize social justice when the various programs already required so many clinical observation hours and hours of course work, and, finally, there was criticism about the expectation to learn more about criticalness, multiculturalism, and social justice. With support from the dean and her ongoing and sometimes private discussions with various coalitions in the College of Education, the unit standards were agreed upon by all College of Education faculty members.

Following the approval of the unit standards, we designed assessments. NCATE requires that the evaluation plan include assessments and management systems to generate data that show how well the unit standards are being met. We rejected this type of assessment, but we focused on the content of the standards and assessments and decided to cope with the narrow form of assessment for the time being. We designed three unit assessments and related rubrics that would evaluate these standards as well as dispositions that reflected a foundation of criticalness. We aligned these unit standards with several other sets of standards as required by NCATE and created a schedule for assessment administration and data analysis. We do not value the quantitative data generated from the rubrics, but it is required by NCATE.

Although we found a way to center the NCATE work on critical education, we did not have any room to move beyond the narrow data requirements.

However, we designed assessments that were as meaningful as possible. For example, the three unit assessments included (1) a reflective essay focusing on the meaning of the unit standards; (2) an oral defense in which each student discusses the meaning of the unit standards and relates them to practice; and (3) an evaluation of a critical service learning project.

We were not hijacked by NCATE; we not only passed the final three standards required for full accreditation but, more important, we created a critical framework for the College of Education. Although we did not agree with the NCATE accountability system, we did not allow it to shift our focus. Even though this work was done with an assessment committee employing ongoing dialogue and feedback, it was obvious that the faculty had limited understanding of the critical theoretical foundation to the vision, mission, standards, and assessments and that an enormous amount of work would be needed to bring meaning to this plan.

Critical pedagogy *across* the College of Education

In order for faculty to make sense of this plan and begin its implementation, the dean: scheduled faculty reading groups which focused on critical pedagogy, dedicated time in faculty meetings to discuss dimensions of critical pedagogy, and offered to purchase various resources to build faculty knowledge of critical pedagogy. There was an expectation that, as faculty became more knowledgeable about critical pedagogy, some degree of criticalness would be represented in their own curricula and course work. In addition, the dean expected search committees to recruit faculty who were knowledgeable about critical pedagogy, who exhibited interested in learning about critical pedagogy, and who demonstrated some level of commitment to social justice and advocacy. During this time an associate dean was hired; this person was expected to have a background in critical pedagogy and be able to support the faculty in their personal and professional development. In addition, a Critical Pedagogy Conference was sponsored by the College of Education where Dr. Peter McLaren, a world-renowned critical scholar, was the featured speaker. There was also support for Dr. McLaren to teach a seminar for the doctoral program. There was encouragement for faculty to learn and interpret the meaning of critical pedagogy and the NCATE plan. In addition, structures were put in place to provide systemic and institutional support.

Tensions manifest

Initially, there appeared to be a commitment to move critical pedagogy forward because we had just passed NCATE and that relieved stress and anxiety in the College of Education. However, as with any new policy, support began to wane when the faculty had to integrate the unit standards into their curriculum and implement the assessment plan. This tension was reflected in various ways. First, while the faculty did not attack the unit standards, they did criticize the implementation of the assessments that were designed to document the focus on the unit standards. After approximately six months, faculty claimed the assessment rubrics were not descriptive enough to make clear judgments of student performance. They blamed the assessment tools and rubrics for not generating meaningful data while never questioning their own level of understanding and expertise in applying the assessment tools. Their solution was to change the assessments and rubrics by: changing the *language* of the assessments to more technical language; removing the critical service-learning project from the assessment plan; and changing the terminology of an oral defense to a response. Second, only two out of six programs critically analyzed their curriculum and strategically embedded critical pedagogy into their course work. Third, several faculty had been hired and only one appeared to have been prepared in critical pedagogy, a few faculty did not have terminal degrees, and a new associate dean was hired without any academic training in critical pedagogy. Fourth, the most recent faculty meeting focused entirely on learning about technology including the Smart Board and a communication tool for students as opposed to previous professional days where the emphasis was on discussing issues related to critical pedagogy. To use a term from the field of statistics, we were "regressing toward the mean," i.e., going back to old practices.

In the end, it was the faculty, not NCATE, who tried to derail the commitment to integrating critical pedagogy across the College of Education by creating obstacles and developing coalitions who would attempt to reduce critical pedagogy to more concrete and conservative notions. However, the critical theoretical foundation and critical unit standards continued to exist and a few programs embraced critical pedagogy to a significant degree. Creating unit standards for the NCATE process can be used to promote critical pedagogy; however, committing to such bold action does not always result in full implementation.

NCTQ and its agenda for teacher education

Despite the inroads we made in reducing the clinical and technical dimensions from the curricula, standards, and policies within the College of Education during the NCATE accreditation process, we are faced with a commercial force that is intent on undoing much of our transformative work. The NCTQ (National Council on Teacher Quality), an organization consisting mainly of business leaders, scholars, and administrators who support the elimination of traditional teacher education programs[1] as well as promote the corporate takeover of K–12 schools, recently called for all administrators across the Chicago area to submit syllabi to their organization. They felt entitled to judge whether these teacher education programs are preparing "effective teachers." They used their connections with the college and university administrators to make it happen.

Unlike NCATE or other teacher accreditation organizations, NCTQ does not give colleges of education the power to determine what unit standards or overall vision they want to guide their programs in preparing effective teachers for K–12 classrooms. Instead, the group has developed criteria that are aligned with its agenda to prepare teachers who will implement corporate, clinical, and technical initiatives in K–12 classrooms, as well as to compel the public to believe that traditional forms of teacher education are the cause of social and economic problems in this country. Among numerous criteria NCTQ uses to gauge whether a teacher education program is preparing students (i.e., teacher candidates) to: learn "scientific" reading methods to foster literacy in K–12 classrooms; effectively implement technology in K–12 classrooms; use standardized assessments to improve instruction; and learn specific behavioral techniques to "manage" a classroom (National Council on Teacher Quality, 2011). Not coincidentally, the organization does not evaluate whether the programs educated future teachers to have a critical understanding of how schools function, an understanding of the relationship between knowledge and power, or an understanding of the "complexities of educational practice and an understanding of and commitment to a socially just, democratic notion of schooling" (Kincheloe, 2004, p. 50). Moreover, unlike NCATE, NCTQ *does* dictate the curriculum that schools of education must follow. For instance, schools of education must utilize a particular textbook to educate pre-service teachers in how to instruct students in developing reading skills in order to receive a high grade from NCTQ (Gabriel, 2011).

Clearly, many of the academic deans were not pleased by NCTQ's major finding: many of the Chicagoland institutions were not doing enough to train teachers to be compliant technicians in K–12 schools. This spurred the deans to write a collective response to the NCTQ's new ratings report. Rather than voice their concern with NCTQ's technical view of what it means to be an "effective" teacher, the higher education institutions' response centered on the *process* of the study. The major contention they had with NCTQ's report is that it is too "narrow in focus and emphasizes static inputs rather than outcomes of actual candidate performance" (Illinois Institutions of Higher Education, 2010). Therefore, the deans' response shows that they are fundamentally aligned with NCTQ's neoliberal agenda for schools: that preparing future teachers to be dutiful technicians ought to be the main priority of schools of education.

The deans apparently got their wish that the NCTQ be more "scientific" in attempting to discern whether or not the 56 Illinois educator preparation programs are preparing teachers to become agents of neoliberalism. After reading the response, NCTQ decided to abandon the evaluation teacher education programs based on reviews of syllabi and materials culled from the institutions' websites. NCTQ has joined with its new neoliberal partner, *U.S. News and World Report*, and broadened the scope of inputs in attempting to determine whether schools of education are producing effective technicians in K–12 schools. These groups will now evaluate "course syllabi, textbooks and reading packets, student-teaching placement information, admissions standards, course requirements, and graduate and employer surveys…to review and rate teacher education in the nation's 1,400 schools of education" (Sawchuk, 2011, p. 4).

Even though our dean has supported the College of Education's vision of "making a salient contribution to the amelioration of injustice and inequality through the preparation of educators who believe all can learn, challenge marginalizing discourses and honor diversity," there is no evidence that she is questioning NCTQ's approach to evaluating teacher training programs She has told the faculty that NCTQ's technical standards must be followed and they need to be "crystal clear in all syllabi." She has never questioned whether NCTQ's standards are in direct opposition to the college's vision for the preparation of educators, nor has she refused to take part in an evaluation process that is antithetical to our college's view of teacher preparation.

Alternatively, some academic deans have started to raise concerns over NCTQ's coercive approach to participation in the NCTQ/*U.S. News and World Report*'s evaluation game. If schools of education do *not* want to take part in the study or fail to supply the neoliberal organizations data to be evaluated, *they will still be ranked* (Gabriel, 2011). Other academic deans have rallie against the type of methodology used to evaluate schools of education. They appear to have little regard for the organization's technical view of education, its control over the curricula, or the fact that it is behind both the elimination of public schooling and traditional teacher education programs. Others, like our dean, are so concerned about making their programs more attractive than their "competitors," that they have supported the entire NCTQ agenda.

Currently, we do not know what will come of NCTQ's second attempt to evaluate our School of Education. The fact that our dean and faculty have willingly infused NCTQ's standards into their courses indicates that they probably will continue to yield to additional mandates from this organization and other organizations that want to commercialize teacher education, promote programmed instruction in K–12 schools, or make teacher educators the scapegoats for the social and economic problems that emanate from neoliberal organizations like NCTQ.[2] Our College of Education, like many others, will probably be more concerned with refashioning its programs to assure a high ranking from *U.S. News and World Report* and NCTQ than preparing future teachers to become critical thinkers who are capable of transforming schools and the world.

Conclusions

The purpose of this essay was to demonstrate how the unit standards developed for the NCATE accreditation process were designed to promote critical pedagogy. Although we shared various questionable faculty responses, the intent is not to criticize them or assume they do not care about students or education. However, their responses are fundamental to understanding the complexity of establishing unit standards that promote a critical orientation to education. Typically, and unfortunately, most faculty members are not prepared in critical pedagogy, have not examined their own personal prejudices and biases, and do not recognize the connections to education. Therefore, making sense of unit standards that speak to critical pedagogy takes leadership, support, learning, and time.

Perhaps it is helpful to conceptualize the struggles involved in this work as typical of what occurs when creating and enacting any new policy. Policies are representations which are developed in complex ways with compromises, and are understood in relation to personal histories, experiences, resources, and contexts (Ball, 1993). Policies are contested; they change their meaning over time, and are not necessarily clear or complete. These struggles over meaning and interpretation occur within a moving discursive frame which articulates and constrains the possibilities and probabilities of enacting the policy. Recognizing the trajectory of policy formulation and enactment as messy and influenced by multiple contexts helps participants to understand the tensions experienced and why there have been so many starts and stops in the process of implementing critical pedagogy across the College of Education.

Moreover, it is important to recognize that even though NCATE promotes a narrow, technical, and neoliberal view of education and requires assessments that include reductionist rubrics, they do not (and should not) dictate the content of our vision, mission, unit standards, or assessments. NCATE representatives and consultants consistently informed us we could speak to our own values and develop our own unit standards, but needed to demonstrate alignment of these values and standards in the assessments and rubrics. While the process is fragile and rife with tensions and struggles, and while we do not support these commercial accreditation schemes, the NCATE process should not interfere with, or obstruct, our view of critical pedagogy in education.

However, the desire of the corporate world to commodify elements that we have generally considered social goods, such as education, is something that critical scholars must be continually aware of and ready to confront. Organizations, like NCTQ and *U.S. News and World Report*, who have a corporatist vision for education, believe teachers ought to be technicians in their classrooms. They wrongly blame teacher educators for the problems that the corporate world engenders; and they must be challenged by critical scholars. If this does not happen, there will no longer be a conversation of how critical scholars can use standards to guide their students to become agents of change. Instead, teacher educators will willfully train future teachers and school leaders to embrace technical forms of teaching, learning, and evaluation. They will unwittingly support the corporations and leaders who benefit from education serving as a commercial, rather than a humanizing, force.

Notes

1. For example, some of the most predominant supporters of free market reform in K–12 schools and in teacher education are members of the National Council on Teacher Quality Advisory Board, including Wendy Kopp, CEO and founder of Teach For America; Fredrick F. Hess, American Enterprise Institute; Michelle Fienberg, founder of the KIPP foundation; Eric A. Hanushek, Senior Fellow of The Hoover Institution; and Michelle Rhee, founder and CEO of Students First and former chancellor of D.C. Public Schools.
2. We were not required to implement the NCTQ's standards in our ED.D Teaching for Leadership program because our program is not designed specifically to prepare students for specific positions in schools. Even if our dean had made the request for us to implement NCTQ's standards, we would have had a discussion with the dean explaining we could not use these standards because they are not consistent with the nature and purpose of the program.

References

Ball, S. (1993). What is policy? Texts, trajectories, and toolboxes. *Discourse* 13, 10–17.

Bartolome, L. (1994). Beyond the methods fetish: Toward a humanizing pedagogy. *Harvard Educational Review,* 64, 173–194.

Brodsky, P. P. (February, 2002). Shrunken heads: The humanities under the corporate model. *Workplace: A Journal for Academic Labor,* 4(2). Retrieved May 22, 2005, from http://www.louisville.edu/journal/workplace/patbrodsky.html

Burbules, N., & Rice, S. (1991). Dialogue across differences: Continuing the Conversation. *Harvard Educational Review* 61, 393–416.

Butin, D. W. (2007). Dark times indeed: NCATE, social justice, and the marginalization of multicultural foundations. *Journal of Educaiton Controversy,* 2(2).

Cochran-Smith, M. (2009). "Re-culturing" teacher education: Inquiry, evidence and action. *Journal of Teacher Education,* 60(5), 458–468.

Fassbinder, S.D. (6, May 2006). The "dirty thirty's" Peter McLaren reflects on the crisis of academic freedom. *Monthly Review.* Retrieved at http://mrzine.monthlyreview.org/2006/fassbinder060406.html

Gabriel, T. (8, February 2011). Teachers' colleges upset by plan to grade them. *New York*

Times. Retrieved from http://www.nytimes.com/2011/02/09/education/09teachers.html?_r=1

Giroux, H.A. (2007). *The university in chains: Confronting the military-industrial academic complex*. New York: Paradigm.

Heybach, J. (2009). Rescuing social jusice in educaion: A critique of the NCATE controversy. Philosophical Studies in Education, 40, 235–245.

Hinchey, P.H. & Cadiero-Kaplan, K. (2005). The future of teacher education and teaching: Another piece of the privatization puzzle. *The Journal for Critical Educational Policy Studies*, 3(2). Retrieved from http://www.jceps.com/index.php?pageID=article&articleID=48

Illinois Institutions of Higher Education (9, November 2010.). Illinois Schools of Education respond to NCTQ report. Retrieved from http://education.depaul.edu/Events/DePaul's_Response_to.asp

Johnson, D.D., Johnson, B., Farenga, S.J., & Ness, D. (2005). *Trivializing teacher education: The accreditation squeeze*. New York: Rowman & Littlefield Publishers.

Kincheloe, J.L. (2004). The knowledges of teacher education: Developing a critically complex epistemology. *Teacher Education Quarterly* 31(1), 49–66.

Kincheloe, J. L (2008). Critical pedagogy and the knowledge wars of the twenty-first century *International Journal of Critical Pedagogy* 1(1).

National Council on Teacher Quality. (2011). NCTQ's standards for rating the nation's education schools. Retrieved from http://www.nctq.org/edschoolreports/national/standardsCompiled.jsp

Porfilio, B.J. & Yu, T. (2006). "Student as consumer": A critical narrative of the commercialization of teacher education. *The Journal for Critical Educational Policy Studies*, 4(1). Retrieved from http://www.jceps.com/index.php?pageID=article&articleID=56

Sawchuk, S. NCTQ. (2011). *U.S. News* launch teacher education review. *Education Week*, 30(18), 4.

Sleeter, C.M. (2008). Teaching for democracy in an age of corporatocracy. *Teachers College Record*, 110 (1), 139–159.

Taubman, P.M. (2009). *Teaching by numbers: Deconstructing the discourse of standards and accountability in education*. New York, NY: Routledge.

Washburn, J. (2005). *University Inc.: The corporate corruption of higher education*. New York: Basic Books.

Wetzel, D.R. (5, February 2010). Alterative teaching certification routes. Retrieved from http://www.suite101.com/content/alternative-teaching-certification-routes-a198503

Contributors

Peggy Albers is a Professor in the College of Education at Georgia State University, Atlanta, GA, USA. She teaches literacy and English education courses and works with teacher education. Her research interests are semiotics, children's literature, English education, and the integration of multimedia into instruction, and she has published widely in *Language Arts, Journal of Adolescent and Adult Literacy, English Education, Talking Points, Journal of Literacy Research, Journal of Early Childhood Literacy*, and *The Reading Teacher*, and has published three books: *Literacies, the Arts and Multimodality; Finding the Artist Within*; and *Telling Pieces: Art as Literacy in Middle Grades Classes*. Her research and writing focus on integration of the arts in literacy. When not teaching, Peggy enjoys studying pottery and art at Callanwolde Fine Arts Center in Atlanta, GA. Her work has been shown and sold at local and state pottery shows.

Wayne Au is an Assistant Professor in the Education Program at the University of Washington—Bothell Campus, and he is an editor for the progressive education magazine and publishing house *Rethinking Schools*. Most recently he is author of *Critical Curriculum Studies: Education, Consciousness, and the Politics of Knowing* (Routledge, 2011) and co-editor of *Pencils Down: Rethinking Testing and Accountability in Public Schools* (Rethinking Schools, 2012).

Victor H. Diaz is a doctoral candidate at Arizona State University, working towards a Ph.D. in Education Policy and Leadership Studies, with an emphasis on Social and Philosophical Foundations of Education. He holds a master's degree from San Francisco State University in Educational Equity and Social Justice, and has taught middle and high school English/Language

Arts and English Language Development for eight years. Additionally, he trains and supports teachers in Teach For America, as well as Arizona State University, where he works as a teaching assistant. His research focuses on teacher education and social justice education, analyzing both within a sociocultural-historical context.

Antonio L. Ellis is a native of Charleston, South Carolina. He is a doctoral scholar in the department of Urban Educational Administration and Policy at Howard University. He holds both a Master's in Religious Studies and Master's in Educational Policy. His research interests are Critical Race Theory in Education and Disproportionality within the Special Education Milieu. He is an emerging scholar and is adding to the body of knowledge in the field of education through book chapters, academic reviews, and conference proceedings publications. Ellis serves as a member of the American Educational Researchers Association and the Northeastern Educational Researchers Association. Antonio loves children and finds joy in acquiring information that leads to student achievement, believing that "All Students Can Learn" within environments that encourages academic achievement.

Danling Fu is a Professor of Language and Culture, in the School of Teaching and Learning, College of Education at the University of Florida. She received her BA in linguistics and MA in English literature and her doctorate in Reading and Writing Instruction. She teaches courses for both undergraduate and graduate students addressing the topics on teaching methods, composition theory/research, writing development and assessment, and literacy/language/culture. She researches and provides in-service and consultancy to public schools nationally, with a special focus on writing instruction and literacy instruction for English language learners. Her publications includes three books: *My Trouble Is My English, An Island of English,* and *Writing between Languages* and more than 60 journal articles, book chapters, and book reviews addressing teaching English language learners and children's writing development. Her recent research focuses on English writing beyond the U.S. borders.

Kathy Garland is Assistant Professor of Secondary Education at Georgia College and State University where she prepares pre-service teachers in a M.A.T. program and teaches graduate-level education courses. Dr. Garland received her Ph.D. in Curriculum and Instruction from the University of Florida. Her dissertation, "Literacy Practices in an English Language Arts Elective: An Examination of How Students Respond to Media Literacy Education," reveals how students develop literacy practices similar to those that are expected with traditional texts. She has taught a range of high school English language arts classes for 10 years, served as English Department Chair, and provided professional development for in-service teachers as a School Instructional Coach. Kathy's research interests include methods for integrating media literacy education with traditional English language arts teaching.

Joshua Garrison is Assistant Professor of Educational Foundations at the University of Wisconsin Oshkosh. Educated at Evergreen State College (B.A.) and Indiana University (M.S., Ph.D.), Garrison holds a doctorate in the history of education. His primary research agenda is the history of childhood, and his work in that field earned him the "Article of the Year" award from the Organization of Educational Historians in 2009.

David A. Gorlewski is an Assistant Professor in the Education Department at D'Youville College in Buffalo, New York, where he teaches courses in curriculum planning, methods, and advanced curricular issues. He has served in public education as a high school English teacher, a staff developer, and a senior level administrator in curriculum and personnel. Publications include *Overflowing but Underused: Portfolios as a Means of Program Evaluation and Student Self-Assessment* (*English Journal*, 2010), and book reviews in *English Journal* (2011) and *Excelsior* (2011). His research interests include portfolios as assessment tools, standards and standardized testing, and school reform.

Julie A. Gorlewski, Assistant Professor of Secondary Education at the State University of New York at New Paltz, has over 15 years' experience teaching secondary English in an inner-ring suburban school district, where she also served as English department coordinator, technology coordinator, and learning center director. She edits a column entitled "Research for the Classroom" for the National Council of Teachers of English publication *English Journal* and is the author of the book *Power, Resistance, and Literacy: Writing for Social Justice* (2011, Information Age Publishers), which was selected for a 2011 Critic's Choice Award by the American Educational Studies Association. She earned a PhD from the State University of New York at Buffalo in the Social Foundations of Education. Her research interests include assessment, school reform, writing and writing instruction, and youth culture and resistance.

Katie Greene is a language arts teacher at Milton High School in Milton, GA, where she has taught ninthgrade composition and literature for six years. Katie earned her Bachelor's degree in Philosophy from Villanova University, her Master's degree in Middle Grades Education from Mercer University, and her Educational Specialist degree in English Education from Georgia State University. She currently serves as the associate chairperson of the National Council of Teachers of English Secondary Steering Committee (2011–2013), and she is the editor of *Connections*, the Georgia Council of Teachers of English state affiliate journal. Katie has served as member of her school's Local School Advisory Council and School Improvement Plan team, and as a fifth grade teacher in Philadelphia as an Americorps volunteer. She has written for such publications as *English Journal, Georgia Journal of Reading,* and

Educational Horizons on the topics of student choice, reflective writing practices, and action research.

Nicholas Daniel Hartlep is a Ph.D. candidate, Advanced Opportunity Program (AOP) Fellow, and instructor at the University of Wisconsin, Milwaukee in the Educational Policy and Community Studies Department. His dissertation research centers on dismantling the model minority stereotype through regression analyses. He has a master's degree and a bachelor's degree in education, both from Winona State University. Hartlep's background is that of a teacher (elementary, middle, and high school). He has written for such publications as *Academic Exchange Extra; Critical Questions in Education; Education Review; International Journal of Arts and Sciences; International Journal of Peace and Developmental Studies; International Journal of Educational Policies; Journal of At-Risk Issues; Journal of Language Identity & Education;* and *Journal of American Culture* among others. He is happily married to his wife, Stacey. They have two daughters, Chloe Haejin and Avery Hana. Hartlep is author of *Going Public: Critical Race Theory and Issues of Social Justice* (2010).

Lauren P. Hoffman is Professor and Director of the Educational Leadership Doctoral Program at Lewis University in Romeoville, Illinois. Her research interests lie in critical pedagogy and how individuals and groups assert their agency in relation to hegemonic forces. Her current work focuses on human rights and capabilities, social activism, and preparing critical teachers and leaders to reveal and resist injustice. She can be reached at Lewis University 100 University Parkway Romeoville, Illinois USA 60446 or hoffmala@lewisu.edu.

Andrea Hyde is an Assistant Professor in the Department of Educational and Interdisciplinary Studies at Western Illinois University–Quad Cities, where she teaches undergraduate and graduate courses in the social and philosophical foundations of education as well as qualitative research methods. She received her PhD from the University of Pittsburgh in Social and Comparative Analysis of Education and holds additional graduate degrees in social science and social studies education. Andrea's research interests include teachers' work and subjective experiences; teacher education pedagogy; the culture of academia; and yoga education and mindfulness pedagogy. As a qualitative researcher, she provides external program evaluation and consultation for Yoga in Schools, which serves mostly urban school districts in Pittsburgh, PA. Andrea is a Yoga Ed™ instructor and certified yoga teacher, who regularly teaches a workshop called Yoga Tools for Teachers to teachers, colleagues, and students.

Patricia Jacobs is a doctoral candidate in the Department of Curriculum and Instruction at the University of Florida. She earned a Master of Arts degree in English Education from Teachers College, Columbia University. She taught

English as a Second Language in Tokyo, Japan, fifth and seventh grade Language Arts at Convent of the Sacred Heart in New York City, and tenth grade English at Columbia High School in Lake City, Florida. Most recently she taught Language Arts Methods in the College of Education at the University of Florida. Patricia's research interests include how to support struggling literacy learners while preparing them with 21st-century digital skills.

Marion (Marty) Mayer is a National Board Certified Teacher in her 35th year of teaching a variety of high school language arts courses. Marty Mayer received her Ed.S. in English Education and Media Literacy from the University of Florida. Her interest in multimodal literacies led her to create Literature in the Media, a full-credit Language Arts Honors elective that was adopted by the Florida Department of Education. The course seeks to create media-savvy users through investigations into the parallels between multimodal literacy and traditional print literacy. In addition to high school, she has taught Digital Photography and Visual Literacy, an online, graduate-level course offered at the University of Florida.

Rosemary A. Millham, an Assistant Professor at the State University of New York at New Paltz, has 28 years of experience in education; 16 years in P–12 classrooms; and 12 as education specialist, science writer, curriculum developer, state liaison, Earth science lead, and research scientist at NASA Goddard Space Flight Center. Her research includes misconceptions, the significance of inquiry in teaching and learning, translating current science into classroom research, and pre-service teachers creating scientific inquiry and research in schools. She writes science and develops curriculum for NASA missions. Ro received her B.S. and M.S. from New Paltz and her Ph.D. at Oklahoma State University. Her memberships include the American Association for the Advancement of Science, American Geophysical Union, National Science Teachers' Association, American Geological Society, and Science Teachers Association of NYS, where she has presented 30 science and education papers, posters, presentations and workshops, and chaired sessions and proposal committees.

Brad J. Porfilio is Assistant Professor of Education at Lewis University in Romeoville, IL, where he conducts research and teaches doctoral students to become critical scholars, social advocates, and multicultural educators. During his doctoral studies, he served as an Assistant Professor of Education at Medaille College and D'Youville College, where he taught courses across the teacher education spectrum and supervised pre-service and in-service teachers from Canada and the U.S. He has published numerous peer-reviewed articles, book chapters, edited volumes, and conference papers in the field of education.

Ted Purinton is Assistant Professor in the Graduate School of Education at the American University in Cairo and the Associate Chair of the program in Comparative and International Education. Previously, he was Chair for the Department of Educational Leadership at National Louis University in Chicago. He is a recent author of *Six Degrees of School Improvement: Empowering a New Profession of Teaching* (IAP, 2011) and co-author of *Making Sense of Social Networks in Schools* with Terry Deal and Daria Waetjen (Corwin, 2008). His doctorate in educational policy and administration was awarded from the University of Southern California.

Lindsey Russo is Assistant Professor of Early Childhood Education at the State University of New York at New Paltz. Dr. Russo earned her Ed.D. in Early Childhood Education at Teachers College, Columbia University, where, previously, she was an instructor and adjunct Assistant Professor in the Department of Curriculum and Teaching. She is the Director of Curriculum Research and Documentation for the Blue School, a private school for children ages 2 through 2nd grade founded by the Blue Man Group and located in New York City. Dr. Russo works with the school and teachers to place creativity, play and authentic assessment at the core of the curriculum. She has published articles, a book chapter, and made numerous presentations on her research interests that include all aspects of play and its relationship to learning within a climate of increased academic expectations and standardization; the role of peer cultures in the preschool classroom; and early childhood teacher education.

Shawgi Tell is Associate Professor of Education in the Department of Social and Psychological Foundations of Education in the School of Education at Nazareth College of Rochester. He has been teaching in-service and pre-service teachers there since 1998. Tell received his Ph.D. in Social Foundations of Education from the University at Buffalo in 1997. His main research interests include education reform, governance, and policy; urban education; and the political economy of schooling. He is currently working on a book on charter schools in the United States and regularly conducts workshops for K–12 teachers on Arab and Muslim students. His classes combine lively lectures and presentations with small-group and large-group discussions and activities where all learn and grow together.

P. L. Thomas, Associate Professor of Education (Furman University, Greenville, SC), taught high school English in rural South Carolina before moving to teacher education. He is currently a column editor for *English Journal* (National Council of Teachers of English) and series editor for *Critical Literacy Teaching Series: Challenging Authors and Genres* (Sense Publishers), in which he authored the first volume—*Challenging Genres: Comics and Graphic Novels* (2010). Additional recent books include *Parental Choice? A Critical Reconsideration of Choice and the Debate about Choice* (Information Age Publishing, 2010) and *21st Century Literacy: If We Are Scripted, Are We Literate?* (Springer, 2009) co-authored with Renita Schmidt. He maintains a blog addressing the role of poverty in education: http://livinglearning inpoverty.blogspot.com/. His teaching and scholarship focus on literacy and the impact of poverty on education, as well as confronting the political dynamics influencing public education in the U.S. His work can be followed at http://wrestlingwithwriting.blogspot.com/.

Studies in the Postmodern Theory of Education

General Editor
Shirley R. Steinberg

Counterpoints publishes the most compelling and imaginative books being written in education today. Grounded on the theoretical advances in criticalism, feminism, and postmodernism in the last two decades of the twentieth century, Counterpoints engages the meaning of these innovations in various forms of educational expression. Committed to the proposition that theoretical literature should be accessible to a variety of audiences, the series insists that its authors avoid esoteric and jargonistic languages that transform educational scholarship into an elite discourse for the initiated. Scholarly work matters only to the degree it affects consciousness and practice at multiple sites. Counterpoints' editorial policy is based on these principles and the ability of scholars to break new ground, to open new conversations, to go where educators have never gone before.

For additional information about this series or for the submission of manuscripts, please contact:

> Shirley R. Steinberg
> c/o Peter Lang Publishing, Inc.
> 29 Broadway, 18th floor
> New York, New York 10006

To order other books in this series, please contact our Customer Service Department:

> (800) 770-LANG (within the U.S.)
> (212) 647-7706 (outside the U.S.)
> (212) 647-7707 FAX

Or browse online by series:
> www.peterlang.com